RECREATIONAL
DRUGS
A DIRECTORY

Prozac   20 mg

RECREATIONAL
DRUGS
A DIRECTORY

Harry Shapiro

COLLINS & BROWN

First published in Great Britain in 2004 by
Collins & Brown
The Chrysalis Building
Bramley Road, London W10 6SP

An imprint of **Chrysalis** Books Group plc

Produced in 2004 by
Salamander Books
The Chrysalis Building
Bramley Road, London W10 6SP

An imprint of **Chrysalis** Books Group plc

1 2 3 4 5 6 7 8 9

ISBN: 1-84340-244-0

Color reproduction by Anorax Imaging
Printed in Italy

In the United Kingdom, United States, and other
jurisdictions world wide, it is a criminal offense
punishable by imprisonment to possess, manufacture,
or supply recreational drugs. This book is designed
to be an educational reference and is not intended
to encourage illegal activity.

Contents

Introduction

The misuse of drugs is a global concern which seems to defy solutions. As a business, the profits from the production and sale of illegal drugs are colossal. The United Nations (UN) calculate that the trade is worth at least $500 billion which puts drug trafficking on a par with oil and arms dealing as one of the world's most profitable industries. During the 1980s, a Colombian drug trafficker had so much cash to deposit in a Florida bank that it was bound to attract the attention of the

authorities—so he bought the bank. According to Drug Enforcement Administration sources after his death, Carrillo Fuentes, a Mexican trafficker nicknamed "The Lord of the Skies" for his use of Boeing jets to transport drugs, spent $20–30 million on every drug operation.

Hardly a day goes by without a drugs story in the media—another tragic death, another drug bust,

another drug-related crime. When asked, parents often put drugs at the top of their list of worries for their children. They feel they know nothing and that any excursion into drugs will end badly. Many young people on the other hand wonder what all the fuss is about—they think they know it all. Meanwhile the media and politicians both seem to be looking for simple answers to what is actually a highly complex subject.

Despite the mountains of research and endless television documentaries, the use of drugs (including alcohol, tobacco, and caffeine) for non-medical or recreational purposes is an often misunderstood aspect of human behavior. The most extensive and solid scientific work on drugs focuses on their chemical compositions and effects on laboratory animals. We also know something about the characteristics of people who use large amounts, seek help, or get into some kind of trouble with drugs because they are the ones most likely to come to the attention of, for example, doctors, drug agencies, and the police, and therefore they are the ones most accessible to researchers.

LEFT: The fact that many drug users often inject means that this method of drug use is a major contributor to the spread of HIV/AIDS on a worldwide scale. Russia has one of the fastest growth rates for HIV in the world and the vast majority of this recorded increase can be attributed to people injecting drugs and sharing their works.

Why be a
drugs worker?

A project worker from Addiction ...

Our clients are usually ...
in extremely chaotic ...
and when they come to ...
often in crisis. Getting ...
engage can be difficult ...

ABOVE: All the research shows that drug treatment works. Because of the nature of addiction, people will relapse, but if somebody with a drug problem goes into treatment, their lives will become more stable with a chance of becoming drug-free.

But information derived from these areas of research doesn't necessarily help much in understanding the "everyday" use and misuse of drugs, nor how social and psychological processes influence the outcome of drug taking behavior. Instead, it can only offer a very rough guide as to what the outcome will be in any individual case.

DRUG, SET, AND SETTING

What happens to an individual when they take a drug is strongly influenced by three factors:

1. The nature of the drug itself

Throughout this book we are discussing psychotropic drugs—drugs which have an impact on the brain and change the way people feel when they take them. Obviously different drugs have different effects—much of the rest of this book is guide to the many different psychotropic drugs which exist in society and the effects they have. They can be grouped roughly into drugs which depress the central nervous system (CNS) like alcohol, heroin, and tranquillizers; those which stimulate the CNS like amphetamine and cocaine, and those drugs which alter our perception such as LSD. Most drugs act on the brain in the way you would expect, but some have paradoxical effects, for example an amphetamine-based drug called Ritalin is used to help calm hyperactive children.

2. Set

What we mean by this is what the person taking the drug expects to happen based on what others have told them or what they have heard, and/or what their past experience has been with a particular drug—these factors may all play a part in determining what happens next time. For example, many people who try marijuana for the first time report that nothing much happened. Only with subsequent use do they obtain the effects they were expecting as if they had to "learn" how to respond to the drug from the reactions of those around them.

How the person is feeling at the time will also have an influence on the experience. So, if somebody drinks alcohol when they feel miserable, they are likely to feel worse. If a person is anxious or depressed before taking LSD, they are more likely to have a bad experience.

3. Setting

Where people use drugs and what they are doing at the time can increase the risks. Young people often take drugs in dangerous places such as near water ways or railway lines, or in derelict buildings to be out of the sight of adults. Apart from these being dangerous places in their own right, if anything goes wrong it will be that much harder for an ambulance to reach them in time. Another problem

BELOW: The quicker a drug gets to the brain, the more intense will be the effects. How the drug acts on the brain will determine whether the user experiences a stimulant, a depressant, or hallucinogenic effect.

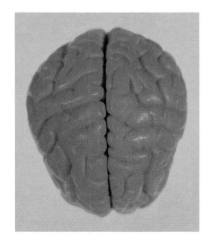

has been the use of ecstasy in clubs where people dance for hours in very crowded and hot environments. This has led to people overheating and some have died of dehydration and heat exhaustion. Again with hallucinogens like LSD, the experience is likely to be worse if the user is taking the drug in unfamiliar surroundings with people they don't know or like.

There are also a range of actions and circumstances which will have the effect of increasing the inherent danger of taking drugs for recreational use.

OVERDOING IT

Taking too much in one go will certainly risk the user having an experience that gets out of control and causes distress or even a fatal overdose. Obviously the more taken, the greater the risk of accidents due to intoxication, including choking on vomit while unconscious.

Anyone taking a psychoactive drug frequently, in high doses, and for a long time, is more than likely to experience a distortion in their perception of and response to their

LEFT: Young people aged between sixteen and twenty-four form the age group who are most likely to engage in a range of risky activities including the use of illegal drugs. Marijuana is the most popular illegal drug but only a small minority of users will go on to use more dangerous drugs like heroin and cocaine.

environment, to the extent that the individual's normal functioning and development are impaired. Social relationships may also narrow down to a small group of people with similar habits, and finding or keeping work and housing may be difficult. As their tolerance and dependence develops, the problems of financing drug purchases can add to the deterioration of diet, housing, and lifestyle, and may result in revenue-raising crimes. Normal desires, such appetite and libido, and reactions to discomfort and pain, may be dulled by the drug, and the resultant self-neglect can damage health. Indirect damage—arising from the lifestyle associated with heavy and, in particular, illegal drug use rather than a direct effect of the drug on the body—is often the most significant, but can sometimes be minimized even if drug use continues. Obviously, heavy use is most likely if someone becomes dependent on the drug, when they will find it hard to stop, despite their health being detrimentally effected.

WRONG TIME, WRONG PLACE

Even in moderate doses most of the drugs (except the stimulants) impair motor control, reaction time, and the ability to maintain attention. These effects can last for several hours. No matter how the person feels, they are not as capable as before, and such activities as driving, operating machinery, and crossing roads become more hazardous to themselves and to others around them. The user will also be less effective at their job.

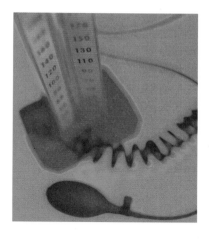

ABOVE: Those who have existing blood pressure and heart problems put themselves at risk by using stimulant drugs like amphetamine, ecstasy, cocaine, and crack.

LEFT: Young people who are caught using drugs can put their education and future careers at risk by having a criminal record.

Even stimulants may impair delicate skills and the learning of new skills, and in high doses will impair performance of tasks they had previously enhanced.

Many drugs also serve to amplify mood, such that if someone is feeling—or is in a situation that makes them feel—depressed, anxious, or aggressive, they could make things a lot worse. Even the drugs (such as alcohol and tranquillizers) we think of as calming people down, can also release aggressive impulses because they weaken the individual's social and personal inhibitions.

13

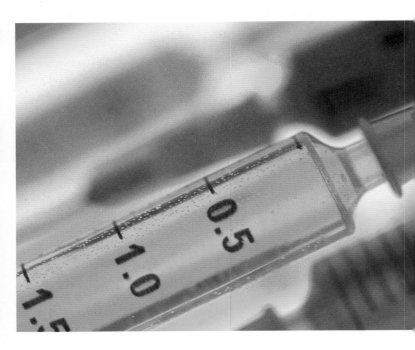

INDIVIDUAL DIFFERENCES

Statements about drug effects are often statements about what might happen in extreme cases, or alternatively about what usually happens with most people. But not everyone is "usual." For instance, some people develop a toxic reaction to a single cup of coffee and the normally insignificant elevation of heart rate caused by cannabis can be painful for people suffering from angina. Glaucoma patients, on the other hand, may find cannabis beneficial but three strong cups of coffee will aggravate the condition. Individuals with pre-existing psychotic tendencies may be "pushed over the edge" by their experiences under the

ABOVE: The most dangerous method of using drugs is to inject them. The risk of overdose is greater because the whole dose is going into the body all at once plus the inherent risk of contracting HIV and hepatitis.

influence of powerful hallucinogens like LSD. Also, the extent to which a drug affects the body tends to vary with body weight, so, in general, less heavy people will experience greater effects and consequently greater dangers from the same drug dose than heavier people will.

Differences determined by gender in response to psychoactive drugs are poorly researched but, for instance, it is known that women alcoholics are more susceptible to liver disease than

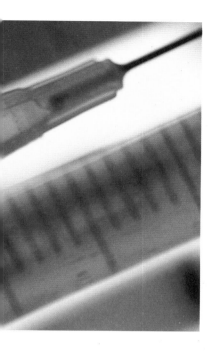

men, which is caused by the physiological differences between men and women. Individual differences in the degree of response to the same amount of a drug mean that dose levels for a given effect quoted in this publication can only be generalizations.

INJECTING DRUGS

Intravenous drug use is less widespread than other ways of using them, but it is also the most hazardous method. Drugs that are injected are mainly of three kinds: opiates, sedatives and tranquillizers, and stimulants (such as amphetamines and cocaine). In turn, these may well be mixed together to combine their different effects.

When injected into a vein, all of the drug enters the bloodstream at once and some is carried directly to the

BELOW: Setting up facilities where users can obtain clean needles and syringes is an effective way of reducing the harm caused by drug use.

NEEDLE EXCHANGE

OPE

The needle exchange is now running out of the basement.

brain, producing a noticeable effect within seconds. For these reasons the onset of the drug's effects (often referred to as the "rush") is quicker and more striking after injection. In general, the short-term effects of injected drugs are along the lines of those taken by mouth, but more intense. Opiates, for instance, produce a sensation of warmth and relief from physical and mental discomfort, but when injected these effects can be magnified into a short-lived burst of intensely pleasurable sensations. Drugs can also be injected under the skin or into muscles, when the effect is more delayed and less intense than with intravenous injection.

The major dangers of injecting are: overdose; infection from non-sterile injection methods (including hepatitis, AIDS, and other diseases transmitted by more than one injector sharing the same needle); abscesses and gangrene caused by missing the vein when injecting; and damage from using crushed-up tablets and other dosage forms not meant to be injected.

For a few people the injection may become as important as the effect of the drug, and if no drugs are available almost anything will be injected. Nevertheless, dependence is not inevitable and takes time to develop.

ADULTERATION AND MISTAKEN IDENTITY

Drugs offered on the illicit market are not always what they are claimed to be, and if the drugs have been illicitly manufactured they are likely to contain any one of a range of impurities or adulterants. Also, the buyer can rarely be sure how strong the substance is, and even if they did know, they wouldn't necessarily know how much to take.

These factors add greatly to the unpredictability of the effects of, and damage from, the use of drugs obtained without the safeguards of medical supervision or the quality control imposed on licit manufacturers.

DOUBLING UP

People who attempt suicide using large amounts of benzodiazepine tranquillizers almost invariably wake up unharmed, but the same dose on top of a large dose of alcohol could easily prove fatal. This example illustrates the point that the effects of drugs which individually depress body functions (alcohol, solvents, sedatives, hypnotics, opiates, and tranquillizers) will add up if they are taken together, so that much lower doses of each could prove to be fatal than would normally be the case. Added to which drugs remain effective for varying

RIGHT: A white pill is a white pill is a white pill. Due to the fact that there is absolutely no quality control on the illicit market, drug users (and often the street sellers as well) have very little idea of what is actually in the drugs that are being bought and sold.

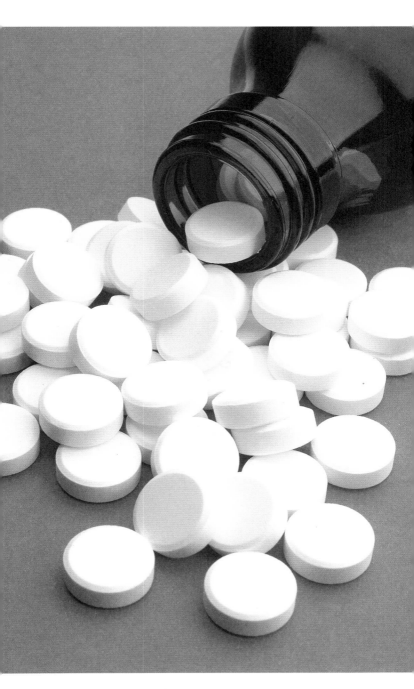

periods of time, often many hours, the two substances don't even have to be taken at the same time to be fatal.

Doubling up on depressant drugs probably causes the most dangerous effects, but complex interactions can occur between other drugs. Doctors and even experienced drug takers make use of these resultant interactions to enable them to "fine-tune" drug effects, but for most people loading one drug on top of another multiplies the risk of a harmful outcome.

All these influences are themselves tied up with the social and cultural attitudes to, and beliefs about, drugs as well as more general social conditions. Even the same person will react differently at different times, so it is usually misleading to make simple cause-and-effect statements about drugs, such as "drug X always causes condition Y." We are all individuals. What might be safe for one person could be dangerous, even fatal, for the next or even dangerous for the same person in a different situation.

RIGHT: Drugs are increasingly a part of our mainstream culture, but most users would draw the line at products that seem to encourage use by young people.

DRUG FAQS

Many of the Frequently Asked Questions about drugs fall under the heading of drug myths. A myth is a popular belief which has limited use as a way of understanding the subject on which it is focused. While there are often elements of truth in all myths, for the majority it could be said that they are based on stereotypical and simplistic images, which have their roots in ignorance and attribute particular characteristics to things and people that are neither supported nor substantiated by much more than hearsay.

Why do people take drugs?

Many reasons have been put forward to explain why people use drugs and why some users become dependent on them. Most theories about the causes of drug use or drug dependence rely upon descriptions of established drug takers. There is very little information about the characteristics of these individuals before they become involved in drugs. However, it is

LEFT: It isn't only humans who look for ways to alter their mood. Scientists have observed a wide range of animals who will avidly seek out plants for their intoxicating effects.

unlikely that either drug use in general or drug dependence is caused by any single factor. It seems that drug use in general is the outcome of interactions between the drug, the personal characteristics of the individual, and their environment. Below (and in no special order) are a few suggestions as to why people use drugs (including alcohol and tobacco).

Genetic

Psychoactive drug use is virtually universal in some form or other right across the globe, and its history goes back to the earliest times of human beings and beyond. There are plenty of examples of animals seeking out the effects of drugs. In the laboratory, monkeys will press the lever for cocaine in preference to that for food; cats go wild for catnip, and the African elephant will travel miles just to get drunk on the fermented fruit of a particular tree. Nothing in nature is

accidental, but nobody has yet come up with a theory as to why we should have the capacity to respond to drugs in the way we do.

More specifically to individuals rather than the whole species, animal research has shown that sometimes there does exist a genetic predisposition to use specific drugs. There is a growing body of evidence that inherited factors can predispose some people to develop alcohol-related problems. Such factors obviously interact with availability, social context, and other important influences on drug use.

Enjoyment

Drugs can be exciting for some as they offer an accessible and often reliable means of obtaining "enjoyable" experiences. Anyone who doubts this should remember that most adults use drugs (alcohol, tobacco, coffee) and appear to accept uncritically that such use is valuable. By their own admission, drug users make it abundantly clear that they take drugs

Self-destructive risk-taking

The obvious dangers of unwise or excessive drug use have led to speculation that sometimes drug taking is prompted by self-destructive impulses. Alcohol dependence, to give an example, has been called "chronic suicide." It has often been observed that chronic drug users appear to have poor self-images and sometimes have quite strong feelings of hostility directed at themselves.

Peer pressure/peer preference

Early experimentation with drugs is often associated with the teenage years. These are the years when young people are increasingly curious about the world around them and are often looking for avenues of defiance to

BELOW: To maintain a regular drug habit is expensive. Even those with money to burn may find the cash runs out in the end.

ABOVE: While it is not the whole reason behind many young people's drug use, it is certain that peer pressure has its part to play. Most young people are desperate to fit in with their friends and may be tempted to try drugs as "dares" so as not to appear out of step.

in the most part because they like it. By definition, drugs alter the user's mental state—often slowing, speeding, or distorting perceptions—and many autobiographical accounts of drug use have been seen to emphasize the appeal of these effects.

21

counteract parental authority. Paradoxically, while striving to be rebellious, young people also want to fit in with their peer group. This has led to a common belief that young people are forced into trying drugs for fear of being left out. While this may suit some parental views that their child would never otherwise have done such a dangerous thing, the reality is often more complex. There may well be some young people who do try drugs under these circumstances, but in the main, young people choose the friends they want to hang out with. If a young person becomes a regular drug user, it is more than likely that he or she has actually chosen to be with a group of peers who share this activity.

Environment

Drug use occurs through all levels of society and material wealth is no protection against drug problems if there is a lack of emotional support and well-being within the family. However, in general, the most serious drug problems are likely to be the product of poverty and deprivation in communities with high levels of unemployment and a whole range of social and economic disadvantage. For young people in such communities, drugs can perform a range of functions; a way of blocking out problems; a daily routine built around

BELOW: Name this drug? Is it marijuana, tobacco, khat, or something that looks like a drug like oregano herbs? Would you buy this?

finding the money for drugs, buying them, and a source of income through dealing in any surplus drugs. This is why the "drug economy" often takes over within an area when the mainstream political, economic, and social institutions have failed the local community.

What are the differences between hard and soft drugs?

Whether or not a drug is labelled "hard" or "soft" will be determined

BELOW: Or what about this pile of crystals? It looks like a large pile of crack cocaine, but it might be speed or ketamine.

in the public mind by the degree to which the drug is believed to cause addiction and how severe the penalties are for its use. Therefore invariably, heroin and cocaine will be regarded as "hard drugs" while cannabis, ecstasy, and LSD will be tagged as "soft drugs." In fact, this is just a shorthand which has no basis in either law or pharmacology. For example, in the US and the UK, the penalties for possession and dealing in heroin, cocaine, LSD, and ecstasy are all equally severe. In these countries the law does not recognize any distinction between for example, heroin and LSD.

While it is true that the onset of addiction is likely to be more swift

than tobacco, many heroin users say that giving up nicotine was far harder than heroin. Not only that but the death toll from smoking tobacco runs into many millions worldwide—far greater than the deaths from heroin use. Conversely, while cannabis and LSD may be regarded as "soft drugs," they can still have serious effects on the mind of somebody who is mentally unstable.

Are all drugs addictive?

It depends on what we mean by addiction. The terms "addiction" and "addict" conjure up all sorts of negative images of people and

dehumanize those they are applied to. Some people even regard addiction as a disease and believe that once people are addicts they will always be addicts, even though there is no real evidence to support this view. People can and frequently do change throughout their life.

Any individual can become psychologically dependent on a drug—or any other activity such as eating, gambling, work, or exercising. To be psychologically dependent on a drug means the person feels that they cannot cope, or cannot face the world, unless they are under the influence of drugs. This kind of dependency has more to do with the person who is using the drug than it has with the drug itself.

In contrast, people can only become physically dependent on certain drugs. Physical dependency comes from the repeated, heavy use of drugs like heroin, tranquillizers, and alcohol. Heavy and continual use of these drugs can change the body chemistry so that if someone does not get a repeat dose they suffer physical

ABOVE: While there is concern about young people's drinking and drug use, the majority are able to have a good time while remaining sensible and not putting themselves at undue risk.

RIGHT: Health experts have issued safety guidelines about drinking alcohol which can help to reduce the risks, but no safety levels for nicotine or tar intake have ever been established.

withdrawal symptoms: the shakes and flu-like effects. They have to keep taking the drug just to stop themselves from feeling ill.

Continual use of drugs like cannabis, ecstasy, and LSD does not result in physical dependency even though people may become psychologically dependent. With other drugs, and particularly stimulant drugs such as cocaine, crack,

amphetamine, and nicotine, there is debate about just how much physical dependence can result. There are no heroin-like withdrawal symptoms, but the psychological feelings of depression can be acute.

Does cannabis lead to other drugs?

This is the so-called "escalation" hypothesis. In the mid-1980s research

from the US revived interest in this idea; specifically it was claimed that cannabis use tends to lead the individual to heroin use, but the arguments are similar for progression to other illicit drugs too.

Most people who use heroin will have previously used cannabis (though only a small proportion of those who try cannabis go on to use heroin). This could be because cannabis actually does (at least for some people) lead to heroin use, but there are other explanations.

For instance, it could be that heroin and cannabis use are both caused by something else in the individual's

BELOW: Millions of transactions like this take place every day of the week in countries all over the world and as you go up the dealing chain the amounts of money become enormous.

personality or background that the researchers have not taken into account. Further more, studies suggesting cannabis might lead to heroin have been done in western societies at a time when cannabis is more freely available than heroin. This could mean that people tend to use cannabis first simply because it was the first drug they came into contact with.

Even if cannabis use did lead to heroin use, there would remain the crucial issue of exactly how this happened. The assumption is that if cannabis leads to heroin, then more cannabis use would result in more heroin use—an argument against legalizing cannabis. But the reverse could be the case.

For instance, it could be that cannabis use involves people in the buying of illegal drugs, making it more likely that they will meet with an offer of heroin, an offer which some will accept. In this example it

RIGHT: Tobacco, alcohol, and over the counter painkillers can seriously affect your health every bit as much as heroin and cocaine.

would be the illegality of cannabis use rather than cannabis use itself that led most directly to heroin use. The implication is that some heroin use might be prevented by legalizing cannabis, even if this meant more widespread cannabis use.

This one example shows that the way any link between cannabis and

heroin works may be as important as whether or not such a link exists in the first place. All that can be said definitely is that:

1. Cannabis use generally precedes the use of other illegal drugs.
2. Cannabis use does not necessarily (or even usually) lead to the use of other illicit drugs.

The lack of proof of the escalation theory is typical of our knowledge about other ill effects sometimes said to be caused by cannabis. There is evidence suggesting a number of undesirable consequences of regular use: mental illness, poor motivation, decreased fertility, impaired development in adolescents, but no

LEFT: Marijuana smoked by itself can harm the respiratory system as any smoked drug can, but the problems are likely to be increased if the drug is mixed up with tobacco.

29

evidence exists which convincingly refutes or confirms these suggestions.

The illegality of cannabis and the fact that most cannabis users do not approach treatment services makes detailed follow-up studies of cannabis users difficult, and laboratory studies cannot duplicate real life situations.

The widespread use of cannabis in western countries has not been accompanied by correspondingly widespread demand for medical, psychological, or social help with cannabis-related problems, but it will never be possible to prove that such problems might not materialize in the future or be found if research techniques improved.

What are the signs and symptoms of drug use?

Many pamphlets and booklets which are aimed at parents have lists of signs and symptoms of drug use. They often include changes in school and work attendance, mood swings, changes in appearance, excessive tiredness, lack of appetite, and so on. The problem is that many of these may be caused by things other than drug use and are often relatively normal behaviors especially among young people.

Unless you happen to be with someone while they are intoxicated or high on drugs you may not see any clear signs and symptoms. Even behavior that seems like intoxication could be due to other things such as mental health problems. The early symptoms of staggering gait associated with physical conditions such as multiple sclerosis could be misinterpreted as drunkenness.

How pure are street drugs?

There is no proper quality control over illegal drugs. It is often difficult to know whether a powder, pill, resin, herb, or liquid is a particular drug. Even knowing what a drug is, the user may have no idea how strong the dose is or whether it also contains another drug or other anonymous substances to bulk it out.

An unusually strong dose of a drug may have devastating effects. For example, a heroin user used to injecting heroin which is forty percent pure could easily overdose and die if they injected heroin at seventy percent purity. Similarly, taking one drug which turns out to be another can be very disturbing, for example an ecstasy pill which was actually a strong hallucinogen.

But while the unknown factor in street drugs can be dangerous, stories about drugs being cut with rat poison and brick dust are exaggerated. Drug dealing is a commercial business. It is not in the dealer's interest to have customers dropping dead from deliberately contaminated drugs and people are much more likely to return to dealers who offer good quality substances.

ILLEGAL DRUGS MAY CONTAIN:

- **Impurities**

  Substances present in the drug as a natural result of the way it was made rather than deliberately added. For example, opiate alkaloids may be present in heroin as a result of refining the opium into heroin.

- **Adulterants**

  These are drugs that deliberately mimic or enhance the effects of the drug being offered. Examples are caffeine and/or ephedrine which are often found in amphetamines or ecstasy.

- **Diluents**

  These are mainly sugars such as glucose, lactose, and mannitol. These are added to bulk out the deal and assist the process of dilution of the drug for injection.

The purity of street drugs and what they contain varies between different countries and regions, or locations within a country, and can also change within a matter of days. Below is only a rough guide to what we know about the purity of different drugs. The purity levels indicated here for different drugs reflect an average purity level for the US and the UK, unless otherwise indicated and for street level quantities of grams and ounces (as opposed to wholesale kilogram weight).

DRUG IMPURITIES:

- **Amphetamine/Methamphetamine**

  The most impure illegal drug available in the UK. Purity may be up to ten percent but is more commonly less than five percent with some samples as low as one percent purity. In the US, methamphetamine is also one of the least pure drug available on the streets averaging about thirty-five percent. However, the smokeable variety known as Ice is (like crack cocaine) much purer, at over eighty percent on average. Amphetamine is often cut with sugars, caffeine, and/or ephedrine and sometimes with paracetamol, Vitamin C, chalk, and talcum powder.

- Cocaine

Purity can vary from twenty to ninety percent with an average of around forty-five to sixty percent. The rest is usually made up of sugars such as glucose, lactose, and/or mannitol.

- Crack cocaine

Usually eighty-five to ninety-five percent pure cocaine freebase and up to 100 percent pure in some samples.

- Ecstasy

The amount of ecstasy (MDMA) in one tablet may vary. Some tablets sold as ecstasy may contain no MDMA and be other drugs. Many ecstasy tablets also contain other drugs—ketamine, amphetamine, caffeine, ephedrine, and the tranquillizer, flunitrazepam, have all be found. Some tablets also contain other ecstasy-type drugs such as MDA or MDEA.

- Heroin

Usually thirty to eighty percent pure, averaging at forty-five to fifty percent pure. The rest is usually paracetamol, other opiate alkaloids, sugars, and sometimes methaqualone or diazepam (valium). Varying purity has often been connected to fatal overdose through injecting heroin when people take a higher purity dose than they are used to.

- LSD

Usually sold as small paper squares, cut from larger sheets which have been soaked in the drug. Most squares do have LSD but fakes with no LSD at all can be sold. The dosage of LSD on one square can vary a lot because the process of dipping the sheets means that as the liquid drug soaks into the sheet it tends to fall to the bottom meaning squares at the bottom of the sheet might have more LSD in them than those at the top.

BELOW: Mood altering drugs like tranquillizers are not meant to be prescribed for months on end. They are only meant to deal with times of severe crisis and trauma; after a few weeks research shows that they are ineffective, but can cause serious withdrawal problems if stopped suddenly.

Drug testing

To try and reduce bad experiences with drugs, a drug testing service has been offered outside some clubs and dance venues in Holland. A user could take the opportunity to have a pill

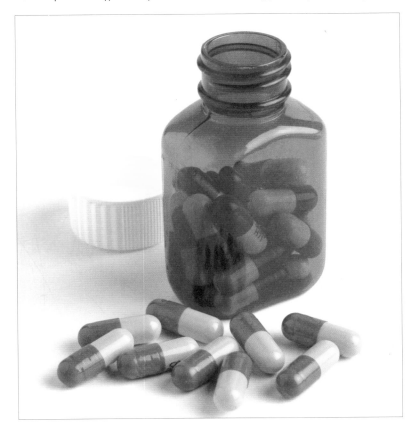

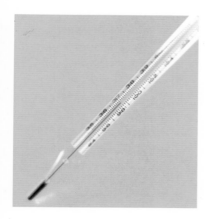

LEFT: Ecstasy effects the body's thermostat and can cause temperature to rise to dangerous levels.

tested using a testing procedure which involved dissolving a tablet in a solution to see what color was produced. This test could not establish the safety of a drug or batch of drugs, but it simply served to help to confirm the identity of the substance or the presence of other substances in the pill.

Why do people die from taking ecstasy?

People die from taking all sorts of drugs, not just ecstasy, and compared with the millions of young people who have tried the drug worldwide, the mortality rate is very low. It is, however, worth focussing on this drug for two reasons:

1. It is the most significant development in youth drug culture for over twenty years and among young people has a relatively benign image.

2. There are still unanswered questions about ecstasy-related deaths. Since the late 1980s, there have more than 200 reported deaths in the UK alone associated with the use of ecstasy and in the US 300–400 since 1994. These deaths have fallen into three categories:

Heat-stroke

Most of the deaths fall into this category and it is no coincidence that most of these have been associated with the use of the drugs in clubs and dance venues. The use of ecstasy by itself will increase body temperature because it appears to interfere with the mechanism of thermo-regulation of the body. This will be exacerbated in the hot club environment. Ecstasy also causes a certain amount of hyperactivity in users. Combined with vigorous dancing for hours on end, this can cause body temperatures to rise beyond the danger limit of 104°F (40°C) with symptoms that include convulsions, dilated (enlarged) pupils, very low blood pressure, and a fast heart rate.

Death is caused by respiratory collapse (breathing failure) resulting from what is called "disseminated intravascular coagulation" (or DIC). What seems to happen is that MDMA somehow reacts with the chemicals that control blood coagulation so that blood coagulates in places it shouldn't, such as the lungs;

subsequently air cannot get through and the person dies. Also, if all the blood-clotting agent has been used up at inappropriate sites, then the blood might not coagulate where it should and there is a risk of haemorrhaging from all the internal bumps and bruises that the human body normally sustains without problems.

BELOW: Drinking lots of water does not protect against the dangers of ecstasy. In fact, drinking excessive amounts of water is potentially life-threatening.

Too much fluid

By now, most of those who go to clubs have got the message about

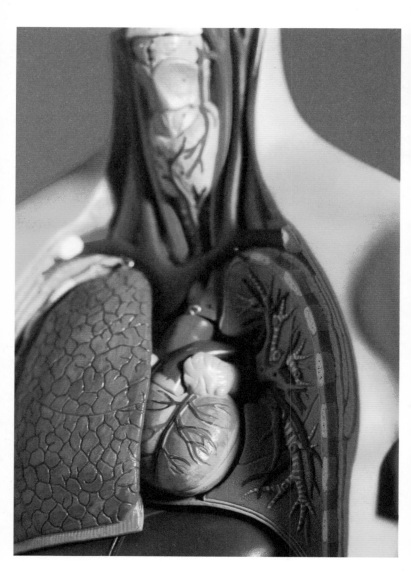

ABOVE: Ecstasy is a stimulant drug which can adversely effect blood pressure and heart rate. There have been some fatalities involving young people who had undiagnosed heart problems and those who know they may have heart conditions should not use any stimulant drugs.

reducing the risks of overheating by wearing loose clothes, "chilling out" regularly, and drinking fluids.

However, there have been deaths from excess water intake, possibly due to a mistaken belief that simply drinking lots of water will offset any side effects of the drug, although not in all cases could the water intake be said to have been excessive. The condition is known as dilutional hyponaetremia.

This condition can arise as ecstasy appears to effect the workings of the kidneys by inappropriately secreting an "anti-diuretic" hormone which prevents the excretion of fluids. Water is retained in the body, especially in the highly water-absorbent brain cells and eventually the pressure shuts down main bodily functions such as breathing and heartbeat.

Symptoms include dizziness and disorientation leading to collapse and coma. Not all of those effected die; there are a number of young people who have been admitted to hospital in this condition, but survived.

Heart failure

Ecstasy causes a significant rise in blood pressure and heart rate which a fit young person can normally sustain. However, a few young people have succumbed to these stimulant effects, sometimes as a result of an undiagnosed heart condition.

Many questions remain about ecstasy deaths. For example, the link between the amount of the drug in the bloodstream and its likely toxic effects is unclear. The literature from research in the US mentions cases where users with high levels of MDMA in their blood have survived "overdoses," but

where a normal dose of around 100–150 mg has caused death.

Yet American psychiatrists have reported using 100 mg of (presumably pure) MDMA with patients in therapy with no ill-effects. The deaths in this country have involved a range of doses from one to perhaps five tablets in one session.

In the UK, there was a recent death of a young girl who died having taking ecstasy from the same batch as her friends. They were fine, she was not. Some scientists have suggested that some of the more mysterious deaths might have been caused because the individual had some genetic deficiency which meant they could not metabolize the drug out of their system.

Does drug treatment work?

As ever in the world of drugs, there are no easy answers, but essentially the answer is "yes," although much depends on your definition of "works"—and there is no one easy route to success. The person with, for example, a long term heroin problem has a long and difficult road ahead of them. They must want to come off heroin, but even so there will be relapses on the way; individuals may travel along the treatment journey more than once. Actually coming off heroin is not the problem—with proper care and support, this can be achieved in a few days. The problem is not getting the drug out of the body, it's getting it out of the mind—not the coming off, but the staying off. A typical treatment journey might start with an assessment of the problem by a doctor or a drugs worker. The

BELOW: Those with drug problems might urgently need treatment, but they must themselves have got to the point psychologically when they want help.

person might go through a process of detoxification, perhaps a period of stabilization on a substitute drug like methadone, and then to a rehabilitation unit for a number of weeks or months to emerge at the end drug free. It may well be that the person returns to drug use and has to start the journey again at a later stage when they are ready.

Another journey might involve detoxification and then attendance of a support group such as at Narcotics Anonymous or Alcoholics Anonymous meetings. The principle philosophy of this treatment is that the person has a "disease" called addiction, that they will always be a "recovering" addict or an alcoholic, and must never touch drugs or alcohol again.

At the other extreme is a form of treatment which stops at the stabilization phase where the person is maintained on methadone for an indefinite period. In some countries this process extends to prescribing the drug of choice, heroin. No such treatment option exists in the US, but it is allowed in some European countries including the UK.

No one treatment can claim a 100 percent success rate, indeed many long term users stop by themselves without ever going near a treatment service. What is important in the drug treatment services is that the user is treated with respect and that there are a range of treatment options available for people with minimum waiting times. Treatment services which try and treat everybody with the same method tend to end up failing most of the people who come to see them. Outside of the service, the best prognosis for success is that the person does not return to their old friends and drug haunts and that they are able to make significant changes in their lives.

OPPOSITE: There have been hundreds of books written about drugs (including this one!) but few people can agree on the "truth about drugs."

ABOVE: A Washington-based research organization calculated that there were more young African-American males in prison (many for drug offenses) than there were in college.

Does drug education stop drug use?

The short answer to this question is simply "no." This is the Holy Grail of drug education—to find a method which stops use in the first place and no such method has yet been found. There are three main aims for all drug education efforts:

- Increasing knowledge
- Raising awareness
- Changing behavior

The first two are relatively easy through drug information-based programs, lectures, films, literature, classroom discussions, and so on. The third is very difficult. Of course, it is impossible to say that no child has ever stopped using drugs or changed their mind about starting because of a drug education program in school. But looking at the rise of drug use amongst young people since the 1960s against the millions of dollars invested in drug education program, it is reasonable to assume that in terms of absolute prevention, any idea that drug education could always prevent use was unrealistic. Back in the 1960s and 1970s, the prevailing view was that you could shock young people into rejecting drugs through the use of film. Some of these films were basic morality tales of how young people with a bright future were ruined by drugs (usually marijuana). Others were medical films which purported to show the physical damage done to the body and the mind by drugs.

A later approach was called *Lifeskills,* a scheme which took the view that it was felt that young people needed to have the personal skills to resist the pressure to use drugs. There were many programmes developed under this banner including DARE (Drug Abuse Resistance Education). This was devised by the Los Angeles Police Department and became one of the most popular drug education programmes in the US, although claims for its success remain controversial.

Over the years, programmes have become more sophisticated, but the research shows that in terms of preventing use, the best that can be said is that some programmes have managed to delay the onset of use.

It remains a matter of some debate whether drug education has in fact been drug propaganda. Some would argue that rather than encouraging young people with the skills to make their own choices—the programs are slanted so that there is in reality only one choice on offer—and that it is to

OPPOSITE: After reclassifying marijuana in 2004, the British government launched a campaign to dispel the idea that marijuana was now a legal substance.

say "no." On the other hand, the school environment is a very difficult one in which to deliver information or skills around such an emotionally-charged subject. Many teachers feel ill-equipped to deliver drug education programs, while head teachers and principals are always keenly aware of the possible political fall-out from drug education involving parents, school governors and Boards, and the local media.

What are the arguments for and against the legalization of drugs?

Why are some drugs illegal? This may sound like a stupid question, but the answer is more complex than might first appear. One answer, of course, is that drugs like heroin, cocaine, or methamphetamine can be very dangerous. So there is a public health imperative which demands that society makes some substances as hard to get as possible. Medical concerns raised by doctors about drugs go back to a time in the nineteenth century when drugs like morphine, opium, and cocaine were perfectly legal ingredients for a wide range of medicines. As newer, safer drugs became available, the case for the legal supply of these and other

CANNABIS
IS
STILL
ILLEGAL

The Police **can** arrest you:

- If you are **Publicly** smoking Cannabis
- If you **Repeatedly** offend
- If Cannabis use has been **Linked** to other problems in the area
- If you possess Cannabis and are close to **Youth** premises e.g. schools

You **will** be arrested if you are aged **17 or under**

drugs diminished and contributed to their final control under the law.

But that isn't the whole story. Everybody knows how dangerous alcohol and tobacco can be, but they are legal. So too are a range of painkillers which can be lethal in overdose or at least cause permanent damage to the liver. In fact, all drugs have the potential to be dangerous if misused, so there must other factors involved in determining what drugs are legal and which are banned. These include those listed over the page.

43

ILLEGAL OR LEGAL?

- What society finds acceptable or has managed to assimilate into the culture. For example, alcohol can cause huge damage not only to the individual, but also to society through drunk driving and violence. Yet the attempt to control drinking through Prohibition (1919–1933) in the US failed mainly because the majority of people did not support it. By contrast, many Muslim countries, some of which have a long tradition of opium and marijuana smoking, ban the consumption of alcohol.

- The degree to which a country's government depends on the revenue from taxation. For example, James I of England was vehemently anti-smoking, but needed tobacco revenues for the financial good of the country.

- The power of vested interests. The tobacco and alcohol industries have been very effective in maintaining their profits and position through their political influence.

- The degree to which religious and moral groups have been able to influence policy. In the nineteenth century in the UK, but even more so in the US, there were powerful middle-class Temperance (anti-alcohol) and anti-drug groups using all their influence to have substances banned because they believed that fundamentally intoxication of any sort was morally wrong and undermined progress in society by distracting (especially young people and the working classes) away from healthy pursuits and employment. This was not just a view in support of capitalism and profits—communist countries took a similarly dim view of drugs and alcohol as undermining the aims of the collective society.

- Racism, too, has played its part in that the association of certain drugs with different racial or ethnic groups in society has prompted a more draconian response.

All of these factors and others came together between 1914–1939 to establish the national and international control system which is largely in place today. During that period, the production, manufacture, supply, and possession of the major plant-based drugs—opium, coca, and marijuana—and their derivatives were all severely controlled with stiff penalties. From the 1960s onwards, as each new drug moved from being recognized as a legal/medical drug to an illegal street drug, so the law has intervened; drugs like LSD, amphetamine, barbiturates, ecstasy, and others. Most countries have a range of enforcement agencies in place to deal with illegal drugs and those who supply and possess them.

So what are the main arguments these days for the maintenance of the laws against drugs?

THE ARGUMENTS:

- Drug use can cause significant harm to individuals and others and so the governing state has a duty to protect its citizens even from themselves which is why some countries have laws to enforce the wearing of seat belts and crash helmets.

- Laws against drugs send out the message from the government that intoxication can have harmful effects on society at large.

- To legalize drugs would make the drug situation far worse because those who are currently frightened off by the law would be tempted to experiment, plus those who are already using drugs would probably use more.

- It is also unrealistic to think that with so much money at stake, organized crime would just walk away if drugs were legalized. Criminals would find another way to be involved and make profits from selling drugs to undercut the legal price. In any case, a drug like cannabis can be grown anywhere so there is every chance that the illicit market would thrive because the legal market would be heavily taxed.

- Those who want to legalize drugs have not answered some key questions. What drugs would be available? Who is going to have access to what drugs? Given how hard it is to regulate the markets for alcohol and tobacco—especially stopping young people from using—how are we going to control the use of a far wider range of drugs?

- People who use illegal drugs know the risks they are taking. People have to take responsibility for their own actions. Some of the reform options like decriminalization would make matters worse. It would do nothing to undermine the illicit market while encouraging more widespread use.

- Legalizers say that alcohol and tobacco cause far more deaths and damage than drugs. Isn't that because they are legal and so widely available? How much more damage would there be if drugs like heroin and cocaine could be more easily obtained? If alcohol and tobacco were currently illegal, it is most unlikely they would be made legal now.

What about the other side of the argument? Ever since drug use became popular among white, middle-class students in the 1960s, there have been calls for the laws on drugs to be relaxed or removed altogether. Most of this effort has been focused on marijuana. There has also been separate campaigning calling for the legalization of marijuana for medical uses. There is strong medical evidence that marijuana relieves the symptoms of a number of medical conditions including glaucoma, a disease of the eye; the pain associated with multiple sclerosis, and the nausea caused by

OPPOSITE: Computer games, CDs, and DVDs are often used as a part exchange for drugs.

chemotherapy treatment for cancer. The legalizers want drugs such as ecstasy, marijuana, and cocaine, controlled and regulated in ways similar to the controls on alcohol and tobacco. But what are the arguments?

Essentially they say that the "War on Drugs" doesn't work. There is no effective way to stop people from wanting to take drugs and all the law does is to put money into the pockets of criminals with all the violence and corruption that goes with it.

WHAT THE LEGALIZERS SAY:

- The State should not be interfering with the rights of the citizen to take drugs in privacy.

- It is hypocritical to have laws against drugs when tobacco and alcohol are legal—and cause far more health damage, especially when any number of expert reports have suggested that moderate use of marijuana is not that risky.

- If drugs were legal, then the government would be able to levy taxes on them which would benefit all of society. The extra funds could be used to help those with health problems caused by drugs.

- At the same time, a major source of criminal income would be reduced. This means at one end, people would not have to steal and rob in order to pay for expensive drugs, and as a consequence, the profits of organized crime would collapse.

- Having legal products would mean proper quality control, so that people would not be using drugs manufactured in unsterile conditions and cut with all kinds of dangerous additives.

- Whatever harm drugs cause, the drug laws make everything worse. Apart from the dangers of contaminated drugs, violence, and corruption—otherwise law-abiding citizens are made into criminals for being caught in possession of drugs and they lose respect for the law.

- The costs of prohibition in terms of actual policing and the costs of crime to society runs into billions of dollars every year including the cost of keeping people in prison. The climate of prohibition stigmatizes users and their families and is a disincentive to seeking treatment.

- It is not necessarily the case that legalizing drugs would mean many more people would use them. During the 1970s, eleven American states reduced the penalties for possessing marijuana and use did not rise dramatically. The only reason why these initiatives were abandoned was because the political climate changed with the arrival of Ronald Reagan in the White House.

- If drugs were legalized, it would be easier to have more sensible drug education in the way that young people are encouraged to drink alcohol sensibly with some government guidance.

How would you control drugs?

Those campaigning for legalization have identified a number of models for controlling the use and distribution of drugs which would vary depending on how dangerous the drug was thought to be:

POSSIBLE DRUG CONTROLS:

- Unlicensed sales—similar to buying ordinary produce in a supermarket. This would seem the least acceptable form of legal distribution, although legalizers argue that the current illegal market, which is unregulated and uncontrolled, is exactly the same and therefore unacceptable.

- Licensed sales—this would mean the shopkeeper would have to have a special license to sell the drugs in the same way that a license is required to sell liquor. It might even be that the government would have a monopoly on sales where drugs could only be purchased from government-owned shops.

- Pharmacy sales—this would allow the public to buy certain drugs from the pharmacist.

- Prescription—this would simply mean that the individual could get certain drugs on prescription from their doctor.

The legalization movement does acknowledge that if all drugs were legalized this would not reduce drug misuse but may reduce some of the harms of having drug use banned, such as using contaminated drugs or having a school or work career ruined by being convicted of a drug offense. They say that organized crime would not disappear, but as drugs constitute such a huge proportion of its income, it would take a long time to find similar profits elsewhere. They also acknowledge that legalization would not deal with the root causes of chronic drug problems like poverty and urban deprivation.

No government has taken the step of completely legalizing any drug which is currently the subject of international controls under the United Nations treaties. Although many people think that Holland has legalized marijuana, this is not the case. The law against marijuana is still in place, it is just that in certain special circumstances, the police have chosen not to enforce the law. That is, when a small amount of marijuana is bought and smoked on the premises of a so-called "coffee shop." The Dutch government do not believe that cannabis use leads to heroin use, but they do argue that having an outlet for the "legal" supply of marijuana, means that young people are less likely to come into contact with drug dealers who might want to sell them other drugs. The statistics seem to show that Holland's heroin population is getting older with fewer young people coming in at the other end—although whether this has anything to do with their marijuana policy is unclear.

Even so, there is controversy over whether or not the Dutch government is breaking the international treaties it has signed. In order to get so many countries to agree, any UN treaty is often worded quite generally, so as not to infringe national sovereignty. With the treaties on drugs, a number of countries have interpreted the treaties as giving each state room for maneuver in deciding how to apply the law. So for example, in a number of European countries including Italy, Spain, Portugal, and Belgium, little or no action is taken against a person caught in possession of a small amount of any drug which is for their personal use.

A number of countries have also adopted various public health "harm reduction" measures. There are measures taken to reduce the collateral damage caused by drug use as part of a realization that simply stamping out drug use is not possible. Such measures include the provision of needle exchange schemes, the prescribing of heroin to users, and the provision of "safer injecting rooms" under medical supervision.

At one time, there appeared to be a international consensus that supported the full maintenance of the Prohibition system. It would seem now that, perhaps with global efforts more focussed on international terrorism, at least in the West, that this consensus may be gradually breaking down. Then again, maybe not. Drug policy, like any other government policy, can be changed if a different government with opposing political viewpoints is elected to power. So for example, Australia, which has been a pioneering country in harm reduction, is looking again at some of its policies. A more right-wing government in Holland is considering restricting the purchase of marijuana to Dutch nationals, and France is now planning to take a tougher line against marijuana use.

BELOW: Young people often find it hard to accept that a drug like marijuana is illegal while adults can legally use drugs which seem much more harmful such tobacco which kills millions of people a year across the planet.

SECTION 1

Depressants

Alcohol
Tranquillizers
Barbiturates
GHB
Solvents
Amyl nitrite
Methaqualone

Depressant drugs can be divided into two main types or categories:

1. Sedative/hypnotics
2. Minor tranquillizers

The word "depressant" actually has nothing to do with depression. It refers to the action of this group of drugs "depress" or dampen down the functions of the brain and other parts of the body's central nervous system

BENZODIAZEPINES

Dalmane 30 mg

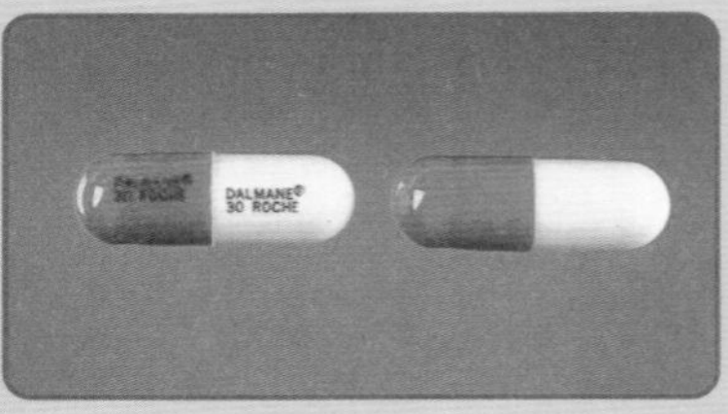

Serax 15 mg

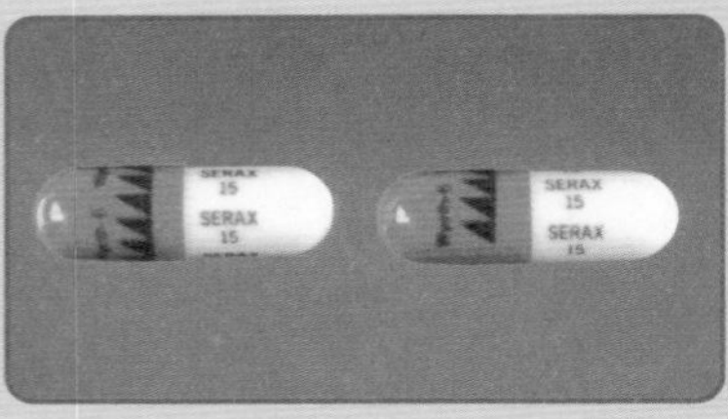

Halcion 5 mg

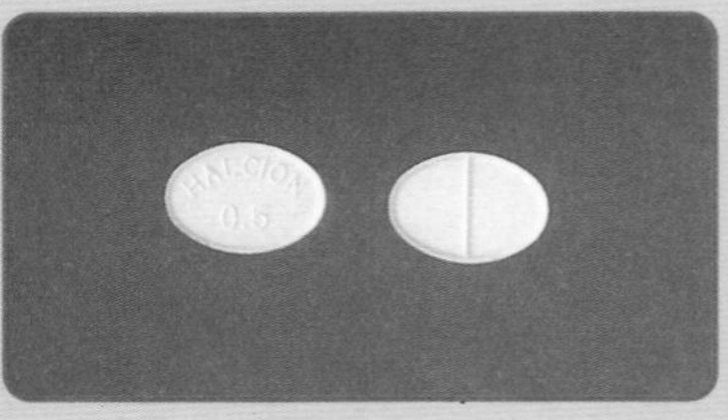

Halcion 25 mg

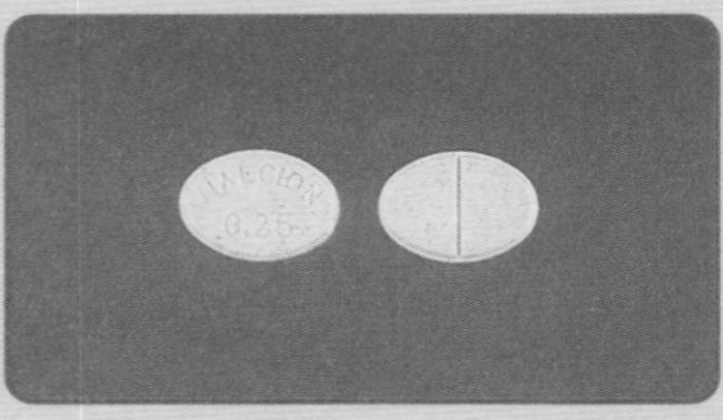

Oxazepam 15 mg

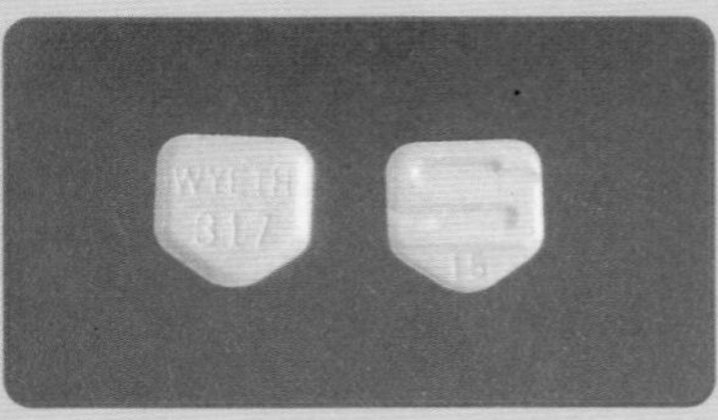

Oxazepam 30 mg

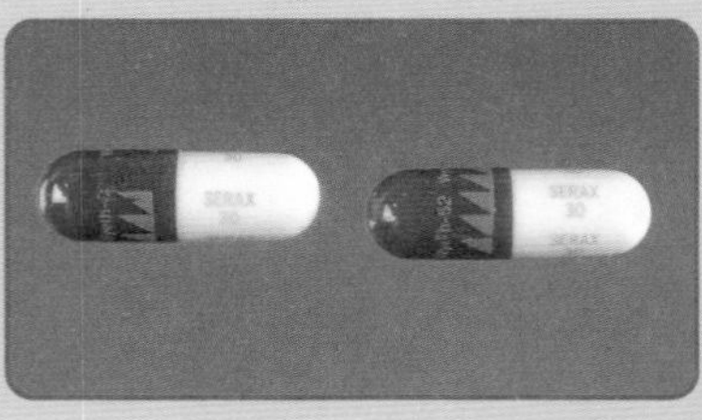

(CNS) by calming people or sending them to sleep. These drugs include alcohol and all the drugs labeled as sleeping pills, the most important of which are barbiturates and benzodiazepines. Other substances which have a similar action on the brain include gammahydroxybutyrate (also known as GHB) and solvents such as glue, aerosols, and lighter fuel which have a record of misuse mainly by young people.

Restoril 15 mg

Restoril 30 mg

Xanax 0.5 mg

Xanax 1 mg

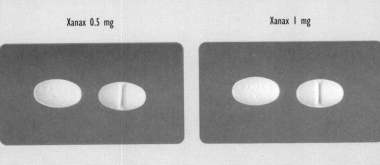

Tranxene 15 mg

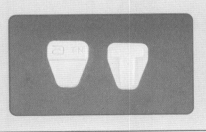

ABOVE: There is a whole range of benzodiazepine tranquillizers. They are useful in helping people sleep and to deal with short-term anxiety and trauma. However, there are millions of people who have become drug dependent.

HISTORY OF USE

The oldest sedative/hypnotic drug is alcohol which dates back to at least 6400 BC and the fermentation of beer and wine. Some historians have traced the making of mead with honey as far back as 8000 BC. Over time, and as with many drugs, scientific progress has enabled the production of ever stronger forms of alcohol such as the distillation of spirits like gin, whiskey, and rum.

Until the nineteenth century, alcohol was the only depressant-type drug available, but with developments in medicine and pharmacology, new sedative/hypnotic drugs were developed. The first of these were paraldehyde followed by chloral hydrate, which is still favored by some doctors because there is less of a hangover feel with this sedative/hypnotic and because there is less respiratory depression during sleep than with the barbiturates. Bromides were also introduced during the nineteenth century including potassium bromide which was used to reduce libido in soldiers.

Barbiturates first appeared in the early twentieth century and became very widely prescribed as sleeping pills. With the advent of

LEFT: Although a depressant drug, alcohol can have the paradoxical effect of making individuals extremely stimulated and aggressive as demonstrated by the number of alcohol related fights which break out in bars and clubs.

benzodiazepine tranquillizers in the 1960s, the prescription of barbiturates began to decline, not least because of the difference between the ordinary therapeutic dose and a lethal dose was worryingly small and overdosing was common in patients. Another sedative/hypnotic drug much in evidence during the 1960s and 1970s was methaqualone marketed as Mandrax in the UK and Quaaludes in the US.

The benzodiazepine tranquillizers, especially diazepam (Valium), revolutionized the prescription of sedative/hypnotics mainly because they were much safer in overdose and there were claims that dependence was far less likely than with older drugs of this type. Such claims proved to be unfounded.

ACTION ON THE BODY

CNS depressants produce a range of effects from mild sedation and relaxation to anaesthesia, coma, and death from respiratory failure. There is great variation between them in terms of the dosages needed for specific effects and the amount of time a single dose is effective in the body.

Low doses produce mild sedation and relaxation, but the actual effects will depend on the mental state of the person who is taking the drug. The psychiatric patient suffering from anxiety will experience some drowsiness and reduced anxiety; the "normal" person will simply feel less inhibited and mildly stimulated. With moderate dose levels, the effects are quite marked—everything from slurred speech to an inability to operate machinery or drive safely. Like alcohol, at these dose levels, some people can become hostile and aggressive, while others will "mellow out" into a pleasant stupor.

Higher doses of sedative/hypnotics are enough to produce anaesthesia, but they are rarely used in these circumstances because of the possible uncontrollable and dangerous side-effects including respiratory collapse.

MEDICAL USES

In the main, these drugs are prescribed to combat chronic sleep disorders and general anxiety and also to deal with times of acute distress and trauma like bereavement. However, one major problem is that tolerance to the sedative effects of these drugs develops quickly and they stop working after only a few weeks of use. Another problem is that while sleep is induced, patients often complain that they do not feel rested. This is because sedative/hypnotics suppress REM sleep, which is the period in the sleep cycle that is important for "a good night's sleep."

MISUSE

The sedative/hypnotic (indeed the drug) which causes most problems in society is alcohol—associated with a whole range of anti-social behaviors

from dangerous driving and domestic violence to street fighting and random acts of delinquency. Alcohol related disease is responsible for four percent of global deaths and disability. There have long been concerns about over-prescribing and extended, repeat prescriptions of benzodiazpeine tranquillizers by doctors long past the period when they were clinically effective. Barbiturates are notorious for the ease which with people can overdose either accidentally or be used as a mechanism for suicide. GHB acts as a sedative/hypnotic and has gained recent notoriety as a major "date rape" drug. The misuse of solvents which have a sedative/hypnotic effect, has been a concern since the 1960s, especially as their use is associated in particular with very young children. Deaths in the UK are still running at one to two a week every year.

Whether or not somebody becomes an alcoholic will depend on a range of factors beyond simply the amount they drink. An individual can be a heavy drinker and possibly be causing physical damage to their body without necessarily becoming an alcoholic. The heavy drinker might confine his or her drinking to social occasions, whereas the person who is drinking to deal with problems may be consuming alcohol first thing in the morning and also drinking alone.

Some scientific research suggests a genetic link in alcoholism, although this might simply be learned behavior

as a child sees alcohol as the way a parent copes with problems. Withdrawal from alcohol (and also barbiturates) can be life-threatening and should only be attempted under medical supervision. Because of their capacity to induce a sense of well-

ABOVE: Mixing depressant drugs is one of the most common means by which people overdose.

being and also problem-obliterating stupor, any of the sedative/hypnotics might well induce a psychological dependence in an individual.

Alcohol

Booze, hooch, liquor

WHAT IS IT?

Alcoholic drinks chiefly consist of water and ethyl alcohol (or "ethanol"), produced by the fermentation of fruits, vegetables, or grain. Beer is about one part ethanol to twenty parts water (five percent or less alcohol), wine is about twice to

four times as strong (nine to twelve percent alcohol), and distilled spirits such as whiskey, rum, and gin are made up of almost fifty percent ethanol, with remaining percentage being water (forty percent plus).

A different kind of alcohol, produced from wood (methyl alcohol), is used in methylated spirits and surgical spirit. Some down-and-out alcoholics ("meths" drinkers) use these products because of their cheapness. Methyl alcohol is extremely poisonous and frequently causes blindness, coma, and death from acidosis.

HISTORY

Early history

The use of alcohol goes back to the earliest days of recorded history. The selective cultivation of grape vines for making wine is believed to originated in the mountains between the Black and Caspian seas (modern Armenia) between 6000–4000 BC. Between 3000–2000 BC, beer making grew in the Sumerian/Mesopotamian civilization (modern day Iraq) with recipes for over twenty varieties of beer recorded on clay tablets. During the same period wine production and trade became an important part of Mediterranean commerce and culture.

LEFT: Intoxication with alcohol is our oldest method of changing the way we feel going back into pre-history when our ancestors would have discovered the joys of eating fermented fruit.

ABOVE: The idea of using alcohol to "toast" somebody's good health and wishing them well, derives from a ceremony in ancient Rome where a piece of toasted bread was dropped into wine.

For as long as there has been alcohol, there have been problems with public drunkenness. There are even hieroglyphics from Ancient Egypt which warn that if anybody fell down drunk in the street that nobody would help them and they would be held up to shame and ridicule. In ancient Rome, it was an offense to be drunk in charge of a chariot.

Europe

It was in Italy around 1100 AD that alcohol was first distilled into "spirits," so named because it was extracted from the "spirit of the wine." From those early experiments, grain alcohol was also distilled during the Middle Ages. At a time when ordinary water was often not fit for human consumption, beer and wine were staple drinks. Alcohol was also believed to have medicinal properties; the Gaelic word "whiskey" means "water of life." In a real sense it was because alcohol kills bacteria and offered some level of protection against the virulent diseases of the day including typhoid, cholera, and all manner of food poisoning.

But there were problems brewing (quite literally) for western society. The enormous social and economic upheavals caused by increasing urbanization coincided with the creation of ever more potent forms of alcohol. Drunkenness was already a crime in England by 1575, but at the same time gin was developed in Holland by distilling grain with the juniper berry and the gin industry grew rapidly in England after it was introduced by English soldiers fighting in the Low Countries. The result in London was rampant drunkenness on a scale never before seen.

United States

Concurrently, the authorities in Massachusetts were attempting to control widespread drunkenness, particularly from home-brews, and to supervise taverns. But by 1860, a total of 138 legal alcohol distilleries were operating in the US producing eighty-eight million gallons of liquor per year. To many this industry was

regarded as a national disgrace, and powerful alliances were formed between moral and religious groups who, over many years of campaigning and lobbying, eventually succeeded in seeing the Volstead Act passed, ushering in the period of Prohibition. There were some health benefits, levels of cirrhosis apparently fell, but the public did not support the Act and it was repealed in 1933. The major fallout from the experiment was to accelerate the creation of organized crime, which learnt about the huge

profits to be made from servicing the vices of the population. Since then, the US, like many other societies, has learnt to live with alcohol and the substantial tax revenues derived from its sale. On the other hand, while fewer people actually die from the effects of alcohol than tobacco, the impact on society at large is arguably far greater. In the US alone, there are between 80,000–100,000 alcohol-related deaths each year.

A recent phenomenon in drinks industry have been Alcopops. These are cocktail-style fruit-flavored alcoholic drinks where the flavor masks the level of alcohol. Although the drinks industry deny these have been targeted at young people, observers claim that these drinks were produced in direct response to the rising use of club drugs like ecstasy at the expense of drink sales. Whatever

BELOW: Alcohol is responsible for substantial amounts of crime. The criminal justice system spends millions dealing with everything from disorderly conduct and domestic violence to drunken driving.

the reason, they have proved to be a huge success.

United Kingdom

In the UK there are particular concerns about the level of binge drinking especially by young women at a time when the licensing laws are being relaxed. Home Office research has shown that alcohol is the root cause of nearly half of all violent crime, and of seventy percent of hospital emergency and accident weekend-night admissions.

The government is trying to attempt to reduce underage drinking through "sting operations" to catch pubs, clubs, and shops selling alcohol to underage people. The industry's lobby group, the British Beer and Pub Association (BBPA), is calling for irresponsible operators to be sacked. The BBPA, which represents half of the pubs in the UK, recently tightened its code to curb various forms of "happy hours" that encourage binge drinking. Local authorities in towns and cities have also been given new powers to penalize licensees who breach the law.

The global situation

Globally, alcohol is a contributory factor to a huge proportion of crimes.

Exact figures vary from country to country, but in many countries alcohol is a contributory factor in sixty to seventy percent of violent crimes, including child abuse, domestic violence, sexual assault, and murder. Alcohol is far and away the leading cause of public disorder, street fighting, and a whole raft of other anti-social behaviors—and there is also the death toll from drunk driving. Alcohol is estimated to cause about twenty to thirty percent of worldwide oesophageal cancer, liver cancer, cirrhosis of the liver, homicide, epilepsy, and motor vehicle accidents.

The World Health Organization calculates that there are around 76.3 million persons with alcohol use disorders worldwide. Unintentional injuries alone account for about one third of the 1.8 million deaths, while neuro-psychiatric conditions account for close to forty percent of the 58.3 million DALYs or Disability Adjusted Life Years. This is the sum of years of potential life lost due to premature mortality and the years of productive life lost due to disability.

Globally alcohol consumption has increased in recent decades, with all or most of that increase happening in developing countries. This increase is often occurring in countries with little tradition of alcohol use within its own population level and few methods of prevention, control, or treatment. The areas of the world with the highest burden of alcohol-related disease are

the states of the former Soviet Union and Central and South America.

EFFECTS

Alcohol is absorbed into the bloodstream and starts to have an effect within five or ten minutes, lasting up to several hours, depending on the amount of alcohol consumed. How much effect a drink has, depends on its strength and how quickly it is drunk, whether there is food in the stomach, and the body weight and mood of the drinker. Since tolerance develops, the effects will also depend on how much the person is used to drinking.

The US National Institute on Alcohol Abuse and Alcoholism (NIAAA) suggests that a safe drinking level for most adults, a moderate alcohol use would be up to two drinks per day for men and one drink per day for women and older people. One drink equals one 12-ounce bottle of beer, one 5-ounce glass of wine, or 1.5 ounces of 80-proof distilled spirits.

After the equivalent of about two pints of beer, most people would feel less inhibited and more relaxed. Emotional reactions range from jovial to aggressive, depending on the circumstances and individual

LEFT: Prohibition in the US did bring down the incidence of liver disease between 1919–1933, but it also fueled the rise of organized crime and the scheme failed because it did not have the support of the people.

predisposition. Somebody who is naturally aggressive could become even more so under the influence of alcohol. The efficiency of mental and physical functioning is reduced. After another two pints, drinkers generally become rather uncoordinated and slur their words a little: emotional reactions can become highly exaggerated and variable. Somebody who was feeling depressed at the start of a drinking bout will often feel even lower as a result of "drowning their sorrows." More drinks might result in staggering, double vision, and loss of balance, followed by unconsciousness. Generally, though, people try to take enough alcohol to feel pleasantly relaxed, and not so much as to lose control of themselves.

There is some evidence to show that moderate drinking might be medically beneficial. Studies have shown that moderate drinkers—men who have two or less drinks per day and women who have one or less drinks per day— are less likely to die from one form of heart disease than are people who do not drink any alcohol or who drink

LEFT: Safer drinking guidelines have been issued by health experts around the world. For men drinking ordinary strength beer, this would be around one to two pints a day.

more. It's believed that these smaller amounts of alcohol can help to protect against heart disease by changing the blood's chemistry, thus reducing the risk of blood clots in the heart's arteries.

In the average adult, alcohol metabolizes out of the body's system at a rate of 0.3 ounces of absolute alcohol—or roughly one pint of ordinary strength beer.

HEALTH RISKS

At higher doses, apart from increased extremes of mood and behavior, drinkers can experience significant memory failure or blackouts where, the following day, they cannot recall part or even all of the previous evening. Heavy drinking is invariably followed by a heavy, drugged sleep from which it can be very hard to wake the person. When they do come round, they are likely to complain of a hangover which is in effect a mild set of withdrawal symptoms.

Mixing with other drugs

Alcohol, more than any other drug, is used in conjunction with other

LEFT: The current record for the world's strongest beer is held by the Boston Beer Co. whose Sam Adams Utopias and Millennium brands are 24% ABV.

substances. Alcohol exaggerates the effects of other drugs which depress the nervous system. Taken with benzodiazepines or barbiturates, for example, it produces a very drunken-like state, which can result in unconsciousness and possibly overdose. Vomiting while unconscious is also a common cause of drug-related deaths. Similar effects are common if drunk with opiates, antihistamines, solvents, and cannabis. Many drug-related deaths may not have happened if alcohol had not been consumed at the same time.

Overdose

Excessive amounts of alcohol consumed at one time can result in alcohol poisoning and death. Many young people who are not used to the effects of alcohol have died in this way, sometimes as the result of games of dare—although these deaths rarely make the front pages. When drunk people pass out, their bodies continue to absorb alcohol. This can push up the blood/alcohol level to dangerous or even fatal levels of 600–900 mg per 100 ml. People are often sick in these circumstances, but because the alcohol has dampened down the vomit reflex, it gets trapped in the lungs and the person can literally drown in alcohol or choke

Long-term use

As with most drugs, effects are related to dose, and some of the extreme forms of physical damage, such as liver cirrhosis are only commonly seen after substantial tolerance has developed and the individual has become heavily dependent (an "alcoholic"). Damage may occur as a direct effect of alcohol in the body, or because of the lifestyle associated with or encouraged by heavy drinking. For instance, alcohol supplies calories but no other dietary essentials; so heavy drinking encourages obesity with its attendant dangers and an inadequate diet with consequent protein and

BELOW: The most expensive whiskey is Macallan Scotch whiskey vintage collection worth $170,000.

RIGHT: Twelve countries have no minimum legal age for drinking alcohol including China, Jamaica, Nigeria, Poland, Thailand, and Vietnam. Officially the highest minimum age of any country is the US at 21.

vitamin deficiencies. In alcoholics, these dietary deficiencies allied with stomach and liver disorders can result in incapacitating brain damage.

Women

At whatever dose level, the effects on women are likely to be more acute because of smaller body size and because they have a larger percentage of body fat which causes higher concentrations of blood alcohol than in men drinking the same amount. Also oral contraceptives slow down the rate at which alcohol is eliminated from the body. Possibly because of the way alcohol is eliminated from the body, women are also at greater risk

of suffering from liver damage, damage to the pancreas, and high blood pressure.

Pregnancy

Women drinking six units or more a day while pregnant may give birth to babies with withdrawal symptoms, facial abnormalities, and lasting retardation of physical and mental development. Cases of this "foetal alcohol syndrome" are rare though. Lesser degrees of regular drinking may result in less serious effects such as lowered birth-weight, but there is little evidence that moderate drinking (for example, up to two units a day) causes significant harm to the mother or baby.

DEPENDENCE

Chronic alcohol consumption increases the body's capacity to metabolize the drug and so more needs to be consumed to get the desired effect.

As with any drug, an individual can come to depend on the effects of alcohol to get them through social occasions or to cope in stressful situations. But with alcohol, physical dependence is more problematic. Once a person has become physically dependent on alcohol, stopping the drug causes severe withdrawal sickness. These symptoms include headache, nausea, abdominal cramps, and even auditory and visual hallucinations. Worse still, the person can suffer major seizures and can die if not treated. The final and most protracted phase is known as the DTs, delirium tremens where the person can appear extremely confused and disoriented with a very high temperature and rapid heartbeat. Hallucinations at this phase can resemble formication—the feeling that insects are crawling all over your skin—similar to amphetamine psychosis. This period can last for three or four days.

Excessive drinking commonly aggravates family, personal, and

financial problems, often contributing to family breakdown, or to repeated violence and other forms of crime associated with a loss of self-control.

THE LAW

Most countries tolerate alcohol drinking with the exception of Islamic countries where it is totally forbidden and harsh punishments await those who break the law. Some states in the US are "dry" and there are by-laws in some British cities which forbid the consumption of alcohol in any public place, such as on the street. The laws that pertain to drinking alcohol relate to: the age at which young people can be served alcohol either by a storekeeper or bartender; the availability of alcohol (for example pub or bar opening times); the permitted blood/alcohol level above which a driver is breaking the drink-driving laws.

BELOW: Although quite rare, babies born to alcoholic mothers may display the symptoms of foetal alcohol syndrome characterized by facial deformities and lasting developmental and physical health problems.

Tranquillizers

Benzodiazepines, sleeping pills, tranx, roofies

WHAT IS IT?

Tranquillizer is the name given to a drug that has the capacity to reduce feelings of anxiety and neurotic behavior. They produce a state of calmness, or tranquillization, and exist as two main categories: major tranquillizers (also known as antipsychotics) and minor tranquillizers (the benzodiazepines). Benzodiazepines have four distinct effects: anxiolytic (reduce stress), anticonvulsant (prevent or relieve convulsions), muscle relaxant, and sedative/hypnotic (induces sleep). They are used to treat a variety of

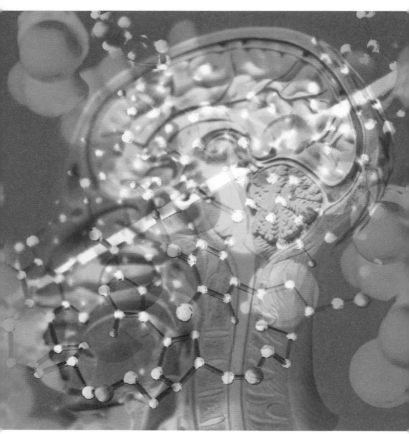

conditions such as anxiety disorders, agitation, muscle spasms, seizures, insomnia, and conscious sedation (pre-surgery).

HISTORY

The first benzodiazepine, introduced in 1960, was Librium (chlordiazepoxide), followed shortly by the arrival of Valium (diazepam) in 1963, with new variations such as temazepam being introduced to the market as late as 1981. The lower fatality rates from acute toxicity and overdose, the more favorable side effect profile, lower potential for abuse, and lower potential for interaction with other drugs all contributed to the wide acceptance of tranquillizers among doctors and increased usage for treatment of anxiety and insomnia.

By the mid-1970s the benzodiazepines became among the most widely used of all prescribed medicines. Indeed, in some countries benzodiazepines were available (and still are, especially in the Middle East and the developing world) without prescription, and usage is even greater than in countries where they remain Prescription Only Medicines (POM). However, although the

LEFT: Due to the reduced risk of overdose, tranquillizers took over from barbiturates as the most prescribed drug for anxiety and sleep problems. Unfortunately, the promise that they would also be less addictive proved false.

benzodiazepines are safer in overdose than the barbiturates they largely replaced, there are continuing concerns about the levels of prescribing where patients may be returning for repeat prescriptions for months or even years on end—long after the drugs have actually stopped working and with little or no further medical assessments.

Over the years, there have been several court cases, both on behalf of individuals and so-called "class actions" where the pharmaceutical companies have been accused of not warning the medical profession, and therefore the public, about the dependency potential of these drugs.

MEDICAL USES

Benzodiazepines act primarily by enhancing the inhibitory effects of the chemical gamma-aminobutyric acid or GABA in the brain, which in effect dampens the brain's activity, as well as indirectly affecting brain chemicals such as serotonin.

Benzodiazepines fall roughly into two categories, the medium-acting and the long-acting. The former include lorazepam and temazepam, the latter chlordiazepoxide and diazepam. Medium-acting compounds last for roughly six to eight hours and are usually taken three to four times a day. The effects of these compounds can often vary in strength. Long-acting benzodiazepines are usually taken once daily, often at night to

Temazepam

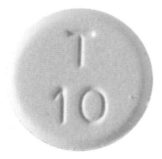

Lormetazepam

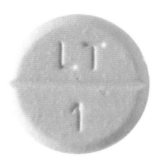

Bromazepam

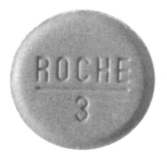

Nitrazepam (Mogadon)

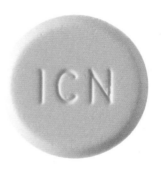

Loprazolam

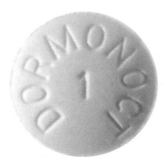

Lorazepam (Ativan)

Clorazepate dipotassium

induce sleep, as they tend to last for longer in the body. Long-acting drugs may take a few days to exert their maximum effect as they build up in the body. Conversely, their effects will take a few days to wear off.

It is the physical characteristics such as onset and duration of action that determine which particular benzodiazepine is prescribed to each patient. Long-acting ones are used primarily as hypnotics and shorter-acting forms are used to treat states of anxiety and are used for seizure control. The main uses for benzodiazepines are:

Anxiolytic

In an ideal clinical environment, these would only be used when the anxiety is so debilitating that it interferes with the patient's lifestyle, work, and interpersonal relationships. In practice, they tend to get prescribed indiscriminately for a host of "stress-related" conditions many of which are unjustified such as for bereavement where it is now thought that the psychological adjustment to the death is inhibited by the use of the drugs

LEFT: Benzodiazepines are the most commonly used anti-anxiety drugs. There are approximately twenty benzodiazepines currently available and they are categorized according to whether they are relatively short-acting (six to ten hours) such as Ativan or longer-acting ones, which can last into the next day, such as Librium and Valium. Together with Temazepam, these top the prescribing list.

and the patient is especially vulnerable to developing dependence.

Benzodiazepines can also be used to alleviate "normal anxiety"—the anxiety felt when under stress, threatened by life's problems, or when nothing seems to go right. In these instances the drug prescribed is used if the stress is understood and the degree of anxiety seems to be in proportion to the stress.

The borderline between the clinical generalized anxiety disorder and normal stress responses is not clear-cut and the use of benzodiazepines to lessen normal anxiety has been criticized as the unnecessary "medicalization" of everyday social problems.

Benzodiazepines can be combined with other medicines and used to treat a host of physical conditions in which anxiety and emotions play a role. In the past this had led to widespread prescription for "psychosomatic illnesses" like high blood pressure, peptic ulcer, and skin disease.

The benzodiazepines used for the "short-term" relief of severe anxiety include diazepam which effects can endure for a fairly long period of time. Shorter acting benzodiazepines such as lorazepam (Ativan), oral or injected, tend to be predominantly used in acute psychiatric inpatient conditions where rapid tranquillization is often desired. Lorazepam is also used to treat panic disorders.

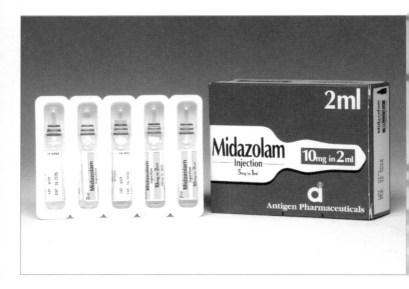

ABOVE: The withdrawal symptoms from benzodiazepines can be very distressing and potentially life threatening with fits and convulsions. These drugs should never be stopped quickly and a doctor should always be consulted.

Hypnotics

Hypnotics are prescribed for cases of short-term, transient insomnia and nitrazepam is the most commonly used. Because the drug's effects last for a long time, it can take a while to leave the body, often producing a hangover effect for the user in the morning.

Other uses

Many of the benzodiazepines are used in the treatment of other conditions. Diazepam is used to help relax muscles or relieve muscle spasm. Chlordiazepoxide, clorazepate, diazepam, and oxazepam are all used to treat the symptoms of alcohol withdrawal. Where as Clobazam, clonazepam, clorazepate, diazepam, and lorazepam are used in the treatment of certain convulsive (seizure) disorders, such as epilepsy.

EFFECTS

The most common effects are the feelings of tiredness and drowsiness, and they are most marked within the first few hours after large doses. Complaints from patients about drowsiness generally recede after the first week, as the body builds up a tolerance for the drug.

HEALTH RISKS

The drowsiness caused by benzodiazepines means that driving, operating dangerous machinery, and

TYPES OF TRANQUILLIZERS

Xanax 1 mg

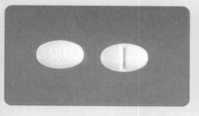

Xanax 0.5 mg

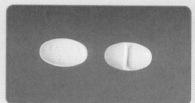

Dalamane 15 mg

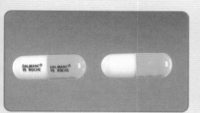

Dalamane 30 mg

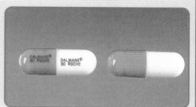

Librium 10 mg

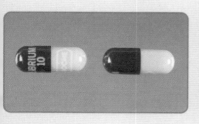

Librium 5 mg

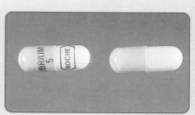

Oxazepam 15 mg

ABOVE: Studies show that tranquillizers, even when correctly prescribed, may interfere with the ability of some users to perform certain physical, intellectual, and perceptual functions. Driving or tasks requiring concentration and co-ordination may be a problem.

similar activities should be avoided. As with many drugs, benzodiazepines can interact with other drugs. Alcohol and benzodiazepines increase each other's sedative action and marked impairment may occur, as do other depressants such as opiates.

The psychological effects of single and repeated doses of benzodiazepines in normal volunteer subjects have been extensively studied; many short-term impairments have been found with respect to fine movements, manual dexterity, intellectual activities, and memory. In anxious people, however, psychological impairment is more difficult to detect because anxiety itself impairs performance.

Occasionally benzodiazepines produce paradoxical, stimulant effects, such as increased aggression and hostility, uncharacteristic petty criminal activities such as shoplifting, sexual improprieties, or offenses such

VALIUM

BELOW: Stanley Adams became famous in the 1970s for exposing Valium manufacturers, Hoffman La Roche who were fined by the European Court.

2 mg

5 mg

10 mg

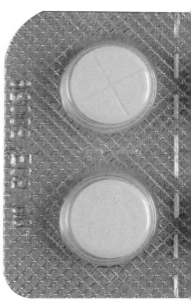

as importuning or self-exposure, and excessive emotional responses such as uncontrollable weeping or giggling. These reactions are most marked in initial anxious patients and are common during the first few weeks of treatment or following an increase in the dosage. Such reactions usually subside spontaneously or after lowering the dosage. Some people are not able to, or simply just don't connect these feelings with taking the drug, which further compounds a confused state.

Benzodiazepines can effect breathing in those who already have respiratory problems such as bronchitis and emphysema. Other side effects which may occasionally be seen include excessive weight gain, skin rash, impairment of sexual function, menstrual irregularities, and, rarely, blood abnormalities.

Most of the side effects lessen over time. However, some impairments, particularly involving memory, may continue, although people can learn to live with this. For example, many people thus effected resort to written lists to jog their memories.

Rohypnol and date rape

Rohypnol (flunitrazepam) has been a particular concern for the last few years because of its abuse as a "date rape" drug. It was marketed in 160 countries, but never approved for use

BELOW: Rohypnol has become notorious as the drug most associated with "date rape" where the victim is sexually assaulted but has no recollection of the attack because the drug induces memory loss.

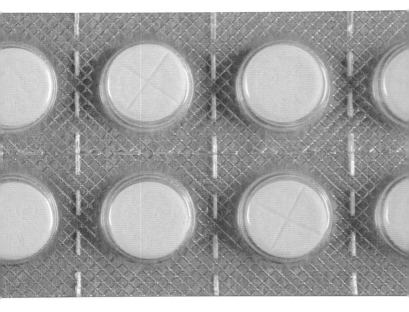

in the US. Ten times stronger than Valium, it can cause paralysis, unconsciousness, and short term amnesia meaning somebody could take the drug and then not recall what happened in the next few hours. The effects begin after only ten minutes and can last up to twelve hours. Higher doses mixed with alcohol can put somebody into a coma for days—and this is exactly what happened to rock singer Kurt Cobain when he mixed rohypnol and champagne just one month before committing suicide. A lethal dose would generally be between seven to fourteen tablets.

BELOW: Although benzodiazepines are safer than previous types of tranquillizer, there is still a high risk of overdose if they are mixed with other depressant drugs.

It was the quick onset of effects, the small undetectable dose needed, the prolonged impact of the drug, and the subsequent amnesia that saw the drug rise to notoriety in the mid-1990s. Women would be given this drug, perhaps slipped into a drink and then wake up hours later, realize they had been sexually assaulted, but have no recollection of what had happened. As the drink would almost certainly be alcohol, the effects were even more potent. Subsequently, because the victim could recall nothing, it made prosecutions very difficult.

In South America Rohypnol was used to rob people. After accepting a drink from a friendly stranger, the unsuspecting and bemused individual would wake up in a nearby alley minus his wallet.

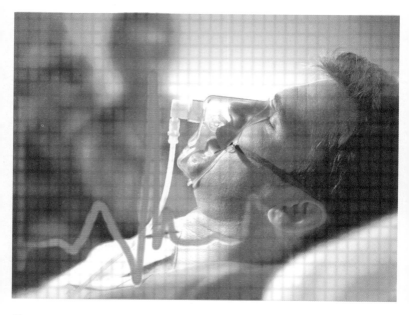

Overdoses

Overdosing with benzodiazepines occurs frequently but death as a result of benzodiazepine use alone is rare. Only in children and the physically frail, especially those with breathing problems, are benzodiazepines hazardous. Those who have taken an overdose become drowsy and fall deeply asleep. However, they are generally rousable and wake after twenty-four to twenty-eight hours.

Long-term consequences

Very few studies have taken the time to investigate whether benzodiazepines continue to lessen anxiety in long-term use. Although people may claim to continue to feel some benefit in being less anxious, the effect of continued use of

ABOVE: Women are advised never to leave their drink unattended or to let strangers buy them drinks as they might be spiked with a date rape drug like Rohypnol.

benzodiazepines may merely be to stop withdrawal symptoms from surfacing. Increasing doubt has been cast on the long-term effectiveness of benzodiazepine tranquillizers. Certainly, when used to induce sleep, benzodiazepines lose their effect in only a few weeks.

Those who inject benzodiazepines and/or share injecting equipment run similar risks to those injecting other types of drugs—namely HIV and AIDS, hepatitis, abscesses, and blood poisoning. The injection of poorly dissolved solid forms of benzodiazepines can block blood

WITHDRAWAL SYMPTOMS:

- psychological symptoms of anxiety: apprehension, mental tension, inattention, irritability, and insomnia.

- bodily symptoms of anxiety: palpitations, tremor, sweating, nausea, stomach cramps, and loss of appetite and weight.

- perceptual symptoms of heightened sensory awareness: sounds seem loud, lights bright. Pain and muscle spasms may be widespread.

- the person feels unsteady and there may be taste/smell abnormalities.

- other symptoms may occur, such a "pseudowithdrawal"—in which the person becomes anxious and apprehensive about the process of withdrawal even before any real reduction in dose has taken place. After withdrawal, panics, phobias, and depression may develop, even though the individual has no previous history of these symptoms.

vessels and may even result in the loss of a limb.

Pregnancy

Benzodiazepines should be avoided during pregnancy wherever possible, as there may be some risk to the baby such as cleft palate and other facial abnormalities. Benzodiazepines also readily pass into the unborn baby's bloodstream and may depress respiration in the newly-born infant. These drugs can also pass into the mother's milk and may then sedate the baby making it sleepy and docile and a poor feeder.

DEPENDENCE

On stopping use, fifteen to thirty-five percent of long-term (over six months) users will have a characteristic withdrawal syndrome, similar to that following barbiturate use and reminiscent of mild delirium tremens—the state of agitated confusion sometimes seen in withdrawing alcoholics. After abrupt discontinuation, especially of doses at

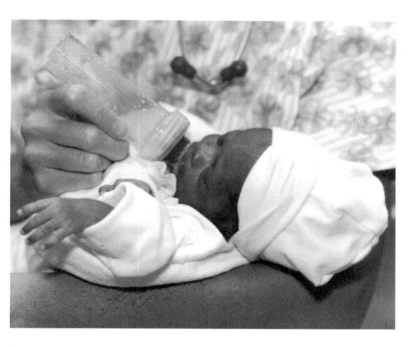

ABOVE: In rare cases, babies of heavy benzodiazepine users may be born with a facial deformity known as a cleft palate.

the upper end of the therapeutic range, a serious illness can come on, with severe paranoid states and confusion and even epileptic seizures that can be life-threatening.

In its mildest and most common form this can represent a "rebound syndrome." For a day or two, or sometimes longer, the person feels jumpy, tense, anxious, and their sleep is poor and broken by nightmares. Panic attacks are common. This happens because the levels of adrenaline in the body have been altered by the chronic use of benzodiazepines. Normally adrenaline is triggered in response to danger (so-called "fight or flight" reactions). If the balance is upset, adrenaline is pumped out when it isn't needed—hence panic attacks. This syndrome merges into more definite withdrawal syndromes. These are characterized by the symptoms listed in the box on the opposite page.

After stopping a benzodiazepine, even after careful tapering of the dose, there may be some delay before the rebound or withdrawal effects can be seen. The delay depends on the drug's rate of clearance from the body, which can take time as benzodiazepines are fat-soluble (and therefore retained in fatty tissue for long periods).

Accordingly, after taking a short-acting compound, withdrawal reactions may occur the next night with grossly disrupted sleep whereas after lorazepam, a medium-duration compound, withdrawal is usually seen within forty-eight to seventy-two hours. After stopping diazepam or one of the other long-acting benzodiazepines, withdrawal may be delayed for up to ten days.

The duration of treatment is an important factor in determining the incidence and perhaps the severity of withdrawal. In one study, patients treated continuously for less than eight months had a five percent incidence of withdrawal reactions. Those treated for longer had an incidence of just over forty percent. If the criteria for withdrawal symptoms are widened to include rebound effects as well, the incidence is much higher and is the rule after treatments as short as four to eight weeks.

Dosage is also an important factor. High-dose users are much more likely to have withdrawal reactions than those maintained on average clinical doses. However, no cut-off point has been identified—patients on even very small doses, such as 5 mg a day of diazepam, may experience symptoms, even after tapering off.

Back in 1980, an expert British medical committee at the beginning of this period "re-concluded that there is 'little convincing evidence' that benzodiazepines were effective in the treatment of anxiety after four months" continuous treatment, but that "the true addiction potential of such drugs was low."

By 1988, the same committee was reporting that benzodiazepine dependency was becoming "increasingly worrying." The committee recommended that benzodiazepines should be used in the lowest possible dose and should not be given for more than four weeks and should be tapered off gradually.

THE LAW

In the US, Rohypnol is the only banned benzodiazepine and its importation is banned. It was the first drug of its type to be more strictly controlled by the United Nations Commission on Narcotic Drugs which oversees the international treaties controlling the manufacture, supply, and use of controlled drugs. In 1996, the US Congress passed the Drug-Induced Rape Prevention and Punishment Act which punishes anyone who administers a drug to somebody without their consent and with the intent to commit a crime. Distribution or importation of 1 g or more carries a penalty of up to twenty years imprisonment.

In the UK, benzodiazepines are a Class C controlled drugs under the Misuse of Drugs Act where it is an offense to be in possession of these drugs without a prescription and unauthorized supply is a serious offense. Benzodiazpines are controlled internationally through the 1972 UN Convention on Psychotropic Substances (signed by nearly 150 countries including all the countries of the EU.) This obliges countries to have in place controls on the possession and supply of benzodiazepines.

BELOW: Despite their legal therapeutic use, many countries have tightened up on the unauthorised supply and possession of tranquillizers.

Barbiturates

sleepers, downers, goofballs, nembies, yellows, seccies, reds, tooeys, blues

WHAT IS IT?

Barbiturates are hypnosedatives, drugs which calm people down (sedatives) and in higher doses act as sleeping pills (hypnotics).

HISTORY

Barbiturates were developed out of barbituric acid discovered in 1864 by the German pharmaceutical company of Beyer. The first medicines were sold in 1903 and since then there have been over 2,500 different kinds of barbiturate on the market. Although barbiturates have pretty much fallen out of favor among both the world's doctors and recreational users, it has been recorded that around four percent of the US population still say they have used these drugs for non-medical purposes, sometimes to counteract the effects of amphetamine or to enhance the effect of heroin.

MEDICAL USES

There are three types of barbiturate, categorized (like tranquillizers) by

BELOW: Barbiturates were discovered by the German chemist Bayer in 1862 on the 4th December, St. Barbara's Day—so the chemist called his new compound "Barbara's Urates."

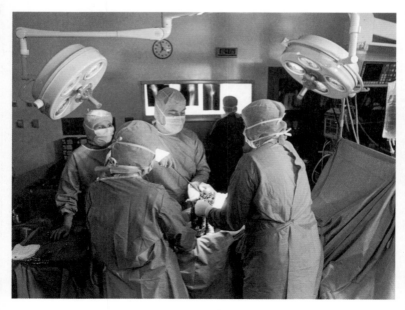

how long they act. Long acting barbiturates work for between twelve to twenty-four hours and include the early types like barbital and phenobarbital used for daytime sedation and mild anxiety. The shorter acting barbiturates like Seconal and Nembutal last for between six to seven hours and are still prescribed for the short-term treatment of insomnia. There are some very short-acting types which cause almost instant unconsciousness and are used in anaesthesia (and also as one of the drugs used in lethal injection executions). It was the shorter-acting ones like Seconal which used to be heavily prescribed as sleeping pills, but they are highly dangerous and have been largely replaced by much safer drugs like benzodiazepines (see the previous section). One barbiturate-type drug, Fioricet, is actually available through online pharmacies.

METHODS OF USE

Barbiturates come in the form of tablets, ampoules, suppositories, solutions, or commonly as colored capsules. They are usually taken by mouth, but may for some specialized medical purposes be injected. Misusers also generally take them

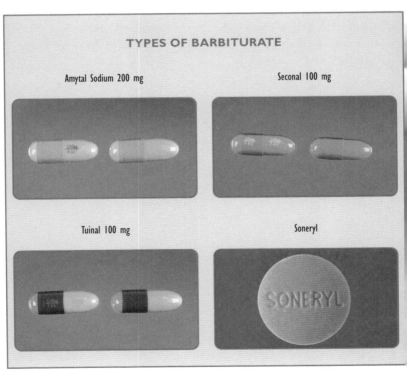

TYPES OF BARBITURATE

Amytal Sodium 200 mg

Seconal 100 mg

Tuinal 100 mg

Soneryl

orally, occasionally with alcohol, but they may also prepare the powders for injection.

EFFECTS

Barbiturates depress the central nervous system in the same way as alcohol and produce similar effects, generally lasting from three to six hours. A small dose (one or two barbiturate pills) usually makes people feel relaxed, sociable, and good humored—a state similar to the feeling aroused after having one or two drinks. With low doses, as with many other drugs, it is possible to "steer" the effect to some extent, but with larger doses this becomes difficult and the sedative effects predominate.

While the desired and common effect is one of pleasurable intoxication or sedation, the result caused is sometimes hostility, depression, and anxiety. When injected into a vein, barbiturates can produce an almost immediate feeling of pleasurable warmth and drowsiness in the user.

HEALTH RISKS

A person trying to keep awake after a moderate to large dose (several pills) will often be clumsy with poor control of speech and body, rendering them liable to accidental injury. There can be extreme, unpredictable emotional reactions and mental confusion, followed by sleep.

Although barbiturates are prescribed for insomnia, regular use does affect sleep patterns; in particular they reduce the amount of REM sleep. This is the period of the sleep cycle where we dream and regular disturbance to this time can cause psychological problems. Heavy users are also liable to bronchitis and pneumonia (because the cough reflex in depressed), hypothermia (because peripheral blood vessels dilate, but the drug blocks normal responses to cold), and repeated accidental overdose (this is due to the mental confusion and tolerance effects, which

means heavy users often take excessive doses.) Prolonged and regular use of barbiturates in the later stages of pregnancy can result in withdrawal symptoms in babies.

Injecting

Most of the hazards discussed are increased if the drug is taken by injection, when infection and a build-up of undissolved tablet in the skin

BELOW: Barbiturates were initially marketed as the new wonder drug, but attracted negative attention when nine members of the Heaven's Gate Cult used phenobarbital to overdose.

tissue may occur. Use of injected barbiturates is possibly the most dangerous form of drug use. Besides the usual hazards, barbiturate injectors especially run an increased risk of overdose, gangrene (if the solution is accidentally injected into an artery), and skin abscesses.

Overdose

Large overdoses cause death from respiratory failure. Deaths of this kind are a real danger among recreational (and other) barbiturate users, as the potentially lethal dose is very close to the normal dose—just ten barbiturate

PP Brings Closure to:

keys to Heaven's Gate are here again in they were in Jesus and His Father 2000 yrs. ago.

ABOVE: Problems with these drugs soon became apparent. They were highly addictive and patients died trying to come off them due to fits, convulsions, and coma during withdrawal. The therapeutic and lethal dose levels were very close and fatal overdoses were common especially if used with alcohol.

pills can be enough to result in a fatal dose. These effects and hazards are magnified if alcohol or other depressant-type drugs have also been taken. Someone already drunk on alcohol might die after taking just half the normally lethal amount of barbiturate pills.

Over the years there have been a number of celebrity deaths involving these drugs both accidental and otherwise including Marilyn Monroe (forty-seven Nembutals), Judy Garland, Jimi Hendrix, and Beatles' manager Brian Epstein. Seconal, in particular, became the drug of choice to numb the effects of all the pressures of being in the public spotlight and all the uncertainties of the entertainment business. Between 1973–1976, barbiturates were implicated in over half of all drug-related suicides. In 1995, the US Food and Drink Administration banned an over-the-counter preparation which combined phenobarbital and theophylline as an overdose risk. In March 1997, thirty-nine members of the Heaven's Gate cult overdosed deliberately on phenobarbital.

DEPENDENCE

After regular use, tolerance and psychological dependence are likely to develop to any sedative, but although more needs to be taken to achieve the same degree of intoxication, the amount needed to cause respiratory failure increases relatively little. Although serious problems of physical dependence are unlikely at normal therapeutic doses, after regular use of higher doses, the withdrawal symptoms can include irritability, nervousness, inability to sleep, faintness and nausea, twitching, and (infrequently) convulsions. After very high doses taken regularly (900 mg a day or more), severe withdrawal symptoms are likely, including, seizures, abnormally decreased blood pressure, delirium, and hallucinations. Sudden withdrawal from very high doses of barbiturates can be fatal and because of this, withdrawal should never be undertaken without proper medical supervision. This process can take up to two weeks, during which the dose is reduced by ten percent each day under supervision. Assuming there are no serious complications, withdrawal effects subside within about a week.

In his novel *The Naked Lunch,* published in 1959, William Burroughs described the chronic barbiturate user like this: "The barbiturate addict presents a shocking spectacle. He cannot co-ordinate, he staggers, falls off bar stools, goes to sleep in the middle of a sentence, drops food out of his mouth. He is confused and quarrelsome and stupid. Barbiturate addicts are looked down on in addict society; 'Goofball bums. They got no class to them'."

THE LAW

In the US, barbiturates appear in both Schedules II and III of the Controlled Substances Act. In the UK, they are controlled as Class B drugs (but Class A if injected) and there are strict limitations on use internationally.

GHB

Liquid ecstasy, liquid X, GBH

WHAT IS IT?

First synthesized in France in 1960, GHB is gammahydroxybutyrate or sodium oxybate—an anaesthetic which primarily induces depressant/sedative effects rather than painkilling properties. GHB is also naturally present in the body in small amounts and in certain ripe fruits such as guava.

MEDICAL USES

In the US, the drug has no recognized medical uses, but in Europe it continues to be used in anaesthesia and for the treatment of insomnia and anxiety and even (as in France) as a drug used at various stages of childbirth, especially to protect the baby from cell damage caused by lack of oxygen (hypoxia). How GHB is

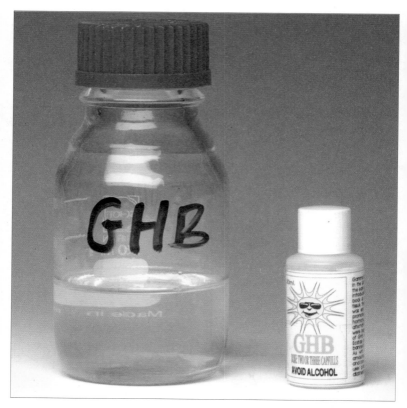

able to do this is still unknown. In the US researchers have applied for GHB to be rated an Investigational New Drug (IND) because they want to test out the value of GHB for a wide variety of conditions from lowering cholesterol to alleviating the symptoms caused by alcohol and opiate withdrawal.

HISTORY

Although its value as an anaesthetic proved limited, the fact that it caused deep sleep made it an attractive commercial proposition as a cure for insomnia and it was sold over the counter in Europe without prescription. The type of sleep promoted by GHB was just the type which aids muscle growth and so GHB became widely available in health food shops and gyms for body-builders. In sub-anaesthetic doses, the drug also creates a dreamy, euphoric state which found favor with dancers at raves—so it became a club drug as well. However, concerns about overdoses and fatalities led to a Federal ban in 1990. In the UK, it became associated with date rape in much the same way as Rohypnol (also known commonly as "roofies"). The profile of the typical GHB user (as researched in the US) reflects the types

LEFT: Illicitly produced GHB comes in small bottles and a capful is roughly one dose. But it is impossible for the buyer to know what the strength of the GHB is in any one bottle.

ABOVE: GHB is another "date rape" drug. Being an odorless, colorless liquid with very little taste makes it virtually undetectable in a drink.

of activities most associated with the drug—white, male body-builders or club-goers aged between eighteen and twenty-five.

METHOD OF USE

GHB is a colorless, odorless liquid with a slightly salty taste, which is sold in small bottles. These bottles might have a warning label advising against drinking alcohol at the same time as taking the contents. It has also been seen in both powder and capsule form.

The typical dose of pure GHB powder is one to three grams dissolved in water or fruit juice. Those with a tolerance to the effects might increase that to four to five grams.

The powder sells for $10–$50 for 100 g and can be dissolved in very little liquid. This means it is impossible for the average user to know how strong the solution is unless you know the original purity of the powder and the amount of liquid it was dissolved in. Part of the reason for the rapid spread of this drug is that it is so easy to produce, requiring only simple chemicals.

EFFECTS

The effects are noticeable from between ten minutes to an hour after taking the drug and have been reported as lasting for as long as twenty-four hours or longer. Like alcohol, in small doses GHB will break down social inhibitions and increase libido. Some users have likened the effect to ecstasy, others to Quaaludes.

HEALTH RISKS

Even at moderate doses, the user might experience blurred vision, impaired physical coordination, and dizziness. Some users can also suffer from caustic burns to the lips and mouth caused when the solvent used to make the drug has not been properly mixed.

At higher doses, the person begins to lose control in much the same way as somebody who is very drunk or high on barbiturates or Quaaludes. Euphoria gives way to powerful sedative effects and there have been

reports of nausea, vomiting, stiffening of muscles, disorientation, convulsions, coma, and respiratory collapse. Because the drug works so quickly, somebody who took too much could be in a coma inside thirty minutes. The depth of coma is measured by the Glasgow Coma Scale where fifteen is a normal reading moving down to three where the person is probably brain dead. Anything below nine is classed as very

serious and will require intervention. A recent study showed that among a group of GHB overdose patients, two-thirds had recorded a GCS score of less than nine and one third were rated as low as three. But although symptoms such as coma can be very frightening for those who witness them, particularly friends and family of the patient, people who have been hospitalized because of these symptoms have made a rapid and full recovery, but remember very little of what happened.

Overdose

In the period 1990–1999, the DEA and the Poisons Control Centers have documented at least 7,000 overdoses and sixty-six deaths. One of those

BELOW: GHB has proved popular with some bodybuilders because it promotes the kind of sleep which is best for protein build-up in the muscles.

ABOVE: Paramedics called to clubs and bars and to deal with GHB intoxicated customers became a regular sight around Los Angeles in the 1990s.

happened in October 1993 when actor River Phoenix collapsed and died outside the Viper Club in Los Angeles. The star of *My Own Private Idaho* had made public anti-drug pronouncements, but Phoenix was a closet rock star and was reportedly attracted to the glamor of "self destruct." He consumed a cocktail of alcohol and drugs including what was then the fashionable drug of the moment, GHB. So ubiquitous did the drug become in such circles that the owner of a high profile nightclub in LA said he was sick of having to call ambulances for people who had crashed out on GHB in the alley behind his club.

users might risk epileptic-type seizures, but these reports are unconfirmed.

DEPENDENCY

Like any drug with sedative effects, there is the potential for physical and psychological dependence. Some withdrawal effects have been reported up to two weeks after using the drug. These symptoms can include dizziness, headache, nausea, vomiting, shaking, amnesia, and some difficulties with breathing.

THE LAW

GHB is a Schedule I drug under the Controlled Substances Act, but a related substance, an industrial solvent, GBL (gamma-butyrolactone) is not. GBL is found in a number of household products. As a commercial product, another industrial solvent BD which converts to GHB once it is ingested, is also legal.

The DEA has banned the illicit use of these substances, but cannot ban the substances themselves. There have been cases where GBL has been sold on the internet with warnings about using it as a solvent only, but these are included to allow them to skirt around the law. It is bought legally online for the same reasons and by the same people who buy illegal GHB. In the UK, GHB is a Class C drug under the Misuse of Drugs Act and many other countries now have controls on possession and sale.

There have been a number of disturbing reports of fatal mixes of GHB and alcohol. Clearly, any dangers will be enhanced from mixing the drug with other sedative drugs and will also be determined by the weight and gender of the person, their general health and so on.

What the effects of long-term use might be are unknown. Some brain research has indicated that long term

Solvents

Glue, lighter fluid, gasoline/petrol, hairspray and other aerosols, marker pens, and similar solvent-based commercial products

WHAT IS IT?

Volatile substance or inhalant misuse (also called "glue sniffing" or "solvent sniffing") is the deliberate inhalation of fumes given off by various solvent-based commercial products in order to achieve intoxication.

The range of possibilities seems endless and young people will substitute one substance for another depending on its availability. The list of substances which have been sniffed by young people is very varied (see the box opposite for a list of just some of these substances).

HISTORY

Use of volatile substances to achieve intoxication is not new—there were crazes for nitrous oxide (laughing gas) and ether sniffing in the nineteenth century (particularly among the wealthy communities and medical students). The sniffing of anaesthetic gas by members of the medical profession has often been reported. It was not until the late 1950s that the modern-day phenomenon of solvent sniffing by young people was first observed. Surveys in the 1990s revealed that around sixteen percent of high school students said they had sniffed solvents at least once. There is

ABOVE: The first reports of glue sniffing came in the early 1960s from the US. Since then it has become a major problem especially among poor minority groups like aborigines and Latin American street children.

particular concern about the use of inhalants by young people from within ethnic groups such as the Native American, Hispanic, and Inuit communities.

METHODS OF USE

Some products can be sniffed directly from their containers. Liquids such as thinners can be poured onto a rag or clothing (lapels and cuffs provide convenient areas for surreptitious sniffing or so-called "huffing"). Glues can also be sniffed in this way, but are more usually poured into a plastic bag

ABUSED SUBSTANCES:

- Balsa wood cement

- Contact adhesive

- Cycle tire repair cement

- Woodworking adhesives

- Polyvinylchloride (PVC) cement .

- Air freshener

- Deodorants, antiperspirants

- Fly spray

- Hair lacquer

- Dust removers (air brushes)

- Commercial dry cleaning and decreasing agents

- Domestic spot removers and dry cleaners

- Fire extinguishers

- Cigarette lighter refills

- "Butane"

- "Propane"

- Nail varnish and nail varnish remover

- Paint sprayers

- Paints and paint thinners

- Paint stripper

- Room odorizers

- Surgical plaster/chewing gum remover

- Typewriter correction fluids and thinners

- Whipped cream dispensers

(usually a chip/crisp bag, freezer bag, or the type available at food store check-outs). Bags are then held closed over the nose and mouth and the vapors inhaled. Air may be breathed into the bag, or the bag may be warmed and pumped up and down which will cause the substance to vaporize more quickly.

In a group of people, the bag (or bags) are often passed around. To increase the concentration of fumes, some users may put their heads completely inside a large plastic bag.

This practice is particularly dangerous if the person falls unconscious and the bag becomes stuck to the nose and mouth, which can then result in suffocation.

Aerosols and butane gas lighter refill containers may be sprayed into a bag and then inhaled or sprayed directly into the mouth by holding the lighter fuel valve between the teeth, or by pressing the teeth against the ball valve found under the plastic nozzle of most aerosols.

ABOVE: Because young people were suffocating by placing a large plastic bag over the head to sniff glue, early (and highly controversial) harm reduction advice was to use smaller bags.

EFFECTS

Inhaled vapors of solvents are absorbed through the lungs and rapidly reach the brain. Feelings include euphoria, dizziness, slurred speech, distorted vision, nausea, and drowsiness. Resultant behavior can be unusually boisterous or emotional depending partly on how the person feels, where they are, and whom they are with. Although the effects of sniffing solvents wears off quickly, some sniffers can remain intoxicated by topping-up the doses.

Many sniffers experience hallucinations, which the user usually has control over. Groups have claimed that they can collectively control jointly experienced hallucinations. Such experiences encourage group solidarity and may make it much harder for individual group members to stop sniffing.

Solvent-related hallucinations can reportedly seem exciting, new, and fun. Even "bad" hallucinations (which seem to be quite common) can be enjoyable in a similar way that images in horror-films are frightening but compelling. Some users like it so much that they may use repeatedly, particularly to avoid boredom or unhappiness.

HEALTH RISKS

At high doses, solvent sniffing can lead to perceptual distortions, delusions, and hallucinations. Most significantly solvents depress the respiratory system—taken in large amounts, breathing can become slow or even stop, leading to coma or

eventually death. Recovery from coma can be generally rapid, although the sniffer may feel drowsy and may have a mild "hangover" (headaches and poor concentration). Traces of some chemicals may be detectable in the body for some weeks after sniffing. Although the intoxicant effect of the substances quickly wears off, the hydrocarbons contained in them are excreted slowly from the body. This may explain why, when neurological effects are evident, these may gradually correct themselves over several weeks.

Deaths

Inhalant misuse is extremely dangerous. There is an ever-present and unpredictable risk of death associated with its use. Many of the recorded deaths have occurred with first-time users.

RIGHT: Sniffers may see pseudo-hallucinations so-called because they know what they are seeing is not real. Groups of sniffers have claimed to see the same illusions.

Most deaths occur as a direct result of substance toxicity. The toxic effects of the substances involved are difficult to determine because of the wide range of complex chemicals involved. Hexane in some glues and lead compounds in some types of gasoline/petrols are examples of the dangerous additives that are to be found in some sniffable products. The issue is further complicated if the substances are being used in conjunction with alcohol or other types of drugs.

If products, such as aerosols and gas fuels, are sprayed directly into the mouth, the sudden cooling of the tissues may cause them to swell and block the airways, resulting in suffocation. Sniffable substances can sensitize the heart to the effects of excitement and exertion, leading to heart arrhythmia (irregular heart beats) and possibly death.

The chances of "sudden sniffing death," as it is sometimes referred to, is further enhanced if the sniffer is

chased or overexcited. Other causes of death include the inhalation of vomit and the use of plastic bags. Accidents are also likely since sniffers may do dangerous things while intoxicated.

Sniffing inflammable products, especially if cigarettes are being smoked at the same time, is clearly risky. Furthermore, much sniffing takes place away from public view, often in potentially dangerous circumstances, such as in derelict buildings and on disused land. In fact, around twenty-five percent of the reported deaths linked to solvent sniffing are caused as a result of solvent-related accidents while twenty-eight percent of deaths are recorded as suicides.

Long-term risks

Overall, it is hard to assess the longer-term health risks. Knowledge of adverse effects and consequences comes mainly from studies in industrial settings where exposure is relatively prolonged but at low concentrations. The high concentrations achieved by sniffing for intoxication can exceed the allowable concentration for industrial purposes by a factor of fifty and are quantitatively and qualitatively different to industrial exposure.

Although the harm resulting from

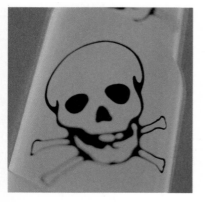

LEFT: In the UK, at least one young person dies from solvent abuse every week. Lighter fuel is implicated in most of the deaths.

ABOVE: Solvent sniffing is mainly associated with younger age groups who do not have the money to buy alcohol or illegal drugs, but use solvents found in every home.

solvent sniffing has not been systematically researched, the following symptoms, although not common, have been observed in individual cases: blurred vision, tinnitus (ringing in the ears), lack of coordination, confusion, muscle weakness, headache, abdominal cramps, chest pain, irritability, belligerence, impaired judgement, and dizziness have been reported.

Those who sniff over a long period may experience nasal bleeding, bad

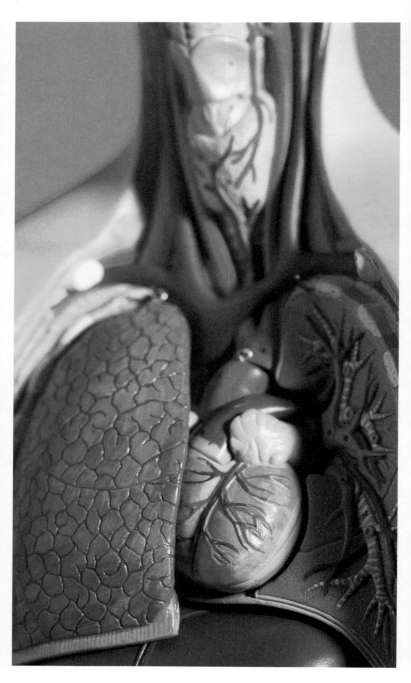

breath, nose ulcers, and eye conditions such as conjunctivitis. Sniffers can become anorexic and there may be general fatigue, loss of concentration, depression, lethargy, irritability, and hostility. Numbness and tingling in the toes and fingers, chronic encephalopathy (inflammation of the brain), and dementia have also been reported after chronic sniffing. Lead poisoning from alkyl-leads used as antiknock agents for car engines have been reported as a complication of gasoline/petrol sniffing.

Brain damage

Chronic abuse of products containing toluene has been associated with permanent organ damage, especially to the kidney, liver, and heart. In one study of chronic toluene abuse, eleven out of twenty-four patients had damage to the part of the brain called the cerebellum. This is the part of the brain that deals with fine muscle movements and may play some part in the learning process. It is not clear whether damage to this area can be halted once the sniffing stops. Memory and attention may also suffer through long term use. However, all research in this area is very tentative because these substances were never meant to be ingested and nobody will

LEFT: Solvents can sensitize the heart to the effects of excitement or exertion leading to irregular heartbeats or even heart failure. Those caught sniffing should not be chased.

ever be able to convince any of the world's ethics committees to grant approval for human research into solvent abuse.

Volatile substances can pass through the placental barrier and enter the foetal bloodstream. At least one study has linked maternal use of toluene with damage similar to that found with foetal alcohol syndrome. Evidence that use of volatile substances can damage the foetus is inconclusive.

DEPENDENCY

Tolerance develops so that after a time a sniffer may have to inhale increasingly large quantities in order to get high. Some susceptible young people, often those with underlying family or personality problems, may develop psychological dependence on the effects of volatile substances. Most misusers tend to stop after a while. In extreme cases however, problem users will seek intoxication on a regular basis, and usually on their own.

THE LAW

Forty-one states in the US have passed some kind of criminal statute relating to inhalant abuse; thirty-one have regulations to do with product formulation, while ten have statutes relating to prevention or treatment. However, there is no Federal law banning the sniffing of solvents because the reality is that because the substances are contained within

perfectly legal substances, any laws are rarely enforced.

In the UK it is an offense for a person to supply or offer to supply to someone under the age of eighteen a substance "if he knows or has reasonable cause to believe that the substance or its fumes are likely to be inhaled for the purpose of causing intoxication." This British law is primarily aimed at irresponsible retailers, but it is difficult to prove that a retailer knew the substances would be sniffed. Because of the

number of deaths associated specifically with butane lighter fuel, retailers must not sell butane gas lighter refills to individuals under the age of eighteen, even if they claim they want it to refill their cigarette lighter. Controls vary in other countries but

ABOVE: Providing the facilities for young people to engage in activities such as sport may help prevent them becoming involved in solvent sniffing.

South Australia, Japan and the Philippines have laws against selling solvents for the purposes of sniffing.

Amyl Nitrite

Poppers plus various brand names like liquid gold, climax, locker room, ram, rock hard, rush, man scent, stud, and TN

WHAT IS IT?

Amyl nitrite is one of three common types of nitrite, the other kinds in this group are butyl nitrite, and isobutyl nitrite. Strictly speaking the term "poppers" applies to amyl nitrite which come in the form of glass capsules or phials that have to be cracked or popped open to release the vapors, hence the street name. Though the slang-name has remained in use when referring to this drug, nitrites nearly always come in small glass screw-top bottles.

BELOW: Somebody once described the effects of sniffing amyl nitrite or poppers as like "being hit in the face with a brick."

Amyl nitrite is a highly flammable, clear to yellow colored liquid that has a sweet and solvent-like scent when fresh but like smells similar to old socks when stale. Poppers are often sold from sex shops, clubs, some bars, and from a few clothes and record shops, also mail order and across the Internet. The fumes are usually sniffed directly from the bottle.

MEDICAL USES

The main medical use employed today for amyl nitrite is as an antidote to industrial cyanide poisoning. It is usually supplied to companies who use cyanide in their manufacturing process. The other alkyl nitrites have no recognized medical use.

HISTORY

The only nitrite with a history of medical application is amyl nitrite. Its ability to dilate (enlarge) the blood vessels was first described in 1859. It was soon identified as a way to reduce blood pressure and ease blood flow. The first report of its use in the relief of angina pectoris was published in the US-based medical journal *The Lancet* in 1867. In 1880, butyl nitrite was also investigated but never put to any medical use.

Amyl nitrite was first marketed as a prescription drug in the US in 1937. It remained so until 1960 when the Food and Drug Administration (FDA) removed the requirement of a prescription and amyl nitrite became an over-the-counter drug. American pharmacists became concerned about apparently healthy young men coming in to buy quantities of the drug. The FDA were alerted and although no ill effects were actually cited at the hearings in 1968, the FDA re-introduced its "prescription-only" status for nitrites.

Once amyl nitrite was removed from general circulation, closely related butyl nitrite products proliferated, marketed as "room odorizers" to circumvent the laws regulating the sales of medicines. All butyl nitrite products were banned in the US in 1988, but the manufacturers used propyl nitrites again to avoid regulation. In 1991 Congress made all nitrite sales illegal if they could be misused as inhalants. From then on production went underground and it is this illicit industry which services demand today.

Recreational use of poppers became popular in the 1950s in showbiz circles in both the US and the UK. Gay men who discovered that the drug's muscle relaxant properties aided anal intercourse and enhanced, and prolonged, orgasms, also adopted poppers. Poppers have also been used as a euphoric trip at dance events. Use began in discos in the 1970s in the US, moving to the disco and then the rave

BELOW: Poppers were marketed as "room deodorizers" because of their strong smell, but they subsequently became very popular within the gay community because one of their effects is that it relaxes the muscle around the anal sphincter aiding anal intercourse.

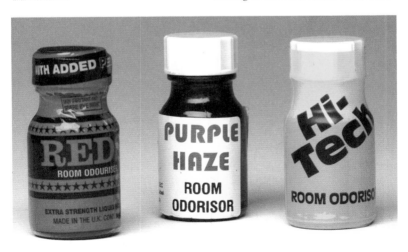

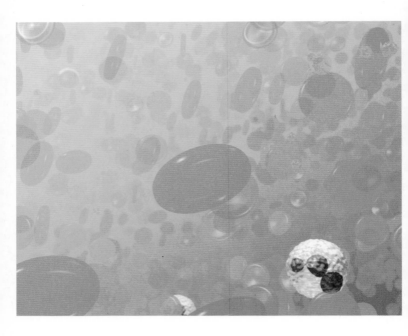

ABOVE: Methaemoglobinaemia is a condition associated with amyl nitrite where oxygen is reduced in the blood causing acute anaemia.

scene in Europe, often in combination with other drugs. The late 1980s and early 1990s saw use of poppers becoming more widespread in the European leisure scene.

METHOD OF USE

Amyl nitrite is produced in 10 ml bottles retailing for about $4–$15 a bottle. There may be some toxicological differences between the various alkyl nitrites, but generally in terms of their effects and the consequences of use, there seems little to choose between them. There are reports of people dipping a cigarette in the bottle and then inhaling deeply through the cigarette which could be highly dangerous if the cigarette happened to be lit due to the drug's highly flammable nature.

EFFECTS

Although not technically stimulants, all the nitrites cause stimulant-like effects because they open up the blood vessels which causes a rush to the head. The effect of inhaling the vapors is almost instantaneous and very short-lived. Users feel light-headed and experience a sense that time is slowing down. People using poppers for sexual pleasure often report a prolonged sensation of orgasm and prevention of premature ejaculation. Poppers also have the effect of relaxing the anal muscles making anal intercourse easier.

HEALTH RISKS

Some of the immediate unpleasant side effects include dizziness, a flushed face and neck, a pounding headache, nausea, and vomiting. One user once commented that the experience of sniffing poppers was like being hit in the face with a brick. Swallowing a large quantity (as opposed to inhaling the fumes) can lead to people losing consciousness. Some deaths have occurred in this way.

One result of having nitrites in the body is the reduction of oxygen in the blood. This is a condition known as methaemoglobinaemia. The level of risk is determined by the percentage of haemoglobin that is converted to methaemoglobin. If levels rise too high the symptoms resemble that of severe anaemia. Thus anybody who suffers from anaemia might put themselves at risk by using poppers. Current literature cites a number of cases of nitrite users admitted to hospital suffering from methaemoglobinaemia. Of these cases most were not fatal and the individuals recovered. Among those who have died, all but one had drunk nitrites rather than sniffed them while another had predisposing heart/blood pressure problems. Users can lose consciousness especially if they are engaged in vigorous physical activity such as dancing or running. Poppers also increase pressure on the eyeball and can prove to be dangerous for people with glaucoma.

Mixing drugs

Poppers are often used in combination with other drugs. Some people say they help boost the effects of drugs like ecstasy and LSD. Combinations of these and other drugs, however, can be dangerous and may lead to unpredictable effects.

Viagra is one drug which is known to cause problems if mixed with poppers. Viagra acts by increasing levels of nitric oxide as well as lowering blood pressure, which facilitates blood flow to the penis. Taking poppers can further increase levels of nitrites and decrease blood pressure to a point where the user runs the risk of passing out or, in extreme circumstances, stroke.

With continual use, tolerance occurs after about two or three weeks. But a similar period of abstinence seems to restore sensitivity. There is no evidence of physical or psychological dependence or any longer-term damage from sniffing poppers, though regular sniffing can result in skin problems around the nose and mouth.

Poppers and AIDS

Probably the biggest controversy surrounding poppers has been the claim that they are implicated in the onset of Kaposi's Sarcoma (KS) in

HIV positive gay men. This was first suggested in the early 1980s when it was revealed that all of the original AIDS cases who manifested KS had also been users of nitrites. Poppers were implicated in two ways, firstly because some of the metabolized by-products of nitrites were shown to be carcinogenic and secondly because nitrites were capable of depressing the immune systems of those using them when compared to non-users.

This evidence, however, is not convincing and further recent studies have not confirmed that nitrites are actually implicated in the development of KS. Even so, poppers are known to impact on the immune system and could be damaging to any individual in an already weakened state due to illness or chronic disease.

THE LAW
Use of amyl nitrites is legal in the US, UK, and across Europe. The sale and manufacture are also banned in the US and UK. These products are technically prescription only medicines, but the reality is that the Internet makes control and regulation by the appropriate authorities virtually impossible.

RIGHT: In the 1980s, before the true cause of HIV was discovered, poppers were implicated in the onset of Kaposi's sarcoma which is a cancer-like disease linked to AIDS that presents in the mouth, nose, and skin.

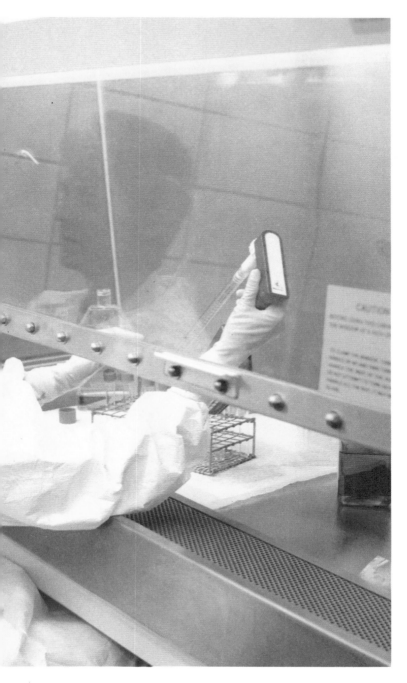

Methaqualone

Quaaludes, 'ludes, mandrax, mandies, sopor

WHAT IS IT?

Methaqualone was a sedative/hypnotic originally developed as a safer non-addictive alternative for barbiturates. It was also marketed as a combination product with an antihistamine called Mandrax.

HISTORY

The drug was developed in India during the 1950s by researchers looking for a cure for malaria. Pharmaceutical companies in the US noted the similarity between this drug and another drug called glutethemide. This was supposed to be the new wonderful, non-addictive depressant until it was found to be even more addictive that barbiturates. So methaqualone appeared on the US market in 1965 under a range of different trade names including Sopor, Optimil, and Quaaludes.

These drugs became very popular on student campuses and in the music business where "'luding out" with methaqualone and alcohol became a regular pastime. In the 1970s, there were nightclubs in New York entirely devoted to Quaalude parties where the only drink available was fruit juice. However, the party was over when more and more reports of overdoses and deaths were coming in—originally from countries like Japan and Germany and then in the US itself.

In 1977, two celebrity deaths brought the situation right into the public eye; actor Freddie Prinz, a Quaalude addict, took twelve of the tablets and shot himself, and Elvis Presley died, reportedly a consumer of a vast array of drugs including Quaaludes. By 1983, the drug was taken off the market for good. Attempts are still made to produce these drugs illicitly, but the process is difficult and underground chemists (based in Mexico) usually end up making mecloqualone, which has a similar effect.

India, where the drug was first discovered, remains the world's largest source of illicit methaqualone and major drug seizures are not uncommon. In September 2000, over two metric tons of Mandrax powder were seized near Hyderabad, the state capital of Andhra Pradesh in central India. And again, in February 2001, 1.4 metric tons of Mandrax tablets were seized by authorities in Bombay. Much of this illicit product finds its way to South Africa which has a serious problem with methaqualone as do many other countries in the surrounding region.

METHOD OF USE
Swallowed as a tablet (see picture below).

EFFECTS
The desired effects occur at low doses—a dreamy state of calm relaxation. Users report feeling mellow; self-confidence, sociability, and libido may increase as the drug reduces inhibition.

HEALTH RISKS
As the dose goes up (or if the drug is taken with alcohol) so the risks are increased. There is marked lack of coordination and motor ability making driving very dangerous. High doses can induce delusions and general disorientation. Overdoses, many of which were fatal, were commonly reported.

DEPENDENCY
It was quickly demonstrated that methaqualone was just as dependence-producing as the barbiturates and withdrawal could similarly be fatal.

THE LAW
In the US, UK, and elsewhere around the globe, methaqualone is placed in the highest category of control. Mecloqualone has similar controls placed on it in the US, but is not reported anywhere else.

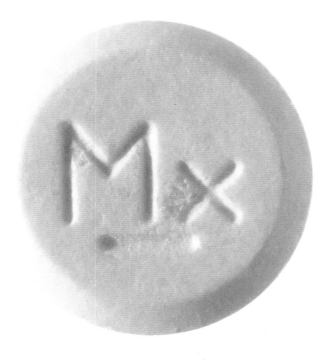

SECTION 2

Antidepressants

Antidepressants

**Tricyclics including amitriptyline (and many other tricyclics);
SSRIs, including fluoxetine (Prozac); paroxetine (Paxil, Seroxat)**

WHAT ARE THEY?

Antidepressants are the drugs that relieve the symptoms of depression. There are three main groups— Tricyclics (TCAs), SSRIs (Selective Serotonin Reuptake Inhibitors), and MAOIs (monoamine oxidase inhibitors). There are almost thirty different kinds of antidepressants available on the drugs market today. These types of drugs all act on specific neurotransmitter chemicals within the brain. Neurotransmitters are released by the brain to transmit signals across the gaps between neurons. Some of these neurotransmitter chemicals, such as serotonin and noradrenaline, also control our mood. In depression,

Prozac by Eli Lilly

Seroxat by GlaxoSmithKline

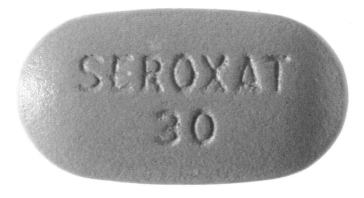

some of the neurotransmitter systems, particularly those of serotonin and noradrenaline, do not seem to be working properly. Antidepressants work by stopping the brain from reabsorbing these chemicals and therefore help the body to maintain higher levels of these active chemicals.

HISTORY

Antidepressants were first created by scientists in the 1950s, and they have subsequently been developed over the years in order to reduce their unpleasant side effects and make them safer in the event of an overdose.

The most widely prescribed antidepressant is Prozac (see image opposite) which has become the new "Valium" of its age. Today many people are reportedly using the drug who are not clinically depressed but just want to "feel better." Prozac is also highly controversial for other reasons. There have been many claims and lawsuits alleging that the pharmaceutical companies producing the drug have hidden evidence that Prozac could drive people to violence and suicide.

In the UK, the Committee on the Safety of Medicines have warned against using many of the SSRIs on the market to treat depression in people under the age of eighteen because of the risk of self-harm, although in this case Prozac was not highlighted as a special risk.

METHOD OF USE

Swallowed as tablets, such as those shown opposite.

SIDE-EFFECTS
Tricyclics (TCAs)

This group of antidepressants commonly cause the individual to from the following: a dry mouth, a slight tremor, fast heat beat, constipation, sleepiness, and weight gain. Those with heart problems are usually told to avoid taking any of the drugs from this group of antidepressants. In addition to these side effects men may experience difficulty in getting or keeping an erection, or delayed ejaculation. Tricyclics are dangerous in overdose and are now generally viewed as an older class of antidepressant and are usually recommended for use only as a second-line choice after the newer breed of drugs such as the SSRIs.

MAOIs

Soon after scientists developed tricyclic antidepressants, another group of chemicals, very different from the tricyclics, were created— these were the monoamine oxidase (MAOI) inhibitors. These new drugs effected the same neurotransmitters (serotonin and norepinephrine) that the tricyclics did, but they also effected dopamine. As a chemical messenger, dopamine is similar to adrenaline. It effects brain processes that control movement, emotional

dopamine), have played their part in sending messages in the brain, they are burned up by a protein in the brain called monoamine oxidase, a liver and brain enzyme. If too many monoamines are absorbed, it leads to a chemical imbalance in the brain. MAOIs work by blocking this cleanup activity. When the excess neurotransmitters don't get destroyed, they start piling up in the brain, and since depression is associated with low levels of these monoamines, it's not surprising that increasing the monoamines ease depressive symptoms.

The major problem is that the MAOI's interact with certain foods—mainly cheese, red wine, and

response, and ability to experience pleasure and pain. Regulation of dopamine plays a crucial role in our mental and physical health.

Once the brain's neurotransmitters, (serotonin, norepinephrine, and

BELOW It could be very dangerous to eat cheese if you have been prescribed MAOI antidepressants.

chocolate and are also known to react with a variety of commonly used drugs with potentially fatal results. They inhibit other enzymes including those in the liver used to break down a variety of drugs such as tricyclics, barbiturates, adrenaline, noradrenaline, ephedrine (used in many common cold cures), many local anaesthetics, and insulin.

SSRIs

During the first couple of weeks of taking this type of antidepressant the patient may often feel sick and also experience heightened levels of anxiousness. Some of the drugs in this particular group can also cause them to suffer from severe indigestion. These types of antidepressants may also interfere with sexual functioning, and there have been the reports of patients becoming aggressive, self-harming, and possibly experiencing suicidal feelings though these reports are rare.

ABOVE: Chocolate too is on the banned list—all these danger foods might react with the drugs to push blood pressure to potentially fatal levels.

PREGNANCY

There is no evidence so far to show that the foetus or newborn will be affected if the mother has been taking antidepressants during pregnancy.

DEPENDENCE

Antidepressant drugs don't cause the addictions associated with tranquillizers. There is tolerance or craving. However, studies have shown that up to a third of people have withdrawal symptoms for a short time when they stop antidepressants. These include stomach upsets, flu like symptoms, anxiety, dizziness, vivid dreams at night or sensations in the body that feel like electric shocks.

THE LAW

In the US, UK, and elsewhere, these are Prescription Only drugs.

SECTION 3

Narcotic Analgesics

Opium
Heroin
Methadone
Fentanyl
Hydrocodone
Propoxyphene
Oxycodone

These are drugs which relieve pain and are produced from two main sources—either from the opium poppy or from synthetic ingredients. Collectively these are known as opioids; those drugs produced purely from the poppy like opium, morphine, and heroin are called opiates. These are the most powerful painkillers ever to be invented.

HISTORY OF USE

The pain-killing effects of opium have been known for thousands of years. The two hundred-year period from 1700–1900 saw a huge growth in the use of patent medicines, many of which contained opium. The most famous one was a liquid mixture of opium and alcohol called "laudanum," so-called because its inventor Paracelsus sung the praises of the concoction as a miracle drug. Opium was a miracle drug in the days before medical science knew anything about the causes of illness like bacteria or viruses. All they could treat were the symptoms of illness— the most distressing of which was pain. During the nineteenth century, ever more stronger versions of opium were discovered. Morphine was first extracted from opium in the

laboratory in 1803; heroin was discovered in 1874. But probably just as significant in the spread of opiate-based drugs used as painkillers (and the dependence problem they caused) was the invention of the hypodermic syringe in 1853. The first major synthetic analgesic to be developed was methadone which was produced during war time in Germany when morphine supplies were restricted. The problems of dependence on these

RIGHT: Most of the world's illicit opium is grown in Afghanistan, Burma, Colombia, and Mexico. The legal supplies for use as pain-killing drugs like morphine, diamorphine, and codeine come from India and Tasmania.

drugs was quickly identified and ever since then, scientists have been searching in vain for an analgesic which is a powerful painkiller, yet non-addictive. This is probably a fruitless task because the link between mind and body dictates that any drug powerful enough to deal with chronic, intractable physical pain will almost certainly blot out the misery of emotional and psychological pain and will therefore be addictive.

During the 1970s, it was discovered that the body actually produced chemicals that are natural-equivalents of these drugs. The first of these to be identified were endorphins, the body's natural opiates. It is believed that acupuncture works by releasing these chemicals from their site in the brain; similarly a phenomenon known as "jogger's high" is experienced by many runners beyond a certain point in a run and is thought to be caused

by the release of the body's naturally
occurring endorphins.

ACTION ON THE BODY

As well as painkilling effects, all these
drugs have a sedative effect on the

BELOW: The hypodermic syringe was perfected in
the nineteenth century—it revolutionized the way
morphine was fed to the brain for fast pain relief.

central nervous system causing both
drowsiness and sleep. Those unused to
the effects will often feel nauseous
when they first use them or even be
sick. These drugs also effect the
digestive system and long-term heroin
users will often be constipated.
However, in terms of physical effects
on the vital organs of the body such as
the brain, liver, kidneys, and heart—

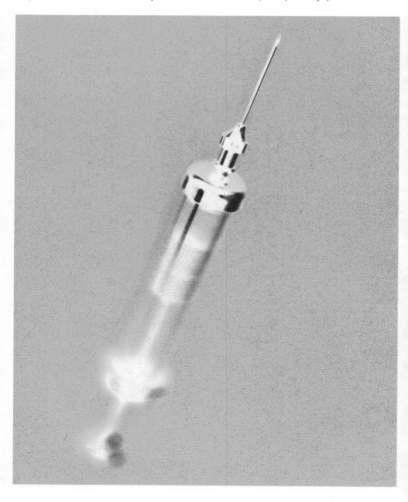

these drugs are relatively safe and do not have the devastating impact over the long term as drugs such as alcohol and tobacco.

MEDICAL USES

Nowadays, the most powerful of the opioids, like morphine, are used in the treatment of serious conditions such as the pain caused by cancer.

The synthetic analgesics have similar painkilling properties as the opiates. They are manufactured for medical use and include powerful drugs like Darvon, Demerol, and Percodan (US), and Pethidine (UK).

MISUSE

The main problem with opioids, which goes back to the earliest days of opium use, has been dependence. For much of the history of these drugs right through to the mid-nineteenth century, dependence was dismissed as an inconvenience and a price worth paying for what was a highly effective remedy for a whole range of medical conditions.

Tolerance to these drugs develops rapidly meaning that increasingly larger amounts of the drug are needed to maintain the effect. Because they are so effective at dealing with physical pain, they also deal very effectively with mental or psychological pain—and this is why it is so easy to become addicted to them if you have those kind of problems. Even patients given these drugs under medical supervision in a hospital environment can become physically dependent on opiates.

If somebody takes opiates for a prolonged period, these opiates then replace the body's natural opiates, the endorphins. Consequently, when heroin or morphine is withdrawn, the body takes time to readjust. This is the unpleasant withdrawal period of sweats and cramps that have been protrayed so vividly in films like *Trainspotting* and *French Connection 2*. Patients being given the opiate for pain control might experience a small amount of physical discomfort after treatment has stopped, but do not become addicted because they do not experience the cravings that make them want to continue taking the drugs.

In modern times, addiction to heroin has presented governments across the world with increasing health, social, and enforcement problems—not only the "end user" countries like the US, UK, and Europe, but also in producer countries such as Pakistan and Afghanistan where injecting heroin has replaced traditional opium smoking among younger people.

Dependence on prescription painkillers is also a major problem, especially in the US. This is a widespread issue that effects all levels of society and even a number of notable celebrities have reportedly been treated for addiction to them.

Opium

WHAT IS IT?

The opium poppy, *Papaver somniferum* belongs to the Papaveraceae family. It is a hardy annual plant and can endure most climates except extreme cold. The main stem of a mature plant is two to five feet tall. The plant flowers after about ninety days growth. Eventually the petals fall to reveal a small, round

green pod which contains the opium. The farmer begins the cultivation process by scoring down each pod with a knife, the sticky opium gum then oozes out and dries on the surface of the pod. The dried gum is then scrapped off the pod. The raw opium is cooked and is often used for smoking by the local population or the process continues to produce morphine by adding chemicals like calcium hydroxide and ammonium chloride, and by taking the mixture through a number of heating and

BELOW: This is an early stage in turning the blue flowered opium poppy into the most powerful physical and mental pain-killer ever discovered.

cooling stages. To produce heroin from morphine requires additional chemicals and further heating, cooling, and filtration processes. The manufacture of heroin will differ depending on whether the end product is for smoking or injecting.

HISTORY
Early times
As an unrivaled painkiller, opium was known and used across the ancient world. It was first described in detail in the early third century BC, but in Sumeria 4,000 years before that description, the image representing the poppy in the Sumerian picture alphabet was constructed from the phrase "joy plant." Because of its apparent "magical" powers to relieve pain and suffering, opium also features significantly in the mythology of ancient Greece. Fertility rites were often associated with opium because the sleep of the poppy was so deep that people appeared to be dead before they awoke—the death and rebirth symbolism linked to the growing seasons and crop cultivation.

The smoking of opium for recreational purposes began in China after the introduction of tobacco smoking introduced in the seventeenth century, but this did not become

LEFT: When the poppy capsule is properly matured, slits are cut in the side to allow the sticky substance to ooze out where it is solidifies and is scraped up by the farmer.

endemic until British-owned Indian opium flooded into the country in the nineteenth century.

Nineteenth Century
In the UK and US during this time, opium was the key ingredient for the array of patent medicines that came onto the market, allowing people who could not afford doctor's fees, self-medication to relieve pain. The American patent medicine industry was worth some $80 million a year by the end of the century. Through a combination of medical concerns, moral outrage, and international politics, opium and its main by-products were brought under legal control in the US in 1914 and UK in 1920. The first International Opium Commission met in Shanghai in 1909 and its deliberations (under different names) culminated in the 1961 UN Single Convention on Narcotic Drugs which still governs international law on opium and all its derivatives.

Modern production
For much of the period from 1920 through to the 1970s, Turkey was one of the main suppliers of opium for the production of heroin. The raw opium was shipped to Lebanon for processing to morphine, then to the heroin laboratories of Marseilles and onto the US. This was known as the French Connection, first exposed by two New York policemen and the subject of a famous film starring Gene

Hackman. Once the French Connection was broken, opium production switched to south East Asia and the region of Burma, Laos, and Thailand known as the Golden Triangle. Most of the heroin produced here is bound for the US, although opium from Colombia and Mexico is increasing its market share. The highest opium yields are from Afghanistan which produces some seventy-five percent of the world market and ninety percent for Europe and the UK.

Opium is still smoked by local inhabitants in the growing areas, but opium has largely been superseded by heroin which is a major problem for Afghanistan, Pakistan, and other countries in the region. There is also a huge market in legitimate opium growing for medical purposes. This is regulated by the UN International Narcotics Control Board. India is world's biggest supplier; Japan and the US are the world's biggest importers. One company in the UK has the monopoly on supplying processed opium (as morphine and diamorphine) to the Health Service.

MEDICAL USES

In its raw state, opium is still used for medicinal purposes in countries like North Korea that cannot afford to import western pain-killing drugs. Opium is used worldwide as a key ingredient in the treatment of

BELOW: Of the twenty alkaloids contained in opium, only codeine and morphine are still in widespread clinical use today.

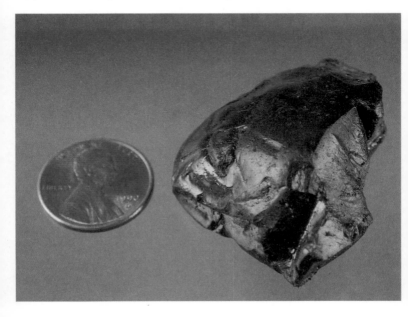

diarrhoea where it is used to suppress coughs. Heroin (diamorphine), morphine, and codeine remain invaluable as effective painkillers.

METHOD OF USE

Opium smokers increase the purity of the raw opium by boiling it in water. The resulting solution is boiled and filtered several times more to extract the maximum amount of the drug. Eventually a black sticky paste remains which is dried and smoked.

EFFECTS

As a smoked drug, the classic opiate effects of euphoria and sedation come on very rapidly as the opium fumes almost instantly cross the blood-brain barrier. Scenes of opium dens in movies give a sense of what the opium experience is all about—a complete sense of being cut off from the world in a semi-hallucinatory dream state.

DEPENDENCY

The attraction this state holds for some people makes opium, like heroin and morphine, very seductive. Needless to say regular use carries a high risk of physical and psychological dependency.

THE LAW

In the US, Opium is a Schedule II drug under the Controlled Substances Act and in the UK and elsewhere it is one of the drugs most strictly controlled.

BELOW: Relative size of two opium poppy capsules to an American cent. But it would take more than that to buy the drugs produced from them.

Heroin

Skag, H , horse, junk, smack, gear, and shit among many other names

WHAT IS IT?

Heroin is the most world's most powerful painkiller. It is one of a group of drugs (the opiates) made from the opium poppy that reduce pain and anxiety. As well as being prescribed as painkillers, opiates are used medically to treat coughs and diarrhoea. Opium is the dried "milk" of the opium poppy. It contains morphine and codeine, both effective painkillers. Heroin is produced from morphine and known as diamorphine. In its pure form it is a white fluffy powder with twice the potency of morphine. Unlike in the UK, doctors in the US are not allowed to prescribe heroin, even for terminal cancer pain.

OPPOSITE: This is so-called black tar heroin from Mexico—now very commonly smuggled over the border into the US.

They can prescribe morphine, but heroin acts faster because, even though it converts to morphine in the body, it is more fat soluable and so gets to the brain much more quickly.

Production

Up until the 1980s, most of the heroin available in the US was from Burma and south east Asia, from the region known as the Golden Triangle. Since then, black tar heroin has come in from Mexico and (together with brown heroin) now accounts for about fourteen of heroin consumption in the US alone. This form of heroin is produced in mobile laboratories situated close to the Mexican poppy fields. The name suggests its consistency—a sticky tar-like substance with a purity of between twenty to eighty percent. Easily the biggest source country for heroin in the US is now Colombia which supplies around seventy-five percent of the heroin consumed. Having already established the distribution networks for cocaine and crack, it was easy for the South American drug cartels to diversify into heroin. For Europe and the UK, the primary source country is Afghanistan.

Heroin is cut with a range of substances to bulk out the weight,

LEFT: In the Far East, different types and strengths of heroin are produced. These variations include brown heroin, which is primarily smoked, and numbered brands like No 3 heroin.

137

these are usually substances such as talc, quinine, and baking powder.

HISTORY

Heroin was first produced in 1874 by C.R. Alder Wright, a chemist based at St. Mary's Hospital in London. He was experimenting with morphine (discovered in 1806), attempting to filter out the addictive properties. After his experiments Wright shelved his new discovery, which was later taken up by Bayer, the German dye manufacturer turned pharmaceutical company. By 1897 Bayer was marketing heroin as a treatment for a range of ailments, including morphine addiction, to over twenty countries worldwide.

By the early 1900s alarm bells began to ring as doctors and pharmacists noticed the increasingly large quantities of heroin-based products their patients were consuming. Not surprisingly, Bayer ceased production in 1913.

In the US, heroin was actually one of the first drugs to be controlled under the Harrison Act of 1914, the earliest Federal law to be enacted against drug use. During the 1920s, the main illegal opiates used were opium and morphine, but after the Second World War, heroin became more widely available, smuggled in from Turkey by organized crime. Heroin use grew worldwide in the 1960s and 1970s especially (but not solely) in areas of acute social and economic deprivation in the US. With the breaking of the "French Connection" in the early 1970s (the mafia supply route from Turkey to Lebanon, Marseilles, and on to New York), new supply routes were established in the Far East. Currently it is estimated that there are around half a million regular heroin users in the US with around two and a half million Americans reporting that they have tried the drug at least once. It is heroin (with crack) which causes most of the problems with illegal drug use

in the US for individuals and their families, the local community, and society at large. Across Europe and in the wake of economic depression in the 1980s, heroin problems have become entrenched. Germany, Italy, France, Spain, Portugal and the Netherlands all have significant populations of chronic heroin users. Despite the image of wealth and secret bank accounts, Switzerland has some of the highest rates of heroin use in Europe while Russia's heroin problem is colossal. Heroin use is a feature of urban Canada and Australia while use among young people is growing in the producer countries themselves.

METHOD OF USE

Heroin can either be sniffed, smoked, or injected. When it is sniffed, heroin is absorbed into the bloodstream through the nasal membrane. When smoked, the fumes are drawn into the

BELOW: Smoking a drug delivers it to the brain almost as quickly as injecting because the smoke can very easily pass through the blood/brain barrier.

lungs and enter the bloodstream very quickly. "Chasing the dragon" is a slang term used to describe a way of smoking heroin by heating the powder and inhaling the fumes through a small tube.

Heroin can also be injected directly into the bloodstream through a vein but some users also choose to inject into muscles or target the fatty tissue just under the skin (known as "skin popping"). As with smoking, the effects of injecting are immediate but stronger, as none of the drug is lost before entering the bloodstream.

EFFECTS

Opiates like heroin are effective painkillers. Like sedatives, they depress the activity of the nervous system, slowing down breathing and heart rate and suppressing the cough reflex. Opiates also increase the size of certain blood vessels (giving a feeling of warmth) and depress bowel activity (often resulting in constipation).

Injecting

When injected into a vein, all the heroin goes directly into the bloodstream in one go. This can

PREPARING BROWN HEROIN

ABOVE: Some people think that to explain how to use drugs more safely sends a message that drug use is acceptable, but these approaches do help to save lives.

LEFT: If people are going to inject drugs, it is vitally important that they do not share needles and syringes. Clean works must be used on each and every occasion.

intensify the initial effects into an almost immediate, short-lived burst of extremely pleasurable feelings, often described as a rush. Other ways of taking heroin give less intense feelings, though after smoking the effects also come on very quickly because the smoke passes rapidly through the blood-brain barrier.

Heroin is the most fast-acting of all the opiates. When injected, it reaches the brain in fifteen to thirty seconds; smoked heroin reaches the brain in

around seven seconds. The peak experience via this route lasts at most a few minutes. The surge of pleasure seems to start in the abdomen; a warm feeling which spreads throughout the body. After the intense euphoria, a period of tranquillity (often refered to as "on the nod") follows, lasting up to an hour. Experienced users will inject between two to four times per day.

"Wrapped up in cotton wool"
Rather than blocking the sensation of pain, heroin makes pain more tolerable by reducing emotional reactions to it. Although pain is still felt it seems to matter less. Heroin cushions the user from the psychological impact not just of pain, but also hunger, discomfort, fear, and anxiety. This relief from suffering is experienced by many people as a positive feeling of well-being, contentment, and happiness. Users talk of feeling "wrapped up in cotton wool" and having all their troubles fade away. People who feel bad about

LEFT: There are plenty of myths about drugs and drug using. Properly trained counsellors are there to set the record straight and help people to straighten out their lives.

The heroin lifestyle

It is hard for most people to understand the attraction of the heroin lifestyle which appears to be little else other than a daily grind of misery and degradation with the ever-present risk of death. However, for those who are unemployed and socially isolated the lifestyle can hold attractions even above and beyond the actual effects of taking the drug. For somebody who has little else to look forward to but the weekly welfare check, becoming a heroin user gives a structure and a purpose (however self-destructive) to everyday life. The user has to find the money to buy drugs, perhaps selling off any surplus, find a means of disposing of stolen goods, has to arrange to meet the dealer, and then goes through the whole ritual of shooting up. Then, once the effects of the drug wear off, he or she has to go through the complete routine over again. There is now not only a reason for getting up in the morning, but the person now has a "social network"— places to go and people to meet.

Al Pacino's first leading role was in a film called *Panic in Needle Park* (1970) where he plays just such an individual. When we see him on the streets, he is not slumped in an alleyway with a needle hanging out of

themselves and feel they have little to live for can find heroin use very attractive. Even at doses sufficient to produce these feelings, the user is usually still capable of functioning adequately. They can usually think, talk, and act coherently. At higher doses sedation takes over and the user becomes drowsy. The initial experience of heroin is not always pleasant. Injecting the drug can make users feel sick, making them throw up, particularly when taking the drug for the first few times.

his arm, but striding purposefully to meet his contacts, like any Wall Street businessman. At one time in the 1980s, the purity level of heroin on the street of New York was down to about three to five percent. Interviewed for a UK television documentary, a New York heroin user confirmed that at that level of purity, it was almost impossible to get addicted—what people were hooked on was the lifestyle.

Staying off

To remain abstinent, a regular heroin user may have to reconstruct his or her life around non-drug using activities and relationships, having first concluded that the reasons for continuing to use heroin are outweighed by the reasons for coming off. This can be very difficult. It is perhaps comparable to a person whose entire social and possibly business life revolves around drinking and the bar, suddenly being told that they cannot drink anymore.

HEALTH RISKS

Although heroin does not damage the vital organs of the body in the way that alcohol does, the regular heroin user is often sick and unwell for much of the time brought on by general self-neglect, poor diet, lack of proper sleep, and the myriad of conditions consequent on being an injecting user (as most regular users are). These range from relatively low-key

problems such as skin abscesses and blood poisoning through to life threatenting illnesses like hepatitis and HIV. Whether they inject or not, heroin users suffer from a high incidence of lung disease (especially pneumonia) caused by repeated drug-induced respiratory depression and decreased resistance to infection. There can also be fatal reactions to impurities injected with heroin. Though heroin is very rarely cut with toxic chemicals, users may develop allergies to some additives or, as has happened in the UK, some may be contaminated with dangerous bacteria that can cause serious, or even fatal, infection. The contamination in the UK was apparently caused because the heroin was buried in the ground for a time before it was sold, and became contaminated with soil bacteria.

Overdoses

Death from overdose is more likely if there are other factors involved, such as the user being under the influence of other depressant drugs like alcohol, tranquillizers, or other opiates. Sometimes a user can lose their tolerance to an opiate, usually as a consequence of stopping and starting the drug. Failure to reduce the dose to match their new tolerance can often result in accidental overdose. It has

RIGHT: Long-term drug injectors eventually use up all the veins in their arms, legs, and feet. They often move to more dangerous sites like the groin or neck.

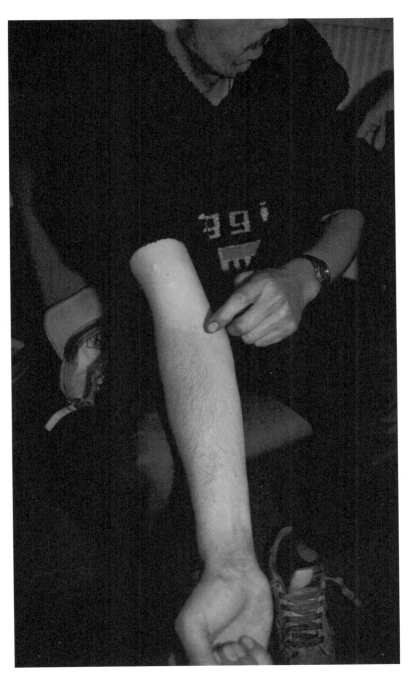

been recorded that a number of newly-released prisoners have overdosed and died because they resumed using heroin at the same dosage as before they were imprisoned. Similarly, a dose of unexpected strength can be too much and cause overdose.

Heroin is sometimes smoked together with crack cocaine. This combination delivers the user an even more intensely rewarding experience than taking either drug alone. "Speedballs" are hugely addictive, ruinously expensive, and highly dangerous; it was just such a combination of opiate and stimulant that killed comedian John Belushi.

Long-term use

The physical effects of long-term heroin use are rarely serious in themselves. They may include chronic constipation and, in women, menstrual irregularity. At higher doses chronic sedation can occur, but at

BELOW: Part of the ritual of injecting drugs is the whole cycle of preparation. The lemon juice in this photo is used to dissolve heroin.

moderate doses addicts can function normally. Women generally remain fertile despite taking large doses of heroin, and pregnancy is possible. The occurrence of diarrhoea during withdrawal may make the contraceptive pill ineffective. It is possible to be a long-term heroin user and still live an active, but none the less troubled, life. Writer William Burroughs was an opiate user for

BELOW: As part of the preparation process, heroin is be heated up in a spoon then drawn up into the syringe. Cotton wool may be used as a filter.

decades, but eventually died of natural causes aged eighty-three.

DEPENDENCE

Heroin is highly addictive. Repeated use for two or three weeks usually leads to tolerance, meaning that larger amounts must be taken to produce the same effects. Users find that they have to increase the dose and/or change their method of use. Injection into a vein maximizes the effects of a given amount of heroin and produces a much more intense, immediate experience. As tolerance develops (and

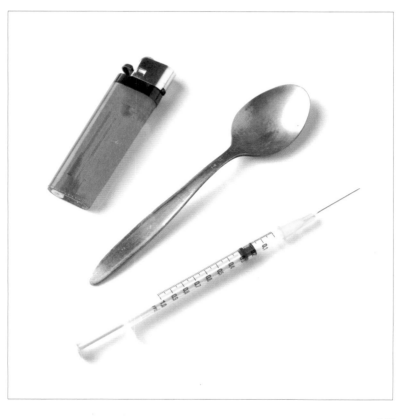

perhaps as money runs short), there may be a tendency to move from sniffing or smoking heroin to injecting. This may make financial sense in the short term but will be self-defeating in the longer term.

Tolerance will build up more quickly if the drug is injected because the effective dose is greater will require larger amounts and more money. If the user is unable to step up the dose to overcome tolerance (due to a shortage of money or supplies), a point will be reached at which this dose will fail to re-create the desired effects for the user. Even if the individual is able to continue increasing the dosage, eventually the same will happen—the person will be using the drug just to feel normal and to avoid withdrawal effects. Many users say that they can never recapture the euphoria of their early experiences. After as little as several weeks on high, frequent doses of heroin, sudden withdrawal results in differing degrees of discomfort. The effects start eight to twelve hours after the last fix and include aches, tremor, sweating, chills, sneezing, and yawning and muscular spasms.

Withdrawal

Withdrawal effects fade in seven to ten days, but feelings of weakness and loss of well-being can last for several months. Abrupt heroin withdrawal is rarely life-threatening and is considerably less dangerous than withdrawal from substances such as alcohol or barbiturates.

The experience of withdrawal effects can be a strong inducement to continue or resume using heroin which then results in a physical dependence. But even after these effects have faded, many users go back to heroin. For this reason it is generally accepted that physical dependence is not as significant as the strong psychological dependence that can develop to the effects of heroin and to the routine and lifestyle of being a regular heroin user.

Pregnancy

Opiate use during pregnancy results on average in smaller babies who may suffer withdrawal symptoms after birth. These can usually be managed with supportive therapy (which may or may not involve giving the baby drugs), until the withdrawal syndrome has run its course, but can be fatal in the absence of medical care. Opiate withdrawal during pregnancy can also result in foetal death, so the preferred option is usually to maintain the mother (and therefore the foetus) on stable doses of opiates until birth or reduce opiates slowly under controlled conditions. Appropriate pre-natal medical care can minimize risks to both the mother and baby.

THE LAW

In the US, heroin is a Schedule I drug under the Controlled Substances Act,

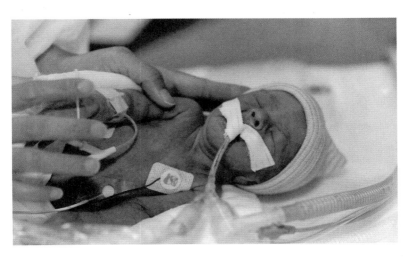

ABOVE: Babies born to women who have used heroin during their pregnancy may suffer from withdrawal symptoms in the first few days of life, but these can be treated with no lasting damage.

meaning it has no recognized medical use in the US and is subject to the most stringent controls. At Federal level, a first offence for dealing 100 g of heroin carries a prison term of not less than five years. Penalties for possession vary from state to state.

In the UK, heroin is a Class A drug under the Misuse of Drugs Act. This means that possession and supply are regarded as serious offences. The maximum penalty for heroin supply is life imprisonment. However, unlike in the US, those doctors who have a special licence are allowed to prescribe heroin to users on a "maintenance" basis. In other words, in order to keep the person off the streets and buying illegal and possibly contaminated heroin, a few doctors are allowed to prescribe pharmaceutically pure heroin. However, these and other doctors who prescribe drugs to users are closely monitored and can be struck off from the medical register if they are found guilty of irresponsible prescribing.

Heroin is strictly controlled in all countries, although some countries such as the Netherlands and Switzerland have also been testing the prescription of heroin to chronic users, similar to the system in the UK. Because of the stipulation of the international treaties, heroin is banned drug throughout the world and appears in the strictest category of all national drug laws. Vietnam, China, Saudi Arabia, and Iran are among those countries that still have the death penalty and these laws have been responsible for the execution of heroin traffickers.

Methadone

Physeptone (UK)

WHAT IS IT?

Methadone is a long-acting synthetic narcotic analgesic with a potency similar to morphine and which mimics the effects of heroin. It is therefore best known as an opiate substitute prescribed to individuals with chronic heroin addiction in order to help them "detoxify." Methadone is useful in this application as it does not produce the "high" associated with narcotic analgesics such as heroin and is therefore believed to be less addictive than the herion it is used to replace.

HISTORY

Methadone was first synthesized by German scientists during World War Two after the US forces and their allies cut off the opium supply to Germany. The scientists discovered the drug while experimenting with a number of different compounds in order to try and find a substitute for morphine, for which their supplies were running low. This same group of scientists also discovered pethidine.

After the war, the American pharmaceutical company Eli-Lilly began clinical trials with what was then called Dolophine—not in honor of Adolf (as has been thought) but probably as a combination of the Latin word dolor (pain) and the French fin (end). At first doctors thought methadone would be a revolutionary new painkiller but by the early 1950s it was hardly being used at all.

In the early 1960s Dr Marie Nyswander and Dr Vincent Dole, a respected American psychiatrist and research scientist, had found that they could not stabilize opiate users on

TYPES OF METHADONE

Dolophine 10 mg

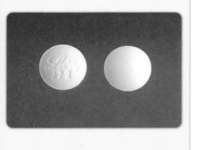

Hydromorhpone 4 mg

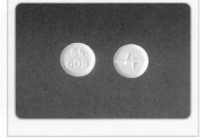

morphine without continually increasing the treatment dose. They reviewed the medical literature in search of possible alternatives and pioneered the radical step of prescribing methadone, which was effective orally, and seemed from pain research and some detoxification experience to be longer acting (they were not able to measure blood levels in those days). They soon found that once they had reached an adequate treatment dose that they could maintain people on that dose for long periods of time.

Methadone Maintenance

Nyswander and Dole were the pioneers of the "Methadone Maintenance Treatment." This innovative treatment was offered only to people with a long history of heroin use and failed treatment attempts. Nyswander and Dole based their approach on the theory that, once addicted, opiate addicts suffer from a metabolic disorder, similar in principle to metabolic disorders such as diabetes. Just as insulin normalizes the dysfunction in diabetes, so methadone was proposed to normalize the dysfunction of opiate addiction.

This new form of treatment spread rapidly in the US but was often implemented in a rigid way that lost some of the characteristics of Nyswander and Dole's original work. Consequently few programs have produced such good results as their

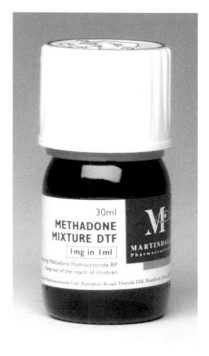

ABOVE: Methadone has become one of the major drugs employed in the treatment of heroin use. It is used to help detoxify users from heroin and to bring some stability to a normally chaotic life.

early work. The ways in which it was implemented in the early 1970s were strongly effected by political and other factors, which resulted in extensive government regulation.

The numbers of patients receiving Methadone Maintenance Treatment (or MMT) in the US rose: in the late 1990s it was recorded that there were about 160,000 patients served by around 800 maintenance programs.

METHOD OF USE

Taken orally once a day, methadone is able to suppress narcotic withdrawal for between twenty-four to thirty-six hours in patients following the maintenance program. Clinic patients usually take the drug in an oral liquid form (available in both sugar and sugar-free formulations) although it is also prescribed as an injectable and it is in this form that it is commonly used as a street drug.

The correct dosage to prescribe to opiate patients is controversial. Dole and Nyswander said that daily doses needed to start at 80 mg to properly stabilize patients and keep them in the program. But many doctors have refused to prescribe methadone at such high levels, claiming that this makes them feel like little more than drug dispensers. In cases where

doctors choose only to prescribe at minimum levels, the user is at risk of getting caught in a negative cycle where they use illicit heroin on top of their prescription. As a consquence they then fail the clinic urine test and are thrown off the treatment program.

EFFECTS

The effects are similar to other powerful opiate drugs, but with two important differences. The first is that the euphoric and sedative effects last longer and users do not experience the intense "rush" reported with heroin use. The second difference is that unlike heroin or morphine, methadone is highly effective when administered orally. These reasons make methadone an appropriate opiate substitute in the treatment of addiction. Methadone can also be used to suppress the withdrawal symptoms for other narcotics and drug cravings.

HEALTH RISKS

Patients can be maintained on stable doses of methadone without undue risk. The main longer-term issues are that the drug itself is dependency-producing and patients do suffer from chronic constipation. However, as well as constipation, there are some other side effects associated with chronic methadone use including

LEFT: Methadone is mainly prescribed in oral doses. This is safer than allowing users to inject and also helps to undermine the drug using lifestyle.

excessive sweating, urinary retention, and sleep disturbance.

In terms of overdose, a 75 mg dose could prove fatal to a non-tolerant adult, but as little as 10 mg can be fatal for children. There have been cases where children have overdosed on methadone left within easy reach.

DEPENDENCY

When taken regularly by high dose users, tolerance can develop rapidly. Both physical and psychological dependence are likely to occur with chronic users, but as the drug is excreted more slowly from the body, the brain is given more time to adapt to the drug free state and so withdrawal, and its symptoms, is less severe. However, this can be seen as a disadvantage from the user's point of view because it makes the whole process of detoxification longer.

THE LAW

In the US because of its medical uses, methadone is registered as a Schedule II drug under the Controlled Substances Act. In the UK, methadone is catagorized as a Class A drug and is similarly controlled elsewhere, although it is permitted to be in possession of the drug with a legitimate prescription. Within Europe, methadone as a street drug is as strictly controlled as heroin but the ability of doctors to prescribe the drug to heroin users differs across the EU. Specialist doctors in Spain, Portugal, Denmark, Belgium, and Italy may prescribe the drug to users, but this is very restricted in France and banned altogether in Greece.

BELOW: Methadone is used to fight opiate addiction to substances such as heroin (below) as it is belived to be less addictive.

Fentanyl

China white, China Girl, TNT, Apache, dance fever

WHAT IS IT?

Fentanyl is a wholly synthetic narcotic analgesic marketed under the name of Sublimaze. It is rated at approximately eighty to 100 times the potency of morphine. Sufentanil (or Sufenta) is an analogue of fentanyl with similar properties is significantly more potent. Sufentanil is five to ten times more potent than fentanyl, which in turn makes it 700 to 1000 times more potent than morphine.

MEDICAL USES

When injected intravenously, fentanyl works very quickly, but the effects will only last for thirty to sixty minutes and is used as a premedication in conjunction with anaesthesia. It is also available as a skin patch for slow-release relief for chronic pain.

HISTORY

Fentanyl was first synthesized in Belgium in the late 1950s. In the early 1980s, attempts were made by underground chemists to make analogues of fentanyl which would be "designed" chemically to put them outside the illegal drug controls. These analogues, alpha-methylfentanyl (AMF) and paraflurofentanyl (PFF) became the first designer drugs. AMF was dubbed "China White" after a particularly pure form of South East Asian heroin. Some of the chemistry was faulty and instead of producing AMF, illicit chemists created another analogue called MPTP.

This new drug actually destroyed dopamine neurons in the brain resulting in a severe, irreversible, and progressive Parkinsonian disease state in the user. Ironically, this progressed medical knowledge of Parkinson's because it demonstrated that external chemicals could cause the disease, and provided medical researchers with the first animal model for Parkinson's. By treating test animals with MPTP, researchers could induce Parkinson's symptoms and the animals could then be used to test whether new drugs were effective against the disease.

Although AMF and similar drugs were banned in the US, there are more than two hundred different versions of fentanyl, some of which were unknown to professional chemists before they appeared on the street. Also, these drugs are fairly easy to manufacture and unlike heroin, do not need to be imported.

METHOD OF USE

These drugs can either be taken intravenously or via intra-muscular injection.

EFFECTS

Users experience intense pain relief and euphoria.

HEALTH RISKS

MPTP, the version which caused Parkinson's disease was called "the walking death" because those who took it could hardly walk or talk and lacked any facial expression. Even with the less potent varieties, there is likely to be muscle rigidity because of the drug's rapid anaesthetic properties. Again, because of the very rapid onset of the effects, users are often only a very small margin away from a potential overdose.

DEPENDENCY

Like other opiates, tolerance will develop to the effects of Fentanyl and there is a risk of physical and psychological dependency with the same effects of a heroin-like withdrawal syndrome if the drug is stopped abruptly.

THE LAW

In the US Fentanyl is a Schedule II drug under the Controlled Substances Act while in the UK, it is a Class A drug under the Misuse of Drugs Act. It would be illegal in most countries to be in possession of illicitly manufactured fentanyl because that would be in contravention of international treaties. The same would also apply if the drug was a legal pharmaceutical product, but the person did not have a legitimate prescription for it.

BELOW: Synthetic painkillers can be even more powerful than naturally occurring morphine.

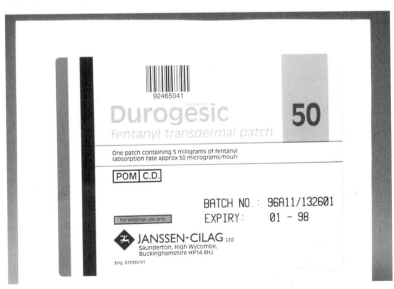

92465041

Durogesic **50**
fentanyl transdermal patch

One patch containing 5 milligrams of fentanyl
(absorption rate approx 50 micrograms/hour)

POM C.D.

BATCH NO. : 96A11/132601
EXPIRY :   01 - 98

for external use only

JANSSEN-CILAG Ltd
Saunderton, High Wycombe,
Buckinghamshire HP14 4HJ

Eng.-215933/V1

Hydrocodone

Vicodin, Lortab (with acetamorphin); Lortab ASA (with aspirin) and many other products

WHAT IS IT?

Hydrocodone is a synthetic narcotic analgesic structurally similar to codeine but much stronger. Five milligrams of hydrocodone is equivalent to 30 mg of codeine when administered orally—and dose for dose, it is almost as potent as morphine. There are over 200 products available in the US that contain hydrocodone. In its most usual product forms it is combined with acetaminophen (Vicodin, Lortab), aspirin (Lortab ASA), ibuprofen (Vicoprofen), and antihistamines (Hycomine). Both tablet and liquid forms of hydrocodone are available.

MEDICAL USES

It is prescribed for treatment of moderate pain and it is also used as a cough suppressant.

METHOD OF USE

Hydrocodone is usually taken orally even by those who misuse the drug, rather than by injection.

EFFECTS

When taken at dosages above the therapeutic level, it produces powerful euphoric and sedative effects.

HEALTH RISKS

Its co-formulation with acetaminophen has also increased the likelihood of acetaminophen-induced hepatic necrosis (a severe and rapidly progressive form of hepatitis which can result in severe liver disfunction and failure) with high/acute dosing. However, slow escalation of dose over time seems to protect the liver during high dose chronic exposures. The lethal dose has been calculated at 500–1000 mg and the risk of overdose is ever-present especially among highly tolerant misusers.

DEPENDENCE

As with all drugs of this type, tolerance develops rapidly and non-medical users will suffer withdrawal symptoms if use of the drug is stopped suddenly. With continued high dosage use, dependence is likely.

THE LAW

In the US, hydrocodone is a Schedule II drug, but the Schedule III status of some of the products has made them available to widespread diversion through forged prescriptions and thefts. (The US has a very high incidence of abuse/use of this drug compared to other countries.)

TYPES OF HYDROCONE

Vicodin 5 mg

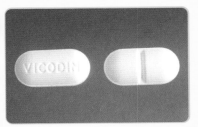

Vicodin 7.5 mg

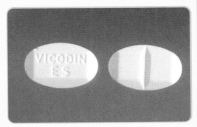

Lortab 2.5 mg

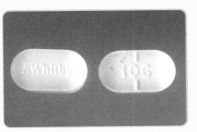

Lortab 7.5 mg

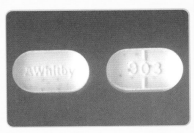

Hydromorphone 2 mg

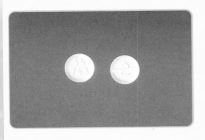

Hydromorphone 4 mg

ABOVE: Pharmaceutical companies are always
trying to develop the non-addictive narcotic analgesic.
But the inextricable link between physical and mental
pain makes it most unlikely that such a product will
ever be produced.

Propoxyphene

Darvon, Darvocet, Dextropropoxyphene

WHAT IS IT?

Propoxyphene is a narcotic analgesic and is structurally a relative of methadone. It is prescribed in two forms—propoxyphene hydrochloride and propoxyphene napsylate—for relief of mild to moderate pain.

Aside from slight differences—the napsylate (or N-form) of propoxyphene is more slowly absorbed into the body and so has a longer duration of action—the two drugs are identical. Both of these drugs can be found in a number of prescription pain medications, including the following:

• Darvon and Darvon-N (propoxyphene only)

• Darvon with A.S.A., Darvon-N with A.S.A. (with aspirin)

• Darvocet, Darvocet-N, Wygesic (with acetaminophen)

• Darvon Compound, Darvon Compound-65 (with aspirin and caffeine)

HISTORY

Propoxyphene was first introduced to the pharmaceutical market in 1957 and was heralded as a safe, non-addicting alternative to codeine. By 1969, it was the most prescribed drug in the US. But its popularity was not to last as in 1972 the manufacturers had to concede that research into the drug concluded that Darvon was actually only half as effective as codeine and might not be any more effective than aspirin.

Despite these claims by the 1980s, the number of reported overdoses began to rise and there were calls for a Federal ban on the drug. In 1989, the Darvon-related death of former NFL great John Matuszak brought renewed calls for a ban and the Federal Food and Drug Administration demanded restrictions on the way the drug was being prescribed.

METHOD OF USE

Propoxyphene is usually swallowed as a tablet, but it can also be injected intravenously by misusers to increase the euphoric effects. While the therapeutic dose is 32–65 mg three or four times a day, chronic misusers can use up 800 mg a day and even a massive 3000 mg a day has been reported.

EFFECTS

When injected, users say that they experience a pleasant state of euphoria, dizziness, drowsiness, and when used in particularly high doses, a heroin-like rush.

HEALTH RISKS

One of the main problems with the Darvon form of propoxyphene, even when used legitimately, is that the margin between the therapeutic dose and the toxic dose of the drug is small—and this becomes even smaller if the drug is mixed with alcohol or other drugs are taken at the same time. In fact, more than ninety-three percent of all propoxyphene-related deaths in 1995 were the result of interactions with other drugs—more than half them involving harmful reactions when mixed with alcohol or Valium.

Paradoxically, the inherent danger of accidental overdose posed by propoxyphene was closely associated with its relative ineffectiveness. Patients took more than the recommended dose because they thought the drug wasn't working and found themselves in hospital—and some never came out.

Compound versions of the drug also present potential problems. Aspirin and acetaminophen are particularly dangerous since they can damage the liver and kidneys when overused. Similarly, heavy doses of caffeine (found in Darvon Compound and Darvon Compound-65) can cause jitteriness, insomnia, and anxiety, which some users relieve by taking

TYPES OF PROPOXYPHENE

Darvocet 100 mg

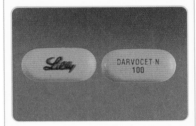

Darvon 65 mg

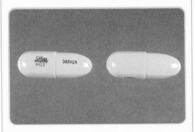

Darvon 65 mg

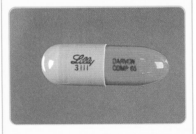

ABOVE: Despite being a relatively mild painkiller, propoxyphene is actually quite dangerous because users think the drug is not working and take too many. Those who survive may have irreversible liver damage.

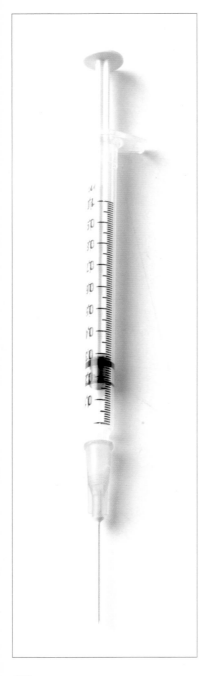

tranquillizers or sleeping pills, this in turn then further compounds the risk of the individual accidentally overdosing.

Injecting

The drug is formulated as a tablet and is not meant to be injected. Darvon is practically insoluble but because the drug needs to be injected for maximum effect regular users face all of the cumulative dangers associated with intravenous use such as the devastating blood-borne viruses like hepatitis and HIV—plus all the inherent problems of injecting tablets. These problems occur because the pill has to be broken down sufficiently to enable it to be injected, but the user will also be injecting themselves with the tablet coating and binding agents that are used to the hold tablets together. This can cause severe damage to the veins and other associated problems such as abscesses and blood poisoning.

Many habitual drug users will resort to taking a combination of drugs like these if there is any interruption in the supply of their usual drugs like heroin and also because they are cheap and easy to obtain.

LEFT: The binding agents which are used to hold pills and tablets together can cause serious damage to a user's veins if drugs which are only meant to be taken orally, are crushed up and used by the addict for injecting.

ABOVE: Dependence on legally obtained narcotic analgesics is one of society's "hidden" drug problems because users often do not regard themselves in the same light as heroin or cocaine addicts and are less likely to seek treatment.

Overdosing

With high doses of propoxyphene, the user may experience confusion, delusions, and hallucinations. Cases of toxic psychosis have been reported to occur with doses of about 400 mg. All of the body's respiratory functions will slow down potentially to the point of respiratory arrest, coma, and then possibly death.

The lethal dose of propoxyphene is around 600 mg and with Darvon (as opposed to Darvon-N) death can occur within an hour of the person ingesting a fatal dose due to the fact that this particular form of the drug is more readily absorbed into the bloodstream.

DEPENDENCY

For the chronic misuser who is injecting the drug, tolerance will develop rapidly and heroin-like withdrawal symptoms are likely to be experienced if the user fails to repeat the dose. Psychological dependence is always a risk when the drug is used in these circumstances, but a feeling of not being able to do without the drug has been reported even at low doses administered under medical supervision and patients have been known to take the drug for years at a time.

THE LAW

It is because of the scale of the use/abuse of narcotic analgesics, such as propoxphene, in the US that means it is more helpful to focus on the US here. Abuse in particular is not much of an issue elsewhere and so it is very difficult to provide any balancing information. In the US, propoxyphene is a Schedule IV drug under the Controlled Substances Act. This means that although the drug can purchased online, there are certain restrictions pertaining to the transfer of a doctor's prescription to make an online purchase. The drug is available in the UK as dextropropoxyphene, and is controlled as a Prescription Only Medicine.

Oxycodone

OxyContin, OxyNorm, Percodan, Percocet, Hillbilly heroin

WHAT IS IT?

Oxycodone is a semi-synthetic narcotic analgesic derived from codeine. It is formulated either as a pure oxycodone or in combination products like Percodan, which has aspirin and caffeine added, and Percocet, which is combined with acetaminophen.

MEDICAL USES

All of these products are prescribed for the treatment of moderate to severe pain. A doctor will only prescribe to a maximum of 5 mg four times a day. It is especially used for the control of post-operative pain and also for cancer patients and those patients who have suffered a serious back injury.

HISTORY

As with so many synthetic and semi-synthetic narcotic analgesics, the hope for oxycodone was that it would prove a safer alternative to morphine. However, the drug is substantially more potent than any other similar drug and so inevitably, it has found a market outside of legitimate medical usage. But this illegal market has not developed in the usual urban wastelands. Instead, a wave of oxycodone swept through large areas of economically depressed, rural areas of the US—including western Virginia, eastern Kentucky, and central Pennsylvania—to the extent that it has been dubbed "Hillbilly heroin." Several states have taken measures to curb distribution and a lawsuit was

TYPES OF OXYCODONE

Percodan 2.25 mg

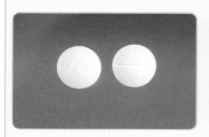

Percodan 4.5 mg

taken out against the manufacturers alleging that they had actively encouraged doctors to prescribe the drug for all kinds of pain, not just for serious intractable cases. Between 2000 and 2002, around 300 non-medical deaths were recorded and attributed to the misuse of oxycodone in the US.

METHOD OF USE

The tablets are formulated so that the drug is released slowly over a number of hours. The idea was that patients only needed to take two tablets a day rather than six or seven, as is the case with other painkillers. However, by crushing the tablets many misusers found' it was possible to get the full hit of the drug in one go.

EFFECTS

At low doses oxycodone can cause feelings of euphoria, sedation, light-headedness, dizziness, slight confusion, and possibly nausea. At higher doses, all of these effects will be amplified and the duration of the effects increased. The user might fall asleep under its influence and breathing will become more labored. Constipation is so frequently reported by patients taking the drug that doctors often prescribe a laxative at the same time.

HEALTH RISKS

The risks increase as the dose is increased. At the very high doses reportedly taken by abusers of the drug, there is a strong risk of casuing overdose, respiratory and cardiac arrest, and coma. For a non-tolerant adult, the estimated lethal dose is 500 mg. Additionally, aspirin and acetaminophen poisoning could result from swallowing large amounts of Percodan or Percocet.

DEPENDENCY

With regular use tolerance develops rapidly in users along with powerful physical and psychological dependence equivalent to that experienced with morphine.

THE LAW

In the US, oxycodone and all of its associated products are registered as Schedule II drugs under the Controlled Substances Act. In the UK and elsewhere, these drugs are usually listed with those drugs most strictly controlled.

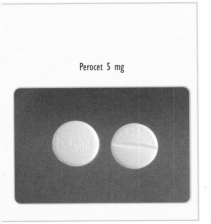

Perocet 5 mg

SECTION 4

Stimulants

Amphetamines
Methamphetamine
Methylphenidate
Cocaine and Crack
Ecstasy
Tobacco
Caffeine
Khat
Anabolic steroids
4-MTA
PMA
STP

Stimulants are those drugs which act upon the central nervous system to produce feelings of well-being, strength, energy, and confidence in the user. Stimulants reduce appetite and ward off tiredness and sleep. The main drugs in this category are amphetamines, the hallucinogenic amphetamines which includes ecstasy, cocaine, tobacco, and caffeine. Khat is also included here as it is chemically a stimulant while other drugs like anabolic steroids and the nitrites ("poppers") have stimulant-like effects.

HISTORY OF USE
Coca (from which cocaine is produced) is a plant found in high altitude south American countries like Peru and Bolivia and for over a thousand years at least, the native population chewed coca leaves to stave off tiredness and reduce hunger while working. During the latter part of the nineteenth century, many patent medicines for hay fever and asthma contained pure cocaine which was isolated from the cocaine plant in around 1860. And of course, Coca Cola famously contained cocaine until new food labelling regulations forced the company to change the recipe. Khat, coffee, and tea are other plant based stimulants with a history in East Africa, the Middle East, and Asia going back centuries, while the history of tobacco is to be found in the Americas.

Amphetamines were developed in the laboratory during the late 1920s. They were first marketed in a spray form intended to combat nasal congestion and then as a range of tablets prescribed in their millions for energy (targeted at people such as truck drivers) and to primarily women to promote weight loss until legislation restricted their use.

The drug MDA is the parent drug of a whole family of substances which have been labelled "hallucinogenic amphetamines," although few in this large group are true hallucinogens. They were developed as part of general pharmaceutical research before the First World War, but the researchers could find little use for them. They were "rediscovered" by a chemist in the 1960s and have been appearing as street drugs ever since. MDMA or ecstasy is one of the most well known drugs in this group.

ACTION ON THE BODY
At low to moderate doses, all stimulants produce a heightened sense of well-being, but the intensity of this will depend on the drug and can range from the mild euphoria of caffeine and tobacco to the overwhelming sensations of crack cocaine. Similarly prolonged use of stimulants will produce feelings of anxiety and discomfort which can range from the irritable and nervous feelings from the ingestion of too much coffee to the full blown paranoia and psychosis of

ABOVE: Coffee, cigarettes, anabolic steroids, methamphetamine, poppers, and crack cocaine are all drugs which stimulate the central nervous system.

chronic amphetamine or cocaine use. Many of the MDA group of drugs produce similar effects to amphetamine, but a few have marked capacity to alter perceptions more akin to the effects of LSD. Anabolic steroids are based on the body's own male hormone testosterone and so not surprisingly will promote feelings of aggression as well as a number of other unwanted side effects.

MEDICAL USES

As the problems with the major stimulants have become known, so their use by the medical profession has declined. Cocaine still has a use as an anaesthetic in eye surgery, while amphetamine-like drugs are used in the treatment of narcolepsy (a condition where the patient continually falls asleep) and Attention Deficit Syndrome in children. Amyl nitrite ("poppers") were formerly the drug of choice for treating angina while anabolic steroids may be prescribed to promote muscle growth in those who have been confined to bed for a prolonged period.

MISUSE

The major impact of misusing stimulant drugs will be on the cardiovascular system—hypertension, erratic heart beat, and possibly heart disease and heart attacks. Where the drugs are smoked like tobacco, crack, methamphetamine, and khat, the respiratory system may be compromised. Psychologically, chronic use of amphetamine and cocaine is associated with paranoia and other forms of psychosis which may also be precipitated by lack of sleep and proper nourishment.

All these drugs have the capacity to induce strong psychological dependence and craving, especially tobacco, amphetamine, and cocaine, proving that the legal status of a drug bears little relation to the dangers of using it.

Caffeine and nicotine

The mildest form of stimulant is caffeine, found in a range of soft drinks, tea and coffee, and some pharmaceutical products like Pro-Plus and some cough and cold remedies. Nicotine is also a mild stimulant, but paradoxically long term smokers who find it hard to give up say that it is the calming and relaxing effects of nicotine which makes it so seductive.

Amphetamines

Amphetamine is a more powerful stimulant; a single dose of powder can last for up to four hours. Ecstasy or MDMA belongs to one branch of the amphetamine family. Using ecstasy to stay awake all night at raves and clubs partly explains its popularity with young clubbers. Amphetamine and drugs with similar effects have been prescribed for obesity and an amphetamine-like drug Ritalin is used to assist those children with Attention Deficit Syndrome. Again like nicotine,

it is a paradoxical effect: one would not imagine that a stimulant drug would be useful in the treatment of hyperactive children.

Cocaine

The most powerful stimulant drug is cocaine and its smokeable variant crack. The speed with which the effects wear off, the intense craving produced by the drug, and the expense of repeat purchases, together account for the significant financial, health, and personal costs of chronic cocaine use to the individual, their family, and community at large.

While people using these drugs often feel they have benefited from the effects, there is no such thing as a free lunch and the rapid high produced by a drug like cocaine is quickly followed by a crash which can cause acute depression and even suicidal thoughts in the user. The use of amphetamine-based diet pills is now strictly controlled because of the severe psychological effects, including paranoid delusions, that these drugs can induce. The stimulant effect of nicotine does little harm when set alongside the immense damage caused by the tar and other ingredients of tobacco products.

RIGHT: The use of substances to improve athletic performance is nothing new. In Ancient Greece, donkey urine was drunk by competitors in the belief that it would make them run faster.

Anabolic steroids

Another group of drugs which fall into this category are the anabolic steroids. These are synthetically produced drugs based on the male hormone testosterone and so, not surprisingly, promote feelings of strength and aggression in the user. They have a limited medical use in promoting muscle growth in those who have been bed-ridden. However, they are primarily known as drugs used to enhance the performance of athletes in sport.

Amphetamines

Speed, uppers, black beauties, whites, bennies

WHAT IS IT?

Amphetamines are synthetic stimulant drugs that act on the central nervous system to arouse and energize the user in much the same as the body's natural adrenalin. There are several different types of amphetamines: amphetamine itself, methamphetamine, dextroamphetamine, and dextromethamphetamine. In terms of effects, there is very little to distinguish one drug from the other; the differences come in the method of manufacture and the relative strength of each.

MEDICAL USES

At one time, these drugs were bought over-the-counter and prescribed in their millions mainly to women as diet pills and as a means of dealing with depression. They were also used in vast quantities by anybody who wanted to stay awake, from students doing exams to long distance truck drivers. There is still a wide range of amphetamine-like appetite suppressant drugs, such as Adipex and Phentermine, available for weight control which can be bought without prescription over the internet despite continuing concerns about dependence. Most of these drugs have been withdrawn in the UK. One that remains in active medical use is Methylphenidate (Ritalin) which is the drug of choice for treating and dealing with hyperactivity in children.

HISTORY

Amphetamines first appeared on the drug market as medicines prescribed for depression and for treating pathological sleepiness (known medically as narcolepsy). In 1932, amphetamine sulphate was marketed by the pharmaceutical company Smith, Kline, and French (SKF) as Benzedrine asthma inhalers and tablets.

During the Second World War, soldiers in all fighting forces were liberally supplied with amphetamines in an attempt to boost morale and combat battle fatigue. An estimated total of seventy-two million tablets were provided to British forces during that period. Following that American soldiers fighting in Korea then took a mixture of amphetamine and heroin to produce the first recorded use of "speedballs."

As restrictions and controls on pharmaceutical products increased, so the illicit manufacture of amphetamine took off—a trade which became associated particularly with motorcycle gangs.

TYPES OF AMPHETAMINES

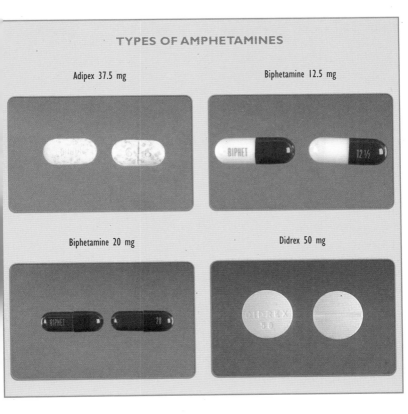

Adipex 37.5 mg

Biphetamine 12.5 mg

Biphetamine 20 mg

Didrex 50 mg

METHOD OF USE

On the streets, the drug is available mainly to users as an off-white or pink powder, usually sold in a small paper wrap. The powder form may be swallowed (often with a drink), snorted up the nose, or it can be dissolved and prepared for injection. Amphetamine is one of the more adulterated drugs and users are frequently sold similar looking drugs like phenyl-propanolamine, ephedrine, or even simply caffeine tablets or powder in its place. Illicitly produced amphetamine often has quite a strong smell, commonly described as "fishy." This rather unusual smell is caused by the presence of various chemicals which are used during the drug's manufacturing process.

EFFECTS

As powerful stimulant drugs, amphetamines produce feelings of exhilaration, increased energy, a sense of well-being, confidence, enhanced ability to concentrate, and a marked reduction in the need for sleep and food. Thus they have found favor as a so-called "functional" drug with many groups including students, athletes, long distance lorry drivers, and recreationally among those wanting to stay awake all night to dance or party. The drug's potential for suppressing appetite and inducing weight loss are particularly valued by people wanting to slim.

Taken orally the effects of a single moderate dose of amphetamine will come on slowly (in about half an hour) and last for about three to four hours. Sniffed amphetamine powder takes effect more quickly—within about twenty minutes—and the more

intense effects can last from four to six hours. If the drug is injected, the physiological and psychological effects are heightened. After a 10–20 mg dose injected into a vein (which chronic users may repeat every one or two hours), users feel a sudden intense sensation or "rush."

The effects of a dosage up to 60 mg, can last from four to six hours and so is far more "cost-effective" than cocaine, the effects of which last only minutes when more of the drug is needed to maintain the effect. Heavy users might consume 250–300 mg a

TYPES OF AMPHETAMINES

Fastin 30 mg

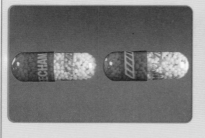

Mazanor 1mg

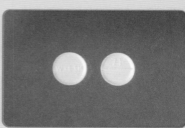

Ionamin 15 mg

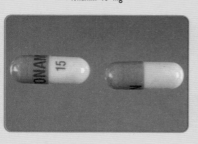

Ionamin 30 mg

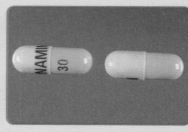

day, although anything up to a 1000 mg daily dose has been reported by some users.

HEALTH RISKS

Taken by mouth at low doses (5–10 mg of pure drug) the physical effects may include increased breathing and heart rate, a rise in blood pressure, reduction of appetite, widening of pupils, dryness of the mouth, diarrhoea, and increased urine output. Amphetamines may also react with certain foods and beverages rich in tyramine, such as Chianti red wine and a number of different cheeses, which can produce headaches and a rise in blood pressure.

Higher doses (of up to 20 mg of the pure drug in a twenty-four hour period) may be accompanied by an intensification of these low dose effects, together with flushing, sweating, headaches, teeth grinding, jaw clenching, and the sensations of a racing heart. The blood may be diverted from peripheral vessels so the users complexion can become pale and their hands and feet may also feel cold.

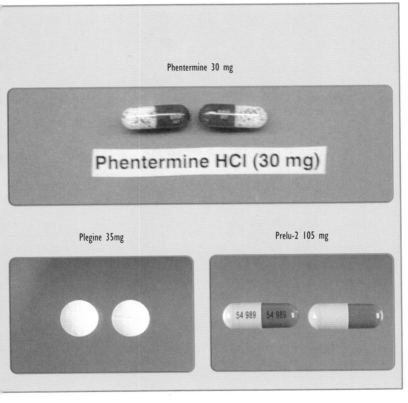

Phentermine 30 mg

Phentermine HCl (30 mg)

Plegine 35mg

Prelu-2 105 mg

54 989   54 989

Amphetamines tend to intensify the users' feelings and emotions about themselves and the world around them. Low to moderate doses do not disrupt thought patterns. Users tend to speak rationally, but can be very talkative and sometimes aggressive. What to the user may be brilliant flashes of insight cogently and forcefully expressed may, to the sober listener, appear nonsensical. Users often find their capacity for concentration increased, but this can merely focus on the compulsive or obsessive attention to a simple task.

Even at low doses a phenomenon known as amphetamine psychosis can occur. This state is characterized by excessive mood swings, agitation, irritability, confusion, and possible bouts of uncontrolled and sometimes violent behavior. With regular use in high doses this condition can become serious. The psychosis wears off once the drug has left the body, usually within a few days.

The stimulant effect does not add to the body's energy resources, but takes from it so the user will feel tired after the upper effects have worn off. It can

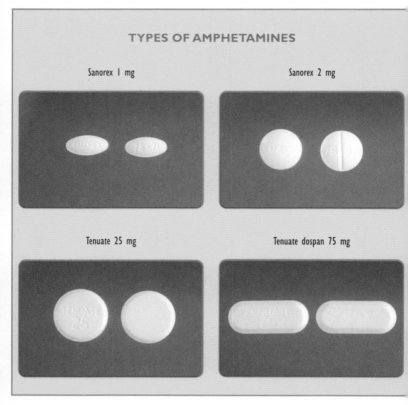

TYPES OF AMPHETAMINES

Sanorex 1 mg

Sanorex 2 mg

Tenuate 25 mg

Tenuate dospan 75 mg

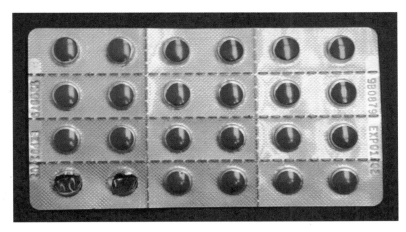

take a couple of days for the body to recover. When the user stops after a "run" of taking the drug there is a rebound effect of extreme tiredness, and sleep that can last up to forty-eight hours. Waking up is often accompanied by hunger and feelings of depression. Lethargy can remain for days or weeks during which the user may experience renewed anxiety or panic attacks.

Overdoses

The tolerance level within each individual will determine the dosage at which a toxic reaction or overdose might occur. This could range from 30–60 mg in a non-tolerant user to 500 mg (half a gram) in a regular user. Naive users have reportedly survived several hundred milligram doses and regular users, doses of several grams. The features of overdosing include muscle spasms, a racing pulse and a high temperature.

ABOVE: There was a time when doctors were prescribing millions of slimming pills to women who were desperate to lose weight. Unscrupulous clinics continue this practice today, despite the health risks.

Although the drug is common among clubbers since the 1960s, there are no recorded ecstasy-type deaths resulting from over-heating. Deaths are usually associated with injecting, either as a direct overdose or complications arising out of using the drug intravenously.

Injecting

Injecting amphetamine can be particularly dangerous as it incurs the risks of overdosing, damage to veins, and infections, including hepatitis and HIV if injecting equipment is shared. The fact that street amphetamine is so impure and mixed with all sorts of bulking agents makes the risk of vein, muscle, and liver damage very real. People who inject amphetamine often

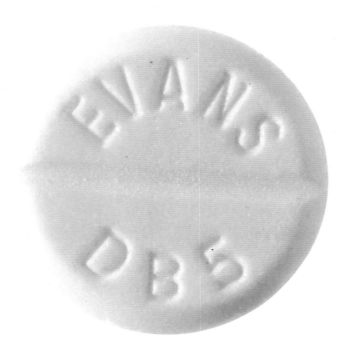

ABOVE: Speed has long been the favored drug of those needing to stay awake for long hours at a stretch such as students studying for exams and long distance truck drivers.

do so more frequently than heroin injectors which in turn compounds the dangers. They are also more likely to be sexually active than heroin users and so more at risk of sexually transmitted infections. The injecting of amphetamine on a long-term basis is often associated with heavy drinking or use of heroin and/or tranquillizers taken to reduce the tension and anxiety caused by amphetamines and smooth the come down. The reverse can also happen— regular amphetamine use can develop as a counterbalance to the sedative effect of alcohol, heroin, and tranquillizers.

Chronic use

Regular users of amphetamine may embark on a session of extended amphetamine use or "run" lasting several days, neglecting food and sleep. As time progresses, initial euphoria and self-confidence may give way to a psychosis marked by abrupt mood changes, possible violence or aggressive behavior, paranoid delusions, and hallucinations of sight, hearing, smell, and touch. The user may actually believe these hallucinations are real or may experience them knowing that they

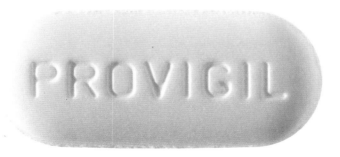

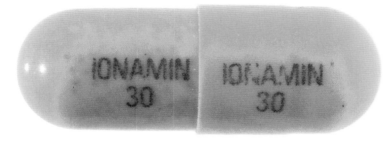

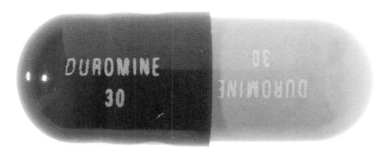

ABOVE: Some amphetamine tablets were
manufactured in combination with a barbiturate,
so that within the same tablet, the stimulant effect
of one drug would then offset by the depressant
effect of the other.

RIGHT: The arrival of ecstasy on the drug scene produced the most significant changes in music and popular culture since cannabis and LSD in the 1960s. Using ecstasy became a lifestyle statement and photos like this defined the nature of youth culture in the 1990s—overheated venues, trance-style dancing, and club drugs.

RIGHT: The arrival of ecstasy on the drug scene produced the most significant changes in music and popular culture since cannabis and LSD in the 1960s. Using ecstasy became a lifestyle statement and photos like this defined the nature of youth culture in the 1990s—overheated venues, trance-style dancing, and club drugs.

are a product of the imagination induced by the drug. Hallucinations of either kind might include unpleasant sensations such as the smell of gas or insects crawling on the skin. There is also a danger that those with latent schizophrenia could have the condition triggered by regular moderate use or even one very large dose. Because amphetamine leaches out the calcium in the body, regular users tend to have bad teeth, compounded by the teeth grinding mentioned earlier.

Heavy use can put strain on the cardiovascular system leading to high blood pressure, irregular heart rhythm, and possible stroke if not discontinued. Injury to the small blood vessels serving the eye can damage the retina. Those who are malnourished as a result of prolonged use may suffer calcium deficiency. Regular use by women may result in both the cessation of menstruation and an interruption of fertility.

DEPENDENCE

Tolerance develops rapidly with amphetamines. Particularly where the drug is being injected, users on amphetamine "runs" may build up to doses of 2 g or more in a vain attempt to recapture the initial "rush."

There is no physical withdrawal syndrome comparable to that experienced by opiate users. However, the feelings of extreme fatigue, hunger, depression, and disturbance of sleep following a bout of prolonged use constitute a pattern of withdrawal effects and dependence, particularly as these feelings disappear with the resumption of drug use.

Even among those who use small amounts, if the drug is taken regularly, marked psychological

dependence can occur in response to the sense of well-being, confidence, and energy induced by the drug. Some people, especially but not only women, may come to rely on amphetamine as part of their quest to stay slim. Regular use is sometimes associated with anorexia and bulimia. There is a high rate of relapse among regular users who stop.

THE LAW

In the US, amphetamines are Schedule II drugs under the Controlled Substances Act. In the UK, it is a Class B drug under the Misuse of Drugs Act. Across Europe, amphetamine is controlled in accordance with the 1972 UN Convention on Psychotropic Substances which means laws are in place to control possession and supply. Amphetamine is not in the strictest category of controlled drug. Furthermore, different countries across the EU have been adopting varying policies as to whether or not to arrest and prosecute individuals for being in possession of small amounts of drugs for personal use. The less draconian response has been applied in Germany, Italy, Spain, Portugal, Luxembourg, and Belgium.

Methamphetamine

meth, crystal, crank, Nazi crank, yabba, speed, ice, glass

WHAT IS IT?

Methamphetamine is a derivative of amphetamine. Since the disappearance of many of the pharmaceutical amphetamine pills and tablets, illicitly produced methamphetamine has become the most widely misused form of the drug in the US and elsewhere. In the US, it comes mainly as a powder and in a crystalline form for smoking. The drug has also become extremely popular in the Far East, along the Pacific rim where the main formulation is a small red pill, known by its Thai name of "yabba" meaning "crazy pill."

HISTORY

Methamphetamine was first formulated in Japan in 1919. It was more potent than amphetamine and easier to manufacture. During the Second World War, methamphetamine was widely used by the military to fight battle fatigue and Hitler was injected daily with the drug (hence one of its slang names—"Nazi crank"). Some historians believe it was this that accounted for Hitler's increasingly bizarre behavior and poor military decisions in the latter years of the war. American supplies of the drug left in Japan after the war caused a localized epidemic of methamphetamine use. The British Prime Minister Anthony Eden also received methamphetamine injections during the Suez Crisis of 1956 which necessitated him staying up for many hours without sleep.

While legitimate pharmaceutical amphetamine was widely prescribed in the 1960s, there were the beginnings of the illicit production of this stronger variety, mainly by motorcycle gangs. The powder trade is now apparently dominated by Mexican gangs who have set up many production sites known as "meth labs" in Mexico and California causing significant pollution problems in the localities in which they are situated through fumes and the dumping of toxic waste. According to the DEA, production of "ice" or smokable methamphetamine is in the hands of Asian gangs based in Los Angeles, who are now increasingly buying powder from Mexican producers to convert to "ice."

The methamphetamine pills found in the Far East were originally imported from Guam, Hawaii, and California, but are now produced locally and some has even been exported back to the US. Because of new laws making it more difficult to obtain the chemicals required to make

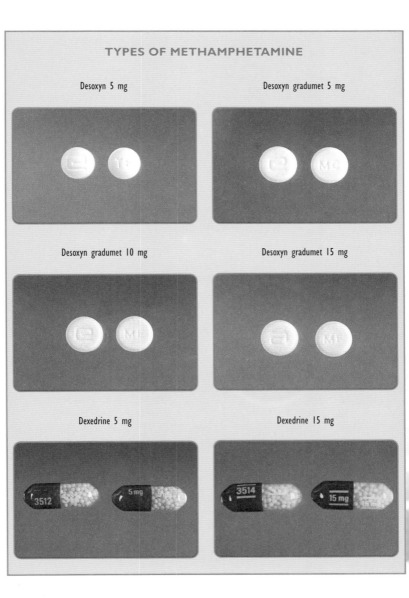

TYPES OF METHAMPHETAMINE

Desoxyn 5 mg

Desoxyn gradumet 5 mg

Desoxyn gradumet 10 mg

Desoxyn gradumet 15 mg

Dexedrine 5 mg

Dexedrine 15 mg

the drug, purity levels have fallen from around seventy percent in 1994 down to thirty-five to forty-five percent in 2001. Overall, all forms of the drug are being used in many regions of the US and misuse of this drug is one of the more worrying aspects of the current US drug scene. An estimated 4.7 million Americans (2.1 percent of the American population) have tried methamphetamine at some time in their lives. The Substance Abuse and Mental Health Services Administration's Drug Abuse Warning Network reports that from 1991 to 1994, the number of methamphetamine-related visits to hospital emergency departments more than tripled, from 4,887 to 17,397.

METHOD OF USE

The powder can be snorted or prepared for injection; "ice" or "crystal meth" is smoked while the red yabba pills are swallowed or smoked. Sometimes the pills are flavored (such as grape and orange) and marked with a variety of logos such as "WY."

BELOW: This is "ice" together with a typical pipe through which it is smoked.

EFFECTS

Immediately after smoking the drug or injecting it intravenously, the user experiences an intense rush or "flash" that lasts only a few minutes and is described as extremely pleasurable. Snorting or oral ingestion produces euphoria—a high but not an intense rush. Snorting produces effects within three to five minutes and oral ingestion produces effects within fifteen to twenty minutes.

As with similar stimulants, methamphetamine is most frequently used in a "binge and crash" pattern. Because tolerance for methamphetamine occurs within minutes—meaning that the pleasurable effects disappear even before the drug concentration in the blood falls significantly—users try to maintain the high by bingeing on the drug. As a powerful stimulant,

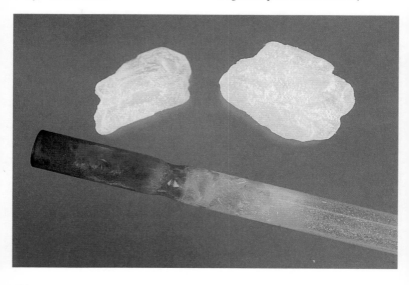

methamphetamine, even in small doses, can increase wakefulness and physical activity, while decreasing the user's appetite.

HEALTH RISKS

Cardiovascular

Methamphetamine can cause a variety of cardiovascular problems. These include rapid heart rate, irregular heartbeat, increased blood pressure, and irreversible, stroke-producing damage to small blood vessels in the brain. Hyperthermia (elevated body temperature) and convulsions occur with methamphetamine overdoses, and if not treated immediately, can result in death. Chronic methamphetamine abuse can result in inflammation of the heart lining, and among users who inject the drug, damaged blood vessels and skin abscesses.

Psychosis

High doses can elevate the body's temperature to dangerous, sometimes lethal, levels as well as cause convulsions. Chronic users can be violent and suffer from anxiety, confusion, and insomnia. They may display a number of psychotic features, including paranoia, auditory hallucinations, mood disturbances, and delusions (for example, the sensation of insects creeping on the skin called "formication"). The paranoia can result in homicidal as well as suicidal thoughts. Psychotic symptoms can sometimes persist for months or years after use has ceased. Many of these psychological disturbances are exacerbated by the fact that binge users can go for days without sleep and proper food.

Poisoning

Acute lead poisoning is another potential risk for methamphetamine abusers. A common method of illegal methamphetamine production uses lead acetate as a reagent. Production errors therefore may result in methamphetamine contaminated with lead. There have been documented cases of acute lead poisoning in intravenous methamphetamine abusers.

Injecting

Those who inject methamphetamine and share needles and other injecting paraphernalia put themselves at risk of contracting HIV and hepatitis. HIV is also an ever-present danger for the methamphetamine user because of increased libido and evidence of rougher, more chaotic sexual activity under the influence of the drug leading to cuts and abrasions.

Pregnancy

Research indicates that methamphetamine use during pregnancy may result in prenatal complications, increased rates of

premature delivery, and some abnormal reflexes and extreme irritability in the newborn.

DEPENDENCY

With chronic use, tolerance for methamphetamine can develop. In an effort to intensify the desired effects, users may take higher doses of the drug, take it more frequently, or change their method of drug intake.

In some cases, abusers forego food and sleep while indulging in a form of bingeing known as a "run," injecting as much as a gram of the drug every two to three hours over several days

until the user runs out of the drug or is too disorganized to continue. Although there are no physical manifestations of a withdrawal syndrome when methamphetamine use is stopped, there are several symptoms that occur when a chronic user stops taking the drug. These include depression, anxiety, fatigue, paranoia, aggression, and an intense craving for the drug.

THE LAW

In the US, Methamphetamine is a Schedule II drug under the Controlled Substances Act. In the UK, the drug is Class B under the Misuse of Drugs Act unless it is prepared for injection and then it is Class A. The fact that methamphetamine is not controlled under the most stringent category of controlled drug reflects the fact that it has very limited medical uses in the control of obesity, narcolepsy and Attention Deficit Syndrome marketed in the US as Desoxyn.

BELOW: An epidemic of methamphetamine use has swept round the Far East Asian countries of the Pacific rim especially Thailand where the drug comes in the form of a red pill called "yabba" meaning crazy.

Methylphenidate

Ritalin, uppers

WHAT IS IT?

Methylphenidate is a stimulant drug related to amphetamine, but milder in its effects. It is best known as Ritalin.

HISTORY

The drug was first patented in 1950 by the CIBA-Geigy Pharmaceutical Company, and was initially prescribed as a treatment for depression and chronic fatigue among other ailments. Beginning in the 1960s, it was used to treat children with ADHD, known at the time as hyperactivity or minimal brain dysfunction (MBD).

Using Ritalin in this way is controversial. Critics say that Ritalin is extensively overprescribed in the US and that the drug is used primarily to control or sedate "problem" children so that they will not disrupt class; that it transforms healthy children into "zombies," stifling their creativity and intellectual energy; and that it can lead children into drug addictions later in life. On the other hand, many parents report that their lives and those of their children have been transformed for the better by Ritalin.

MEDICAL USES

According to most estimates, more than seventy-five percent of Ritalin prescriptions are written for children diagnosed with ADHD, with boys being about four times as likely to take Ritalin as girls. Ritalin is also prescribed for mild depression and narcolepsy in adults.

Exactly how it works is unclear. It may have something to do with neurons in the brain. Instead of being balanced as they should, some of the neurons work overtime while others are under worked. For some reason, Ritalin stimulates the neurons that are not working as they should. The area of the brain that tells one when to pay attention to certain activities and to ignore other ones is "lazy" in ADHD sufferers. Ritalin stimulates those

LEFT: Although a stimulant, Ritalin has the paradoxical effect of calming hyperactive children.

neurons so that the child can pay attention and focus. Therefore while it calms down those children with ADHD, it would act like an amphetamine for those children without the condition.

EFFECTS

When used to treat ADHD, children appear calmer and more directed and controlled in their daily lives with an increased attention span.

HEALTH RISKS

Some of the more unwanted effects include weight loss, rashes, stomach pains, and insomnia. If used by young people non-medically as a recreational drug, then they run risks similar to those of amphetamine users.

DEPENDENCY

Children on Ritalin medication do not appear to develop tolerance to the drug. However, where the drug is misused by young people or adults, all the warnings about dependency that are cited for amphetamine apply.

THE LAW

In the US, methylphenidate is a Schedule II drug under the Controlled Substances Act, while in the UK it is listed with amphetamine as a Class B drug under the Misuse of Drugs Act. Ritalin is a controlled drug across Europe and unlike in the US and UK, its use to control the behavior of young children is largely outlawed.

TYPES OF METHYLPHENIDATE

Ritalin 5 mg

Ritalin 10 mg

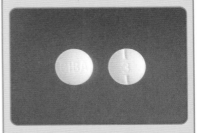

Ritalin 20 mg

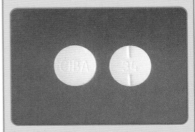

ABOVE: Ritalin for Attention Deficit Disorder is highly controversial. Some experts say that normal childhood behavior is being drugged while parents of ADD children say their lives are much improved.

Cocaine and Crack

Cocaine: Charlie, C, snow, blow, dust, flake, nose candy, toot
Crack: base, stones, rocks, wash

WHAT IS IT?

Cocaine is a naturally occurring, strong stimulant drug made from the leaves of the coca shrub. These plants are native to the mountainous regions of South America, more particularly in the countries of Peru, Colombia, and Bolivia. Crack cocaine is a smokeable form of cocaine which has manufactured into small lumps, known as "rocks"—they are usually about the size of raisins (see page 196 for an illustration).

MEDICAL USES

Cocaine is still used as a local anaesthetic, particularly for nose and throat surgery. It is also the ingredient of a pain-killing medicine rarely used these days called "Brompton's Cocktail." This is a combination of cocaine and morphine or methadone,

BELOW: Imitating our logo-obsessed society, this cocaine is branded with the mark of a certain dealing network to indicate to customers that they are buying a "quality" product.

where the cocaine is used to help to maintain mental functioning in the patient (often a cancer sufferer) while the narcotic analgesic does its pain-killing job.

HISTORY

Early history

Native South Americans have chewed coca leaves since at least 2500 BC as an aid to work. The cocaine in the leaves reduces tiredness and suppresses hunger. Coca also played an important part in social and religious life.

The conquering Catholic Spaniards of the sixteenth century were initially hostile to coca partly because they believed it to be symbolic of native "pagan" religion. However, they changed their minds when they saw the effect coca appeared to have on

ABOVE: With both cocaine and crack the intense craving produced by the drug keeps the user coming back for more and more.

the work performance of their new slaves toiling in the silver and gold mines and on plantations. Taxing coca also provided a useful source of revenue for the church.

Cocaine was successfully isolated from coca leaves around the middle of the nineteenth century and became the main ingredient of a number of patent medicines of the time, used to alleviate the symptoms of hay fever, asthma, and similar conditions. Cocaine's anaesthetic properties were put to use in eye surgery. Sigmund Freud was a champion of the therapeutic potential of cocaine (including promoting it as a cure for morphine addiction) but later changed his mind when he saw what long term use did to one of his close friends. Once the medical honeymoon period with cocaine was over, it became controlled drug in the US in 1914. Cocaine became the focus for Hollywood drug scandals in the 1920s, but then little was heard about cocaine until the late 1960s. Licit supplies had dried up, illegal production was in its infancy, and amphetamine was the stimulant of choice at that time.

In the UK and Europe, coca and cocaine-based preparations were very popular in the nineteenth century. In the UK, cocaine was actually controlled in 1916 during the First World War before opium and morphine (1920) because of concerns that prostitutes were selling the drug to soldiers on leave. Berlin during the 1920s experienced a cocaine epidemic, but like the US, cocaine became rare elsewhere until its come back in the 1970s and 1980s. In the UK, rates of cocaine use have been increasing ahead of other illicit drug use.

Modern history

Cocaine reappeared in the US as an expensive recreational drug used by the entertainment industry, especially rock musicians and film stars,

RIGHT: Crack was the most serious drug problem to hit the US in a generation. It thrived in areas of acute social deprivation providing huge profits for street gangs as the intense craving produced by the drug kept the people reusing.

acquiring the image of a "champagne drug" through the 1970s and 1980s when the arrival of crack changed the image of cocaine from one of white affluence to black poverty and violence. Currently in the US, there are about three million occasional

users with 1.3 million reporting use in the last month, and around 500,00 in the last week (mainly crack). At one time it was estimated that nearly ten percent of the American population had tried cocaine at least once. Americans spend more than $32 billion a year on coke, although that is reckoned to be an underestimate.

METHOD OF USE

Cocaine powder

In the US the most common form of cocaine is a white crystalline

powder—cocaine hydrochloride. Most users chop around 10–35 mg of cocaine into "rails" about one to two-inches long with a razor blade or credit card before snorting it up the nose, often through a rolled banknote or a straw. It also sometimes made into a solution and injected.

Crack

For a time, the new cocaine fashion was freebase, a smoked version of the drug which could be quite dangerous to prepare as it required the use of heated inflammable solvents. By the mid-1980s, a far more convenient way of smoking was devised, known as

crack, the preparation of which required little more than bicarbonate of soda and a microwave. Crack (the name deriving from the sound the drug makes as it burns) is usually smoked in a pipe, glass tube, plastic bottle or in foil and sometimes mixed with tobacco and/or cannabis in a joint. It can also be prepared for injection. The drug became very popular and enormously lucrative for the dealers for the following reasons:

1. On a "hit" by "hit" basis, the drug was relatively cheap if you compared a $5 rock with $70 gram of cocaine The effects are extremely intense and immediate for the user.
2. The effects wear off within fifteen minutes so those who enjoy the experience and want to repeat it over a period of time, will need large supplies.
3. The drug is ready to use. The freebasing process has already been done. In this respect, crack has been seen as one aspect of today's "fast food" society.

EFFECTS

When cocaine is sniffed the effects peak from anywhere between fifteen to forty minutes and then diminish, meaning the dose may have to be repeated every twenty minutes or so to maintain feelings of euphoria and strength. All these intervals are reduced with crack—euphoria is felt almost immediately, the effects peak in about one to five minutes and wear off inside fifteen minutes.

Like amphetamine, cocaine in all its forms produces feelings of well-being,

LEFT: The fashionable face of cocaine use in the 1970s and 1980s—the popular consensus was that cocaine was not addictive.

193

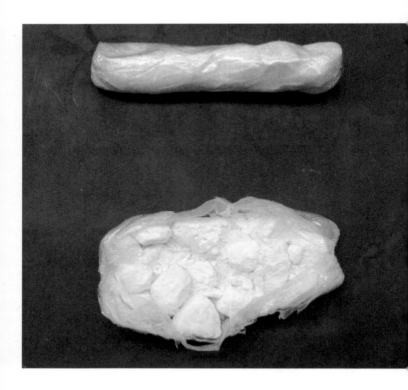

ABOVE: Celebrity coke deaths and the huge response to 800-COCAINE, the first official cocaine help line, proved that regular use could cause serious health problems.

exhilaration, indifference to pain and fatigue, and a sense of greater physical strength and mental capacity. Cocaine users are often very talkative. It is for these effects that cocaine has found favor with those who feel they have to be in top form to cope with highly stressful situations such as are often found in the business or entertainment worlds. However, laboratory tests on humans have failed to confirm that things really do "go better with coke."

In other words, users think they are performing better under the influence of cocaine even when they are not.

Regular cocaine users claim that the cocaine "high" is "smoother" than that achieved with amphetamine. Again, however, experienced users under laboratory conditions fail to differentiate between injected doses of cocaine and different types of amphetamines. By way of illustrating the relative impact of smoking over sniffing cocaine, one user told a drug worker it was comparable to the difference between smoking the highest grade marijuana and rubbing it on your knees.

Sexual activity

Cocaine has the reputation of improving sexual performance and responsiveness. Low doses can delay orgasm and heighten pleasure. However, at high doses or with continued use, sexual desire may diminish and men may have difficulty getting or maintaining an erection.

HEALTH RISKS

The most common physical effects of cocaine and crack use are a dry mouth, sweating, loss of appetite, and increased heart and pulse rate. Any cold, numb, or burning sensation in the nose is due to cocaine being an anaesthetic. When sniffed, cocaine has the effect of contracting the blood vessels in the nose. As the drug wears off and proper blood flow is resumed, users often experience many of the symptoms of a bad cold, runny nose, inflammation, and general nasal

ABOVE: A key factor in the spread of crack cocaine was the ease of manufacture.

irritation. Those who smoke crack suffer from chronic coughing, wheezy breathing, and a partial loss of voice.

Large doses or a run of quickly repeated doses over a period of hours

BELOW: Crack is easy to conceal—dealers will walk around with small wraps in their mouth which they will swallow if they are confronted by the police.

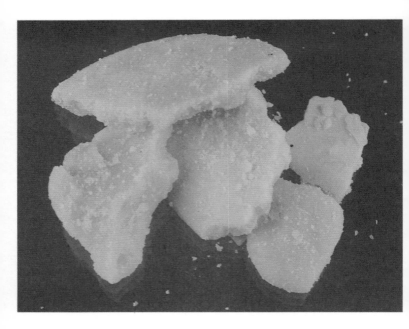

can lead to anxiety and panic. In extreme cases this can descend into paranoia and perhaps hallucination. As with amphetamine psychosis these effects usually diminish as the drug is eliminated from the body.

Most cocaine users will only experience moderate increases in blood pressure and mild heart pounding. However, when the drug has been used repeatedly over several hours or in one very large dose, blood pressure and pulse rate may shoot up and the heart start skipping beats. This can cause cardiac arrest and/or respiratory collapse.

Overdose

Exactly what constitutes a lethal dose of cocaine has not been clearly

ABOVE: The main effect of using crack is that it makes you want to take more. Chronic users may binge, stopping only when the money runs out.

established. Death has been known to occur after injecting as little as 20 mg whereas one researcher has noted the case of a man who regularly smoked 14 g of freebase a day for three weeks.

Taking cocaine with other stimulants such as amphetamine or ecstasy can further increase heart rate and blood pressure to a point where the user can become very anxious, overheats, or collapses. Taking ecstasy on top of cocaine is particularly dangerous, especially if the user is attempting to regain the high of the cocaine by eating or snorting ecstasy pills or powder. Unlike cocaine, ecstasy takes a while to take effect, which can sometimes tempt the user to increase the dose before they actually "come up." If too much is taken, the user may overdose resulting in anxiety, overheating, vomiting, and possibly coma.

Mixing drugs

Cocaine is often taken in combination with other drugs. Drinking alcohol while under the influence of cocaine can result in increased intake of alcohol. Combining cocaine with the use of other drugs can have often create unpredictable and sometimes disturbing effects. One particularly dangerous use of cocaine is a "speedball," a mixture of injected cocaine and heroin. This combination is said to greatly increase euphoria but has resulted in a number of fatal overdoses. Cocaine is also dangerous if taken with some hypertensive drugs and certain anti-depressants. When taken with monoamine oxidase inhibitors (MAOIs) cocaine use can result in dangerously high blood pressure. Other issues which can be associated with long-term habitual use often include some of the following problems:

LONG-TERM PROBLEMS:

- digestive disorders, dehydration, and anorexia—all associated with loss of appetite, erratic eating patterns, and inadequate nutrition

- loss of sexual desire

- heart problems such as abnormally rapid heart rate and irregular heart beat

- damage to the membranes lining the nostrils if regularly sniffed. The tissue separating the nostrils may become perforated, which requires surgery, but this condition is actually much rarer than is generally believed

- abscesses, swelling, and blood clots may occur if injected. Sharing needles increases the risk of contracting infections such as HIV

- longer-term respiratory problems can prevail if smoked

- financial difficulties may result after continual use, with the user losing possessions, property, and possibly relationships. as a consequence

- chaotic lifestyles can develop as a consequence of addiction and problematic use. This can include crime and the day-to-day pursuit of the drug and money to buy it

Chronic use

With constant, frequent use, increasingly unpleasant symptoms develop. Euphoria is replaced by an uncomfortable state of restlessness, nausea, insomnia, and weight loss. If use is continued, this may develop into a state of mind similar to persecution mania. Regular users who do not use sufficient amounts to become psychotic may nevertheless appear constantly nervous, excitable, and be unnaturally suspicious of other people. Confused exhaustion due to lack of sleep and food is not unusual. All of these effects generally clear up once the use of the drug is discontinued, although full recovery may take several months.

DEPENDENCE

It is said cocaine and crack are not physically addictive like heroin in that stopping its use does not lead to strong physical withdrawal symptoms that are typical of heroin withdrawal. While this is true, it is misleading to

RIGHT: Crack pipes can be made out of tin cans. The drug is placed in the hole at the top and ignited and the fumes are drawn through the straw.

define and therefore measure the existence of physical addiction using withdrawal symptoms associated with heroin use alone. Each drug has it own unique physical effects, which in the case of cocaine are very powerful. A chronic user of cocaine or crack will become very tolerant to the drug and their body will also be very used to the drug keeping them awake and functional. Once the user stops, which can prove very difficult for a regular or chronic user, they will very quickly start to feel tired, panicky, exhausted, and unable to sleep, often causing extreme emotional and physical distress. This can manifest itself in symptoms such as diarrhoea, vomiting, the shakes, insomnia, anorexia, and sweating, which for some people can prove unbearable. Many chronic users are well aware of these symptoms and, in an attempt to avoid them as well as ensuing fatigue, are very reluctant to stop its use.

Crack

As far as crack is concerned, claims have been made that, unlike cocaine, it is instantly addictive making

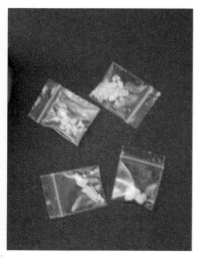

ABOVE: There is a high level of reported violence associated with crack cocaine. Users can become paranoid and drug-related gun crime is rampant.

and if so how quickly it happens, will vary depending on the individual user's mental state and circumstances.

Pregnancy

Cocaine and crack use have been associated with abnormal foetal development. Cocaine can cause problems during pregnancy in that it constricts the blood vessels, so restricting the blood flow carrying necessary maternal nutrition and oxygen to the foetus. Maternal use of cocaine has therefore been implicated in spontaneous abortions, separation

occasional or intermittent use impossible. Certainly, crack appears to induce an intense craving in some users which can rapidly develop into a "binge" pattern of drug use. As long ago as 1980, even the literature of America's drug subculture warned about the seductive powers of smoking cocaine.

However, studies of people who have ever used crack show that nowhere near all go on to daily, dependent use and that when this happens it usually takes a few months. To become a dependent user of cocaine hydrochloride would usually take longer. For both crack and cocaine dependency is not inevitable. Whether people become dependent,

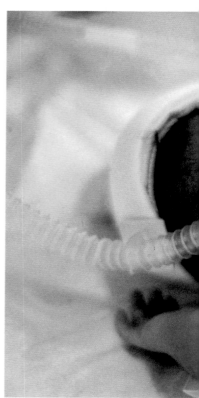

of the placenta (abruptio placenta), and stillbirth. Gastro-intestinal birth defects have also been suggested as a consequence of cocaine use in pregnancy. Other complications often associated with maternal drug use (irrespective of the drug) can include premature birth and low birth weight.

"Crack babies"

Much has been made of so-called "crack babies," those born supposedly "addicted" to crack. Media stories have suggested that such babies may die, having "lost the will to live."

However, medical evidence given to US Congressional hearings on cocaine and crack babies indicates that such claims are erroneous and that the cocaine-addicted infants usually get over the drug in about one or two weeks. It is true that during this period, such babies will be irritable, difficult to comfort, and may feed

BELOW: There has been much media hysteria surrounding alleged mortality and long-term developmental damage to so-called "crack babies" which has been challenged by doctors and is not borne out by the clinical evidence.

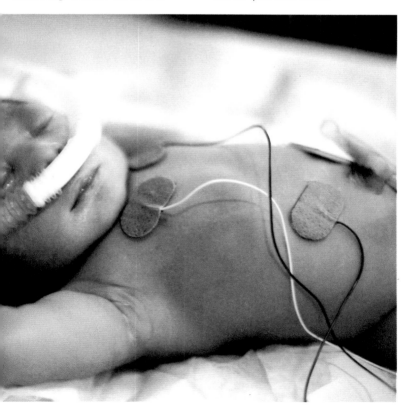

poorly. This may well hinder the mother-baby bonding process, which could already be compromised if the mother and baby have been separated by the baby's stay in hospital.

Reviews of the literature questioned the validity of much of the evidence that alleged to show long-term damage to children of crack users during their pregnancy. The impact of poverty, community violence, inadequate education, and unemployment are often far more significant factors. There have also been case reports suggesting that children may be effected by passive inhalation of cocaine smoke.

BELOW: Every year, the US Customs, the coastguard, and the DEA seize tons of cocaine either as it enters the US or as it is being transported from South America. However, both the demand and the supply seem limitless.

Symptoms can include nausea, motor coordination problems, and seizures. However, the symptoms subside with no apparent lasting damage.

THE LAW

In the US, cocaine and crack are Schedule II drugs under the Controlled Substances Act. The panic which ensued with the arrival of crack saw a controversial change in the law introducing far higher penalties for selling crack than powdered cocaine. There is a minimum mandatory sentence of five years for possessing 5 g of crack; for a similar sentence for possessing cocaine powder, the quantity would be 500 g. A second arrest for the possession of 5 g of crack would earn the individual no less than ten years in prison. Critics have declared that this discriminates against the black community because

ABOVE: Once drugs are seized they are either immediately destroyed or they may be held as evidence if the smugglers have been caught.

the individual caught on the street possessing and selling crack is more likely to be black, whereas most crack and cocaine users and the regional wholesaler who supplied the powder for conversion to crack, are more likely to be white. Calls to amend the law have so far been rejected by the US Congress.

In the UK cocaine and crack are controlled as Class A drugs under the Misuse of Drugs Act. It is illegal to be in possession of either crack or cocaine or supply them to other people. Maximum penalties for possession are seven years imprisonment plus a fine and for supply life imprisonment plus a fine.

BELOW: There are few places left to hide drugs where the enforcement agencies will not find them. Suspect cars will be stripped down to the rivets.

Ecstasy

XTX, E, and a whole range of names related to the physical appearance and color of the tablets and the logos stamped on them such as Calvin Klein, Mitsubishi, Motorola, and Nike among others

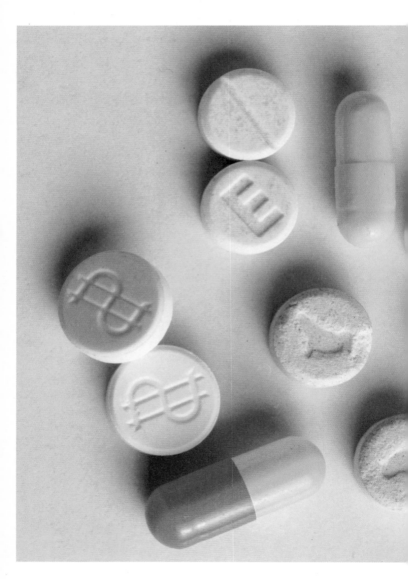

WHAT IS IT?

Ecstasy a member of a family of drugs headed by MDA. Ecstasy is known chemically as 3, 4, methylenedioxy-methylamphetamine or MDMA. It is classed as a hallucinogenic amphet-

amine, because its effects are likened to a mixture of amphetamine and LSD, though Ecstasy is rarely hallucinogenic at normal dose levels. Other drugs in the MDA family include MDEA, MMDA, MBDB, MEDA, and 2CB. They, as well as Ecstasy, are usually made from the oils of natural products such as nutmeg, crocus, saffron, and sassafras.

These drugs vary widely in their potency and effects. Those listed above are relatively mild. Others included in the MDA family like PMA and DOM are much more potent and are chemically synthesized drugs.

MEDICAL USES

As a Schedule I drug, the US authorities deem that Ecstasy has no medical uses. However, up until its Federal ban in 1985, Ecstasy was in use by a number of psychiatrists and therapists. Its capacity to induce empathy in users made it useful in helping, for example, married couples see the other person's point of view in marital therapy sessions. Recently, a research organization called "The Multidisciplinary Association for Psychedelic Studies" (MAPS) has received Federal approval to conduct research into the potential use of Ecstasy in post-traumatic stress

LEFT: There are as many designs and shapes on ecstasy pills and tablets as there are illegal chemists to make them. Those pills stamped with fashionable logos are very common on the illicit market.

situations. There was also some limited use of ecstasy being employed by doctors for therapeutic purposes in the Czech Republic and Switzerland.

HISTORY

MDMA was first made by two German chemists around 1913 as a part of a general research program conducted by the pharmaceutical and

research company Merck. Little interest was shown in the new drug and it was largely forgotten about until 1939 when it was tested on animals during research on

ABOVE: Most deaths from ecstasy have taken place in environments such as these where individuals have become overheated and dehydrated and have not taken enough breaks from dancing nor regularly sipped water.

adrenaline. In 1941, the drug was applied to new tests as a relief for Parkinson's disease, but it was rejected when one of the patients participating in the test progam experienced increased rigidity.

MDMA (and other drugs in this family) were also tested unsuccessfully by the US military in the 1950s in their search for Cold War "truth drugs" to use on enemy agents. But the real architect of the modern MDMA phenomenon was a Dow Chemicals scientist named Dr. Alexander Shulgin.

ABOVE: Although ecstasy was a street drug in the US during the 1970s, it did not make an impact on drug use among young people until the mid-1990s when the UK and European-style dance culture became big news.

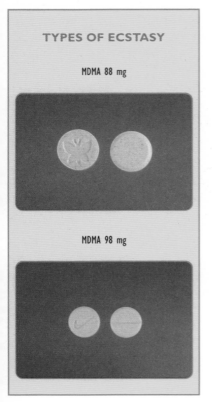

TYPES OF ECSTASY

MDMA 88 mg

MDMA 98 mg

"The hug drug"

Alexander Shulgin had invented a particularly profitable insecticide and as a reward for this he was given a lab and free reign to conduct any research that took his fancy—which in his case, was to discover new hallucinogenic-type drugs and test them on himself and volunteer friends. When the company discovered what he was researching, Dow quietly dispensed with his services, but he carried on and one of the many drugs to come out of his lab was "rediscovered" MDMA.

Eventually the drug hit the streets in the 1970s and was dubbed "the hug drug." In the 1980s, ecstasy was freely available over the counter in clubs and bars until a Federal ban in 1985. But "E" made little impact in the US, until the rave culture came across from the UK and Europe bringing ecstasy in its wake—one of the rare examples of an illegal drug craze being "imported" from Europe to the US. Ecstasy became ubiquitous at raves and dance venues across the US creating a tidal wave of media and political concern and prompting new laws to tighten up on both the drug and the venues where it was being used.

Not just raves

However, the drug has now escaped from the international club scene and has formed part of the lifestyle of not only many young people, but those in older age groups who experienced the drug in their youth and are carrying on using it, much in the way many people use Prozac, a drug which actually shares some chemical similarities with ecstasy.

Although the official statistics show a slight decline in use among school students, generally, ecstasy may now be only second to marijuana as the illegal drug of choice in countries such as the US.

METHOD OF USE

MDMA usually comes as a pill or capsule that is swallowed. As a powder (either in crystal form or as a crushed pill) it can be snorted, smoked in a joint, or swallowed either by dabbing and licking it off the finger or dissolving it in a drink. There is a huge range of colors and designs for the drug which sells for around $20–$30 a pill. Inevitably with illegal

drugs, there is no quality control and what passes as MDMA may include a range of other drugs including caffeine, ephedrine, amphetamine, ketamine, or close relatives of MDMA such as MDA or MDEA.

EFFECTS

Ecstasy is effective at a single dose level of 75–100 mg. The effects begin to take hold after twenty to sixty minutes and can last for several hours. As with many other drugs, the experiences induced by ecstasy, whether bad or good, often depends on what mood the user is in before the drug is taken, what they expect to happen, and the friendliness or otherwise of their immediate surroundings.

At moderate dose levels most users report a mild euphoric "rush" followed by feelings of serenity and calmness, and the dissipation of anger and hostility. The drug appears to stimulate empathy between users, but there is no evidence that ecstasy is

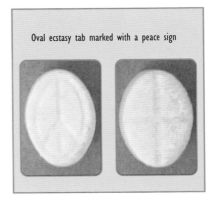

Oval ecstasy tab marked with a peace sign

ABOVE: This is 2CB—a hallucinogen related to ecstasy also known as Nexus or Brom, or by chemists as 4-Bromo-2,5-Dimethoxyphenethylamine. It made its emergence on the dance scene as an alternative and a complementary drug to ecstasy. The drug is sold either as a white powder or as small pills.

really an aphrodisiac. In this respect it tends to enhance the sensual experience of sex rather than stimulate the desire for sexual activity or increase sexual excitement. Again, at moderate dose levels there is heightened perception of surroundings without the visual distortions and illusions associated with the use of LSD. Ecstasy is to some extent psychedelic without being truly hallucinogenic. However, some sensitive individuals may experience

visual imagery, particularly in what they may refer to as in "the mind's eye." Typically at high doses, when the eyes are closed, users can experience colorful and dynamic hallucinations.

Some people who took the drug originally as a means of overcoming social awkwardness not only reported that the drug had cured their shyness, but their enhanced social skills remained after they had stopped taking the drug.

HEALTH RISKS
At normal dose levels, the pupils become dilated, the jaw tightens and users often grind their teeth. Some people may feel sick, begin to sweat, the mouth and throat will feel dry,

and blood pressure and heart rate will rise. Most people will lose their appetite. There can be some difficulty with blurred vision and body co-ordination making it potentially dangerous to drive or operate machinery.

Once the drug has worn off there may be some after-effects, or comedown, similar to those experienced by amphetamine. Ecstasy effects levels of "feel-good" neurotransmitters in the brain such as serotonin. In a comedown these chemicals fall to levels that can make the user feel anxious, depressed, paranoid, tired, and experience dizzy spells. These negative effects can typically last for around a period of three days, reaching their peak in the last day.

The "mid-week flu" is all too familiar to many weekend clubbers, who can do little or nothing to avoid it. The best that can be done is to aid recovery with plenty of rest and healthy drinks and food such bananas and nuts. These contain not only vitamins and minerals, but also brain chemicals such as 5-HTP, that aid the production of the "feel-good" neurotransmitter serotonin.

Higher doses

At doses above 200 mg or if the drug is being used repeatedly over a few days, all these effects may be experienced more acutely. The comedown may last for many more

TYPES OF ECSTASY

Trumpets

"E"

Rastafarian

TYPES OF ECSTASY

"X"

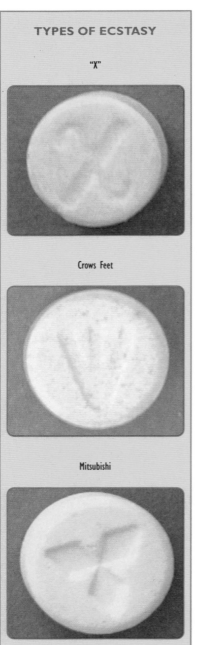

Crows Feet

Mitsubishi

days, even weeks, leaving the users feeling depressed, anxious, tired, and emotional. Most of the bad experiences with the drug have been reported by people using higher doses over a period of time and include anxiety, panic, confusion, insomnia, psychosis, and visual and auditory hallucinations. Generally, these effects disappear once the drug is stopped, but they can leave the user in a weakened mental and physical condition for a while.

Mixing drugs

Many ecstasy users take other drugs while under the influence of "E." While combining drugs can have both dangerous and unpredictable effects many users find that their drug experiences are enhanced. As far as current authorities know there is no reported increase in risk associated with combining ecstasy with cannabis or tobacco smoking. However, some of the dangers of combining ecstasy with other drugs include:

1. LSD could increase the possibility of a bad trip especially if large quantities are taken or the user is already anxious. LSD taken after ecstasy can prolong the trip and keep the user awake for longer;

2. Amphetamines or cocaine could increase the risk of overheating, particularly if the individual is dancing non-stop and there will

be a greater risk of harm for people who suffer from heart or blood pressure problems.

3. Alcohol increases the risk of overheating because alcohol acts as a diarectic and leaves the body dehydrated and unable to cool itself properly.

4. Ketamine is a hallucinogenic anaesthetic which could result in a very unpleasant trip with increased risk for people who have heart or blood pressure problems. Also, if someone who has taken ecstasy needs medical assistance for any reason, use of an anaesthetic like ketamine may complicate matters.

Deaths

There have been about 300–400 ecstasy-related deaths in the US since the mid-1990s. Most people die because of the combination of a drug which affects the temperature regulation in the body and the hot environment of a dance venue pushes body temperature to dangerous levels. (For more details on this, see pages 34–35.) In the UK, there have been around 200 ecstasy-related deaths, but very few across Europe as a whole.

Long-term use

Some long-term users have reported increased susceptibility to minor ailments such as colds, flu, and sore throats. Women may find that their periods are irregular and heavier with ecstasy use while others may have no periods at all while using it.

There is some evidence of a link between repeated ecstasy use and liver damage. Generally, the research suggests that people should not take ecstasy if they suffer from heart disease, high blood pressure, glaucoma, epilepsy, or are in poor physical or mental condition. More specific warnings sate that women with a history of genito-urinary tract infection should not use the drug.

There is no conclusive evidence that ecstasy has any effect on the foetus or causes problems in the newborn, but given the effect on the circulatory system, it would be advisable to avoid the drug during pregnancy.

Mental health problems

Research conducted on animals has found that regular or heavy ecstasy use can cause changes in brain chemistry and can result in damage to particular nerve endings (serotonin terminals) in the brain, some of which may be permanent.

Research on small samples of humans has also suggested that long-term ecstasy users may have persistent lower levels of serotonin compared to people who have not used ecstasy. The extent to which this happens, how long these effects last for, and the implications for the individual's mental health are not clear. The important issue to be recognized here is the link between these physical aspects of the brain and brain function. The nerves apparently damaged by regular ecstasy use are thought to be involved in memory function and low serotonin levels associated with depression. Studies that have looked at both nerve damage and brain function have found a link between recent heavy ecstasy use, slightly lower levels of serotonin (measured as density of serotonin transporters), and reduced memory recall. These findings have to be treated with care however. Similar studies show that with time these effects can be negligible or, despite some changes in serotonin levels, brain activity is not affected.

Results inconclusive

To be sure whether or not regular ecstasy use can lead to long term mental health problems, researchers would need to conduct a longitudinal study involving a control group of non-users examined perhaps over twenty years. Such a study would have to take account of the extent of ecstasy use, other drugs used at the time (both ecstasy type drugs and other legal and illegal drugs), many lifestyle factors, and evidence of mental health problems before using ecstasy. One study found that from a sample of non-, ex- and current regular, ecstasy users, the current users had the worst memory. Despite sophisticated statistical analyses, the study could not rule out the effects of other variable factors such as higher cannabis, amphetamine, and cocaine use among ecstasy users on the test results as well as the differences in the individual and their lifestyle that makes them more likely to take ecstasy in the first place.

The UK has had nearly twenty years experience with the drug and although the kind of study outlined here has

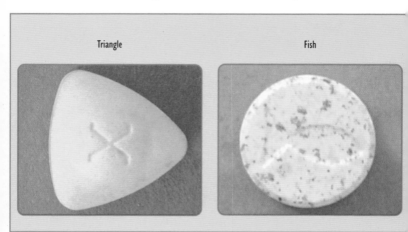

Triangle   Fish

not been conducted, even so there is no anecdotal evidence that those who were using Ecstasy in the mid-to-late 1980s are suffering any higher levels of depression or other mental conditions than the late thirties/early forties population at large. Overall, the degree to which Ecstasy causes serious and permanent "brain damage" is a highly controversial point of discussion.

There are clearly risks involved in using ecstasy, but scientists appear keen to rush into print with the latest (invariably government-funded) "bad news" about the drug. Research findings about the possible long-term consequences using brain imaging techniques which have been challenged by the scientific community, have nonetheless featured in government sponsored anti-ecstasy media campaigns. This dubious relationship between "objective" research and politics took a severe

knock when the main research facility conducting government-funded research into ecstasy had to publicly withdraw findings which sensationally linked the drug to Parkinson's Disease. It was discovered that rather than being given ecstasy, the laboratory monkeys had been given methamphetamine instead.

DEPENDENCY

Tolerance develops to the effects of ecstasy meaning that regular users may find themselves taking stronger doses to achieve the desired effects. There is no physical dependence or heroin-like withdrawal symptoms. However, some users may become psychologically dependent on use of the drug and the whole party experience. Regular use may lead to periods of fatigue, anxiety, and depression. As experienced with regular amphetamine use, the temptation may be to continue or increase use in an attempt to relieve these unpleasant experiences.

THE LAW

MDMA and all the other drugs in this group are Schedule I drugs under Federal law in the US. The advent of ecstasy as a club drug has prompted political action against venues frequented by young people. The US Congress is considering two bills that would hold music bands, DJs, bartenders, promoters, venue owners, radio stations, and others liable if a

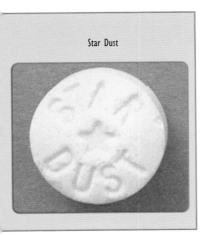

Star Dust

patron uses drugs at a nightclub or concert. The Ecstasy Awareness Act (H.R. 2962) would throw anyone in jail who "profits monetarily from a rave or similar electronic dance event knowing or having reason to know" some event-goers may use drugs there.

Similarly, Section 305 of the CLEAN-UP Act (H.R. 834) makes it a federal crime—punishable by up to nine years in prison—to promote "any rave, dance, music, or other entertainment event, that takes place under circumstances where the promoter knows or reasonably ought to know that a controlled substance will be used or distributed."

In 2001, harsher federal penalties for MDMA offenses went into effect, treating MDMA more seriously than

LEFT: Despite some well-publicized drug deaths, ecstasy has a relatively benign image and is often associated with simply going out and having fun by younger users.

In the UK, ecstasy is a Class A drug under the Misuse of Drugs Act and there have been various pieces of legislation aimed at preventing large rave gatherings and also targeting club owners. Ecstasy is strictly controlled in most countries across the world. As an analogue of amphetamine, it is controlled worldwide under the laws of the 1972 UN Convention on Psychotropic Substances and so few countries had to introduce new legislation in order to control the drug when it became popular.

BELOW: Ecstasy can push body temperature to dangerous levels but drinking excessive amounts of water can potentially be fatal.

cocaine and almost as seriously as heroin. Inevitably states differ in how they treat possession and dealing, but such has been the furore over "E," that some states have imposed harsh penalties for ecstasy, including Illinois where anyone convicted of possessing the equivalent of fifteen doses of MDMA must serve a term of four years in a state prison.

Tobacco

WHAT IS IT?

Tobacco is a plant that comes in two varieties, nicotiana tabacum and nicotiana rustica. Tobacco is grown in over 125 countries, on over four million hectares of land, a third of which is in China alone. Since the 1960s, the bulk of production has moved from the Americas to Africa and Asia: land devoted to tobacco growing has been halved in the US, Canada, and Mexico, but has almost doubled in China, Malawi, and Tanzania.

The raw leaves of the plant are dried and shredded and then rolled into cigarettes or cigars, or packaged as pipe or chewing tobacco or as snuff. In addition to nicotine, tobacco smoke contains some 4,000 different gases and particles, including "tar," a conglomeration of many chemicals, which is especially harmful to the lungs. Among the harmful gases in tobacco smoke are nitrogen oxide, carbon monoxide, and cyanide. More than forty carcinogens—chemicals capable of causing cancer—have been identified in tobacco smoke.

HISTORY

Early history

The peoples of the pre-Colombian Americas first used tobacco. Native Americans cultivated the plant and smoked it in pipes for medicinal and ceremonial purposes.

Christopher Columbus brought a few tobacco leaves and seeds with him back to Europe, but most Europeans didn't get their first taste of tobacco until the mid-sixteenth century, when adventurers and diplomats like France's Jean Nicot—for whom nicotine is named—began to popularize its use. Tobacco was introduced to France in 1556, Portugal in 1558, Spain in 1559, and finally England in 1565.

As with most new substances, tobacco was originally hailed for its supposed medicinal benefits. But in England, there was a fierce dispute about just how beneficial it was, especially when use moved from the Royal Court to the ordinary people. However, by 1625 tobacco's revenue advantages had led even King James—until then a fanatical opponent—to

LEFT: Tobacco was smoked by South American Indians long before the arrival of Europeans. It was an important part of religion and ritual and much stronger than the tobacco now found in cigarettes.

219

ABOVE: In the nineteenth century, tobacco was mainly chewed. The invention of the cigarette created massive wealth for the industry.

accept its widespread non-medical use and to regulate the trade of tobacco in the interests of the British colonies in the US.

The first successful commercial crop was cultivated in Virginia in 1612 by Englishman John Rolfe. Within seven years, it was the colony's largest export. Over the next two centuries, the growth of tobacco as a cash crop fueled the demand in North America for slave labor.

Growth in smoking

By the end of the nineteenth century, tobacco use was common in North America, but the quantity of tobacco that each individual used was still relatively small and it was primarily chewed rather than smoked. A

targets of the ads—smoking by women was considered impolite—and cigarettes were portrayed as a product for the rugged and powerful. With the rise of the Women's Suffrage movement in the UK and the move away from "Victorian values" in the 1920s, however, the tobacco companies began to fashion campaigns that encouraged women to smoke.

First health warnings

With the dramatic growth of tobacco use in the West came the first articles in the scientific and medical journals addressing the health effects of smoking. In 1930, researchers in Cologne, Germany, made a statistical correlation between cancer and smoking. Eight years later, Dr. Raymond Pearl of Johns Hopkins University reported that smokers do not live as long as non-smokers. By 1944, the American Cancer Society began to warn about the possible ill effects of smoking, although it admitted that "no definite evidence exists" linking smoking to the occurrence of lung cancer. At the time, the general public knew little of the growing body of statistics.

That changed in 1952, when Reader's Digest published "Cancer by the Carton," an article detailing the dangers of smoking. The effect of the article was enormous and widespread. Similar reports began appearing in other periodicals, and the smoking

number of factors contributed to a twentieth-century surge in tobacco use. The invention of the safety match made it safe and easy to light up and the revolutionary cigarette-manufacturing machine made it possible to produce pre-rolled cigarettes in great quantities.

The advent of the mass-circulation newspapers and magazines made widespread advertising of cigarettes possible. Initially, men were the sole public began to take notice. The following year, cigarette sales declined for the first time in over two decades.

The tobacco industry responded swiftly. By 1954 the major US tobacco companies had formed the Tobacco Industry Research Council (TIRC) to counter the growing health concerns. On the advice of the TIRC, tobacco companies began mass marketing filtered cigarettes and low-tar formulations that promised people a "healthier" smoke. The public responded and soon sales were booming again.

BELOW: Nineteenth century tobacco advert when many companies in the southern states were selling the product.

The next big blow to the tobacco industry came in the early 1960s, with the formation of the Surgeon General's Advisory Committee on Smoking and Health in the US. Convened in response to political pressures and a growing body of scientific evidence suggesting a causal relationship between smoking and cancer, the committee released a 387-page report in 1964 entitled "Smoking and Health." In unequivocal terms, it concluded "cigarette smoking is causally related to lung cancer in men." It said that the data for women, "though less extensive, point[s] in the same direction." The report noted that the average smoker is nine to ten times more likely to get lung cancer than the average non-smoker and cited specific carcinogens in cigarette smoke, including cadmium, DDT, and arsenic as causative elements.

Stricter tobacco controls

The control of tobacco is well documented for the US. In 1965, the Congress passed the Federal Cigarette Labelling and Advertising Act requiring the surgeon general's warnings on all cigarette packages. In 1971, all broadcast advertising was banned. In 1990, smoking was banned on all interstate buses and all domestic airline flights lasting six hours or less.

In 1994, Mississippi filed the first of twenty-two state lawsuits seeking to recoup millions of dollars from tobacco companies for smokers'

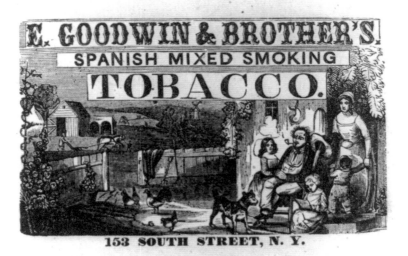

E. GOODWIN & BROTHER'S
SPANISH MIXED SMOKING
TOBACCO.

153 SOUTH STREET, N. Y.

Entered according to Act of Congress, in the year 1848,
BY E. GOODWIN & BROTHER,
In the Clerk's Office of the District Court of the United States for the
Southern District of New York.

Medicaid bills. Then, in 1995, President Clinton announced FDA plans to regulate tobacco, especially sales and advertising aimed at minors.

Since then, there have been legislative moves to make public spaces including bars and restaurants, smoke free zones. In other countries too, such as the UK, it is becoming increasingly difficult or even impossible to smoke at work, on public transport, and in public buildings. In 2004 the Irish government implemented a complete ban on smoking in all public areas, a move which the British government is considering. There are ever-stricter controls on tobacco advertising and

ABOVE: The mass circulation newspapers spread across the country by the expanding network of railways relied heavily on tobacco advertising for its revenues. Now such advertising is increasingly banned.

sponsorship of sport across the whole of the European Union.

Smoking worldwide

According to the World Health Organization (WHO), global consumption of cigarettes has been rising steadily since manufactured cigarettes were introduced at the beginning of the twentieth century. While consumption is levelling off and even decreasing in some countries (like the US and UK) worldwide more

Every cigarette we smok
fatty deposits sti

We'll hel

ABOVE: Bans on advertising, health campaigns, and increasing levels of taxation are all ways in which governments try to encourage people to stop smoking. The latest moves are to ban smoking in public places, as has happened in Ireland.

people are smoking and smokers are smoking more cigarettes. The recorded numbers of smokers will increase mainly due to expansion of the world's population. By 2030 there

224

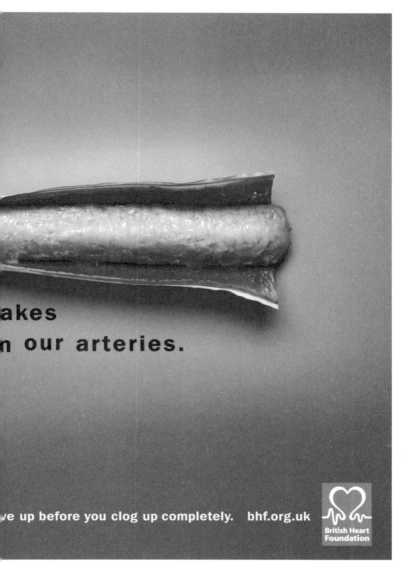

akes
n our arteries.

ve up before you clog up completely.   bhf.org.uk

British Heart
Foundation

will be at least another two billion people in the world. Even if prevalence rates fall, the absolute number of smokers will increase. The expected continuing decrease in male smoking prevalence will be offset by the increase in female smoking rates, especially in developing countries.

Tobacco companies are producing cigarettes at the rate of five and a half

ABOVE: There have been substantial damages paid out by the tobacco companies to those who have claimed that they were never given the information that smoking could seriously damage their health.

trillion a year—nearly 1,000 cigarettes for every man, woman, and child on the planet. Cigarettes account for the largest share of manufactured tobacco products—ninety-six percent of total

Soviet Economies (631 billion), and Western Europe (606 billion).

Worldwide there are 4.2 million premature deaths from smoking every year. The WHO calculates that no other consumer product is as dangerous, or kills as many people. Tobacco kills more than AIDS, legal drugs, illegal drugs, road accidents, murder, and suicide combined.

Smoking and health in the US

There are approximately forty-seven million smokers in the US. About twenty-three percent of adults smoke and about thirty percent of adolescents.

Tobacco use is the leading preventable cause of premature death in the US. It is estimated that directly or indirectly, tobacco causes more than 400,000 deaths in the US annually, a figure that represents nearly twenty percent of all deaths in the US. These deaths have been attributed to a number of conditions defined as tobacco-related, including heart disease (115,000 deaths), cancer (136,000), chronic pulmonary disease (60,000), and stroke (27,000).

METHODS OF USE

Manufactured cigarettes consist of shredded or reconstituted tobacco processed with hundreds of chemicals. Often with a filter, they are manufactured by a machine, and are the predominant form of tobacco used worldwide. Cigars are made of air-

value sales. Asia, Australia, and the Far East are by far the largest consumers (2,715 billion cigarettes), followed by the Americas (745 billion), Eastern Europe and Former

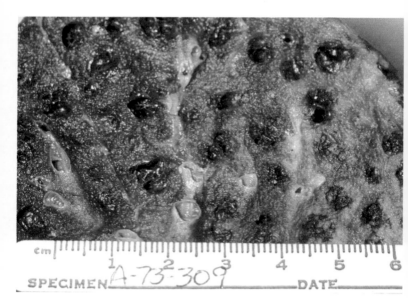

cm | 1 A-73-309 2 3 4 5 6

SPECIMEN————————————————DATE

ABOVE: The devastation of lung disease. According to the American Lung Association nearly 6,000 children under eighteen years of age start smoking every day. Of these, nearly 2,000 will become regular smokers—that is almost 800,000 annually.

cured and fermented tobaccos with a tobacco wrapper, and come in many shapes and sizes. Pipes are made of briar, slate, clay, or other substances—tobacco is placed in the bowl and inhaled through the stem, sometimes through water.

Snuff was very popular at one time, where a "pinch" of snuff, a pulverized tobacco preparation, was inhaled through the nostrils. Now, however, it is mostly placed in the mouth ("dipped"), where the nicotine it contains is slowly and directly absorbed into the bloodstream.

Chewing tobacco (an entirely American fashion) is taken in a similar way.

EFFECTS

Cigarette smoke consists of droplets of tar, nicotine, carbon monoxide, and other gases. The lungs absorb nicotine and other substances, so how much is absorbed depends on how much smoke is actually inhaled rather than "puffed."

Nicotine is a drug with complex effects on brain activity. It is absorbed through the lungs rapidly enough for each inhalation to have an almost immediate and separate effect. Nicotine levels build up over smoking a cigarette and then rapidly decline until the next "smoke." Immediacy of impact is thought to contribute to the attraction of smoking, while the rapid decline permits frequent use.

Although tobacco is a mild stimulant, it is paradoxically used for its calming effects, to alleviate stress and anxiety, but also to maintain performance in the face of fatigue or monotony. Users smoke as a relaxant on most occasions, though most smokers say they are more likely to light up in the company of others who do likewise. Its appetite suppressant qualities make the drug additionally attractive to those concerned about their weight.

One or two cigarettes will lead to an increase in pulse rate and blood pressure, reduce appetite, lower skin temperature and produce symptoms of stimulation and arousal. While regular smokers experience satisfaction on inhaling, first-time users can often feel sick and dizzy.

HEALTH RISKS

The more one smokes, the more likely one is to suffer from heart disease, blood clots, heart attacks, lung infections, strokes, bronchitis, bad circulation, lung cancer, cancer of the

BELOW: Evidence from tobacco industry files reveals that executives knew in 1964 that nicotine was addictive, but they withheld that information for thirty years. During that time, nine million Americans died from tobacco use.

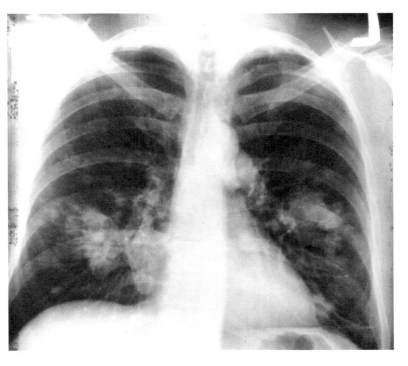

mouth and throat, and ulcers. Few will get all of these effects, but everybody who smokes is more likely to suffer from each.

Lung cancer is the disease most closely associated with smoking. Risk of irreversible damage to the lungs increases with the number of cigarettes smoked per day, the number of years of smoking, and the earliness of the age at which one started. However, if no irreversible damage has yet occurred the lungs clear themselves once smoking has stopped and it is believed that the ex-smoker can eventually regain normal health and life expectancy.

Since the 1950s, increased use of filter tips and decreased average cigarette strength may have contributed to a reduction in lung cancer. However, recent evidence suggests that although "low tar" or "mild" cigarettes have lower tar levels, smokers simply tend to inhale deeper and more often, to the extent that any benefits are cancelled out.

Although cancer is the disease most closely related to smoking in the public consciousness it is actually not the biggest smoking related killer. As an example, every year in the UK around 114,000 people die as a result of smoking, of these 30,000 die from cardiovascular disease. Smoking actually kills more people worldwide from cardiovascular disease than from cancer and more than a third of almost five million deaths attributable

to smoking globally are due to cardiovascular disease.

It is not only smokers who suffer the adverse effects of tobacco. Increasingly the phenomenon of passive smoking has been recognized whereby non-smokers inhale smoke involuntarily. Some of the smoke they inhale is known as "side stream smoke"—the smoke that smoulders off the end of a cigarette, cigar, or pipe. This smoke has neither passed through a filter nor through the lungs of a smoker and is therefore extremely potent, containing more tar, nicotine, particles, and gases than inhaled smoke. Side stream smoke can cause respiratory distress and allergic reactions, as well as lung cancer. Recognition of passive smoking has been one of the main driving forces behind the increasing prohibition of smoking in public places.

Pregnancy

It has been recorded that women who smoke beyond the first months of pregnancy tend to give birth to smaller and less mature babies, which may then cause difficulties after the birth. These mothers also run a slightly increased risk of spontaneous abortion and increase the (still very small) risk of losing the baby around the time of birth.

It has also been proven that women who smoke and take oral contraceptives are ten times more likely to suffer from diseases of the heart or circulatory system than women who do neither.

DEPENDENCE

The most striking aspect of cigarette use is the extent of dependence and regular use. People who begin to smoke tend to increase their consumption until they smoke regularly. If they stop, they may feel restless, irritable, and depressed.

Globally, more people are regular users of tobacco than any other known drug. Large tobacco corporations have been forced into admitting that tobacco is addictive—a fact they have apparently known for many years, but kept secret. Court cases have been heard and are being planned in pursuit of damage claims against the companies both in the UK and US. Some of the tobacco companies have offered out of court, blanket compensation deals to protect themselves from further litigation.

THE LAW

No country bans tobacco smoking outright, but many countries do have restrictions on the age below which tobacco products cannot be sold; locations in which tobacco can be smoked; and the level of advertising and sponsorship allowed to the tobacco companies. Some countries, especially the UK, also demand that health warnings appear on packaging.

BELOW: On present smoking patterns, about fifty million children and teenagers in China today will eventually be killed by the habit. Of these, about half will die in middle age.

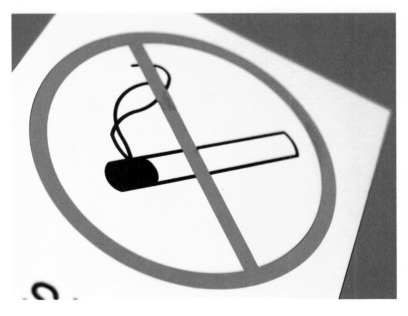

Caffeine

WHAT IS IT?

Caffeine is a stimulant which acts on the central nervous system making people more wakeful and active. It is the most commonly used stimulant drug found naturally in range of plants which as beverages are popular the world over—coffee and tea, cocoa beans and kola nuts. Coffee is grown in many areas of the world including

Africa, Arabia, Central and South America, Java and Sumatra, and the West Indies. Tea is mainly grown in India, Sri Lanka, China, Indonesia, and Japan. Most of the world's cocoa beans come from West Africa. Caffeine is also a common ingredient in many soft drinks.

MEDICAL USES

Caffeine is produced in the laboratory as the ingredient for a wide range of over-the-counter analgesics and headache pills and a drug for stimulant purposes in its own right, for example British products like Pro-Plus.

HISTORY

Coffee was introduced into England in 1601 and popularized on medical grounds. Later "coffee shops" spread as a forum for male social and political activities, provoking governmental licensing restrictions and suppression.

Tea generally contains less, but can contain almost as much caffeine as instant coffee. It was introduced into Britain, again as a medicine, in 1661, but soon became popular as a "pick-me-up." Despite opposition, by the late 1700s tea had ousted coffee as the national beverage and had become

LEFT: The recent plethora of real coffee outlets that have sprung up in many British towns and cities has substantially increased the nation's caffeine intake.

one of the country's chief sources of revenue.

Coffee came to the US in the mid-1660s, although tea was the favored drink until 1773 when the colonists revolted against the heavy tea tax imposed by the UK. The Boston Tea Party changed American drinking habits forever in favor of coffee.

Offering tea or coffee is now a customary form of hospitality to visitors, and there can hardly be a restaurant or café in the world that does not provide one or the other, or both. Caffeine pills are often taken as a "keep me awake" pill, whilst driving, at work, or as a general stimulant. Students are renowned users of caffeine, in any form, to aid them through heavy study loads at exam times. With up to 50 mg in each caffeine tablet, it would be easy for someone to add as much again to their caffeine consumption from beverages. Tablets available online contain as much as 200 mg. Some athletes also allegedly use the drug as a legitimate performance enhancer, typically in the form of a caffeine suppository. Some regard the drug as a slimming aid, but there is evidence to suggest this is not the case. In the US, for example, the drug has been banned from use as an additive to slimming products.

EFFECTS

Coffee is the strongest of the beverages; one strong cup of "real" coffee may contain caffeine equivalent to the minimal stimulant dose. Soft drinks also generally contain less caffeine than coffee, but, because of their lower body weight, children consuming a full can could ingest the caffeine equivalent of four cups of coffee.

Each cup of brewed coffee provides an average 115 mg (drip method) or 80 mg (percolated) of caffeine, instant coffee about 65 mg, tea 60 mg, and a can or bottle of soft drink from 30 to 50 mg, all with wide variations depending on the amount used and the method of preparation. These compare with the standard stimulant dose of 200 mg.

Caffeine is an indirect nervous system stimulant in that it "prevents" the brain from slowing down, therefore not actually stimulating the brain, just letting it function effectively. In moderate doses (150–250 mg), the drug allays drowsiness and fatigue and postpones the onset of sleep, helping prevent boredom and tiredness interfering with performance on manual and intellectual tasks.

HEALTH RISKS

With the advent of many new coffee outlets, especially in the UK, selling freshly prepared strong coffee, caffeine intake has risen considerably in recent years.

The effects of coffee are evident within an hour, lasting three to four hours. Afterwards, there can be a "let-down" effect of increased fatigue.

Larger doses impair performance, especially where delicate co-ordination of movement is required. There are increased feelings of alertness, or sometimes of anxiety. Physiological effects can include increased heart rate, raised blood pressure, increased excretion of urine

(these diminish with repeated use), constriction of blood vessels in the brain (relieving some types of headache), and increased breathing. Coffee—even decaffeinated coffee—increases stomach acidity.

Higher doses

The consumption of 500–600 mg of caffeine a day can cause feelings of

ABOVE: The two most important species of coffee are Arabica—which accounts for over seventy percent of world production—and Robusta.

anxiety and restlessness. After more than one gram of caffeine is taken at one go (say the equivalent of fifteen cups of instant coffee), the physiological effects may become pronounced enough to cause

abnormally increased sensitivity and sensory disturbances (like ringing in the ears and light flashes), together with insomnia, muscle tremor, abnormally elevated heart rate and breathing, and gastrointestinal complaints such as nausea, vomiting, and diarrhoea. The individual may also experience restlessness and excitement which can then progress to delirium. Death from a caffeine overdose is possible but very unlikely and very rare—for example, it would normally take the consumption of over 100 cups of coffee to reach that level of toxicity.

Long-term use

Evidence that heavy, long-term coffee drinking increases the risk of peptic ulcer, heart disease, or certain cancers is inconclusive, and adverse effects are likely to be infrequent and generally slight. However, individuals suffering from ulcers, high blood pressure, or anxiety may find that excessive caffeine/coffee consumption aggravates their condition.

OPPOSITE: Hot chocolate first came to Europe from Mexico in 1528, followed by tea in 1610, and coffee from the east (1615).

Pregnancy

The safety of caffeine consumption during pregnancy is controversial. Some studies suggest that modest caffeine intake of less than two average-sized cups of coffee per day presents a slight risk to the baby but others do not. There is stronger evidence that larger daily amounts of caffeine during pregnancy may increase the risks of miscarriage,

BELOW: Whatever method is used, decaffeinated coffee must contain less than 0.1 percent caffeine to comply with European regulations.

ABOVE: Colonists in Boston became aware of tea in 1670, but it was not on sale until 1690.

premature delivery, and low birth weight, but again there is no solid proof of this. On balance it would seem that a modest intake of caffeine is unlikely to cause any problems during pregnancy.

DEPENDENCY

People consuming levels of caffeine equivalent to that of seven or more cups of strong coffee a day may feel chronically anxious and irritable, and experience muscle tremor and headache. The stimulant effect may also cause chronic insomnia, but all of these disturbances will clear up once the individual's caffeine intake is reduced or stopped.

Tolerance develops in many people (but not all) of the physiological effects of caffeine, and there is a well-established withdrawal syndrome, noticeable after regular use of about

370 mg a day. On discontinuing, the habitual user feels less alert and relaxed, more drowsy and irritable, and may experience headaches which can be severe. Regular drinkers often feel tired and irritable if they miss their usual morning coffee. Dependence, mainly psychological, can develop to the extent that people find it hard to stop drinking coffee, even for medical reasons.

THE LAW

Caffeine is not subject to any legal prohibitions on its manufacture, sale, distribution, or possession. The medicinal products containing caffeine will be subject to the pharmacy and over-the-counter regulations of different countries.

BELOW: Whether it's tea or coffee, millions of people around the world cannot face the day until they have had their caffeine fix.

Khat

Abyssinian tea, African salad, catha, chat, kat, quat, qat, quadka

WHAT IS IT?

A green leafy plant, which grows ten to twenty feet high, it is cultivated throughout eastern Africa and the Arabian peninsula at altitudes of 1500–2000 meters. There are several varieties of khat, but two are generally available: *Miraa* chiefly from Kenya and the *Harari* from Ethiopia. *Catha edulis*, is commonly known as *qat* or *qaadka* in Somalia, or *chat* in Ethiopia, but it is now referred to consistently in the literature as "khat."

Khat contains two known pharmacologically active stimulant substances, cathinone (aminopropiophenone) and cathine (norpseudoephedrine). Cathinone is the main active ingredient. Its concentration in the fresh leaves ranges from 0.3 to 2.1 percent, depending on the origin and variety of the plant. Cathine concentrations range from 0.7 to 2.7 percent. The active ingredients start to deteriorate two days after the plant has been harvested, meaning it must be consumed fresh. The youngest leaves near the top of the plant are the most potent and are often wrapped in banana leaves after harvesting to retain their strength. Khat is also available dried, crushed, or in powder form. However, traditional users of the drug choose to eat only fresh leaves as the dried plant contains no (or very little) active chemicals.

Out of Africa

With the migration of refugees from north eastern Africa to the US, Russia, and elsewhere, it became more convenient to access the active ingredient of khat, cathinone, first as an easily exportable paste for smoking, then as a synthetic manufactured substance produced illegally in the US. The drug, formulated as methcathinone has also found its way into the US via Russia where it was spread by motorcycle gangs especially in rural areas during the early 1990s, although now it has been largely overtaken by methamphetamine and ecstasy.

MEDICAL USE

The medical use of khat dates back to antiquity, when Alexander the Great reportedly used it to treat his soldiers for what was recorded as an unknown "epidemic disease." In the Harar region of Ethiopia, khat is widely believed to effect 501 different kinds of cures; these equal the numerical value of its Arabic name: ga-a-t (400+100+1).

HISTORY

Khat has been chewed or drunk in the Muslim cultures of Somalia and Yemen for centuries, where it has been

ABOVE: Grown at altitudes above 1,500 meters in two main varieties across eastern Africa and Arabia, khat is tightly packed in banana leaves to keep in the moisture until it is consumed.

considered a rival to coffee. It was also mentioned in an Arab manuscript in 1333. In modern times, khat was such an important commodity that its daily export to Aden lay behind the founding of Ethiopian Airlines. Some homes in the growing regions have special rooms for khat chewing and it has been estimated that in the Yemen, many people spend over one third of their family income on the drug.

BELOW: A bust of Alexander the Great—despite medical use going back centuries, excessive use of khat among men can cause both health and financial problems for families.

METHOD OF USE

The fresh leaves, twigs and shoots of the plant are chewed like tobacco then retained in the cheek and chewed intermittently to release the active drug which give the stimulant effect. The dried material, which is much less effective, can be made into a tea or paste. Khat can be smoked or sprinkled onto food. A bundle of forty twigs has a street value of around $30–$60 per kilogram.

EFFECTS

Khat is predominantly a stimulant in effect. A typical khat chewing session

is said to be the equivalent of ingesting a moderate 5 mg dose of amphetamine sulphate. Following mild euphoria and talkativeness, users have often reported calming effects, and a reduction in appetite.

HEALTH RISKS

Due to the fact that it is chewed, khat effects the oral cavity and the digestive tract. Inflammation of the mouth and other parts of the oral cavity, with secondary infections, is common in khat users. There is evidence that excessive use of khat can lead to other health problems, such as heart disease and loss of sex drive in men. Stomach irritation and constipation can precipitate hernias; khat consumption also interferes with the absorption of iron and other essential minerals.

Of particular concern is the risk of oral cancer, reportedly prevalent among khat chewers in Yemen. Prolonged and excessive use can bring on psychological problems such as depression, anxiety, and irritation, sometimes leading to psychosis.

Many Somalis (and people from other khat using cultures) do not acknowledge the problems that have been identified with khat. This may be related to the fact that in their home countries most chew on a social or moderate basis. Once abroad in a strange country, some users have escalated their consumption as a reaction to changed circumstances and the frustrations of life as a refugee.

Synthetically produced methcathinone is full of adulterants from the manufacturing process including sulphuric acid and highly toxic chemicals like toluene, potassium permanganate, and sodium dichromate which is toxic to the heart, brain, skin, and kidneys.

DEPENDENCY

Long-term use of methcathinone can bring with it many of the problems of chronic methamphetamine use including malnutrition, muscle wasting, a general collapse of personal hygiene, and a range of psychological problems including habitual dependency.

THE LAW

In the US, while the plant itself is not illegal, the active chemicals are; cathinone (and synthetic methcathinone) is a Schedule I drug under the Controlled Substances Act, cathine is classed as a Schedule IV drug. Khat is also illegal in Canada, Norway, and Sweden, but currently legal in the UK and most of the rest of Europe, and also legal in Africa and the Middle East.

In the UK the khat plant itself is not controlled under the Misuse of Drugs Act, but the active ingredients, cathinone and cathine, are Class C drugs. Cathinone may not be lawfully possessed or supplied except under a license for research, though cathine may be prescribed.

Anabolic Steroids

'roids, juice

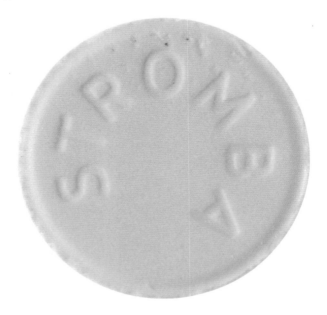

WHAT IS IT?

Anabolic steroids (AS) are synthetic derivatives of testosterone, one group of hormones which occur naturally in the body and are responsible for the development and functioning of the male reproductive organs.

MEDICAL USES

These drugs have limited medical uses including the following:

1) It is often employed as a treatment of persistent anaemia where the red blood cells are unable to regenerate effectively;

2) To assist protein build-up in people

ABOVE: Some of the anabolic steroids used by body builders and athletes, such as Stanozolol, have been formulated for veterinary use only.

weakened after surgery or through long-term confinement.

3) To replace testosterone in those men who have had the testes removed following surgery for testicular cancer.

HISTORY

Doping in sport

The current history of non-medical use of AS apparently began in 1954 among Russian weightlifters and their American counterparts at the weightlifting championships in

Vienna. In 1956, the drug company Ciba developed the first oral AS, methandrostenolone, and many American athletes used this drug before the Melbourne Olympics of that year. By the time of the Mexico Olympic Games held in 1968, using steroids to build strength was an open secret in the world of athletics and it has been reported that their use was rife among strength and track and field athletes. The International Olympic Committee banned steroids in 1980, but the use of steroids in competitive sport continued to grow through with increasing amounts of public and media attention, most notably when Canadian sprinter Ben Johnson was stripped of his 100 meters gold medal during the 1988 Seoul Olympics.

A lot of media attention has recently focused on the discovery of a new previously undetected AS—Tetrahydrogestrinone or THG. This is a designer AS used only so far by elite athletes—"designer" in the sense that it was designed to escape detection by the sporting authorities. It was created by modifying two other known

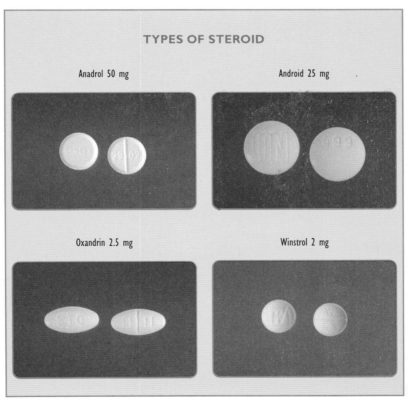

TYPES OF STEROID

Anadrol 50 mg

Android 25 mg

Oxandrin 2.5 mg

Winstrol 2 mg

steroids, trenbolone and gestrinone. Trenbolone has become one of the most popular steroids on the black market over the last few years. The modifications made the drug undetectable with normal testing procedures.

Body building

Outside of sport, the main group of users have been those involved in bodybuilding. This might be specifically to obtain the kind of body "sculpture" deemed necessary for bodybuilding competition, for more general fitness or cosmetic purposes, or for functional/occupational reasons such as those engaged in acting as

BELOW: Many steroids on the market are manufactured to look as if they come from legitimate pharmaceutical companies, but most are fake.

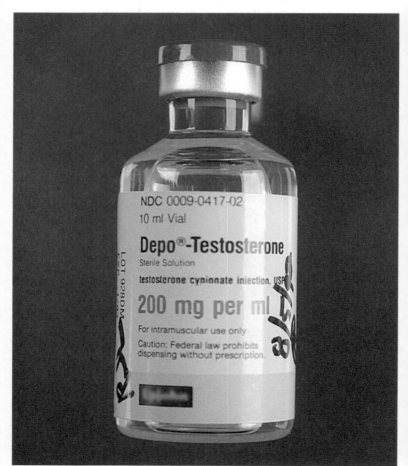

bodyguards, doorkeepers at places of entertainment, or even police officers. The other main group studied has been American high school students with sub groups including members of the gay community and those who model clothes in the fashion industry.

BELOW: Some needle exchange programs see so many steroid clients that they have set up separate facilities to supply clean works.

Overall, it has been estimated that in the US alone, there are more than one million current or former AS users.

METHOD OF USE

Steroids come in both oral and injectable forms with many different varieties on the market, each one sold under several proprietary names including Nandrolone, Stanozolol, Sustanon, Boldenone, and

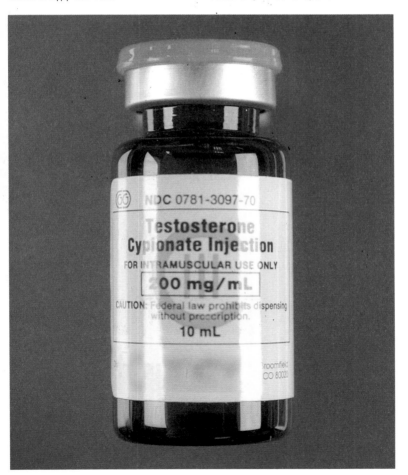

ABOVE: Testing for the use of performance enhancing drugs has become one of the most controversial issues in sport.

Testosterone. Most steroids used non-medically are counterfeit, prepared by illegitimate pharmaceutical outfits, but in illicit laboratories. The Internet has made anabolic steroids easily available across the world, transcending any national laws.

Steroids are used in a cycle for up to twelve weeks (although this period can vary) followed by a rest period

and such cycles might be repeated two or three times a year. Steroids are frequently taken together in often complex combination regimes during the cycle (referred to as "stacking") and sometimes in a pyramid fashion where dosages are increased to a maximum dosage and then tapered off towards the end of the cycle.

EFFECTS

Because these drugs are based on male hormones, it is not surprising that users report they feel "wired up" and

aggressive. Women users report an increase in sexual drive.

ABOVE: Drugs in sport became worldwide news when Ben Johnson lost his gold medal in 1988

HEALTH RISKS

There are many side effects of using AS reported by both men and women—these include acne, male pattern baldness, and the build up of breast tissue on men. AS use can cause high blood pressure and other heart conditions including heart failure and strokes and serious kidney and liver damage, even cancer of the liver ("Wilm's tumor"). In women, the voice can irreversible deepen and breast tissue reduce. Long-term use of steroids can cause sterility in men and there is an association between AS use and prostate cancer.

Adulterated drugs

Given that there is no quality control throughout the illegal drug market generally, it is not surprising that this applies equally to the market in anabolic steroids. Sometimes this lack of quality control can have fatal consequences. Unconfirmed reports indicate that perhaps up to three British bodybuilders died of cardiac arrhythmias recently when they took a counterfeit of the drug Anabol which had been wrongly manufactured to include 2 mg of the bronchodilator Clenbuterol for which the normal dose is 0.02 mg. Other samples were also said to include amphetamine. Another bodybuilder who took the same drug was admitted to hospital with all the symptoms of MDMA (Ecstasy) overdose including muscle cramps, sweating, nausea, headaches, and paranoia.

Another potential problem is that injectable drugs made in illicit laboratories may not be sterile and

BELOW: There have been cases of extreme acts of violence and even murder committed under the influence of anabolic steroids—so-called "roid rage."

251

generally anybody who is injecting AS runs the same risks as any other intravenous drug user, namely hepatitis and HIV/AIDS.

Where young people are using these drugs, there is a danger that growth many be stunted because AS "trick" the long bones in the leg into believing that growth is complete and the ends of the bones close off preventing any more growth.

Psychologically, AS can cause serious problems with aggression and sexual violence in men. There have even been some cases where men have committed murders under the influence of so-called 'roid rage.

DEPENDENCY

Withdrawal symptoms have often been reported, which respond when steroid use is resumed. Symptoms reported include depression, tiredness, anorexia, insomnia, decreased libido, hot and cold flushes, sweats, nausea, and increases in pulse rate and blood pressure. This suggests at least an element of physical dependency.

It is likely that those who use steroids can become dependent on the achievement of sought after effects as much as anything to do with the body/drug dynamic. Those who have achieved an improved body image through use of AS (with concomitant feelings of power, self-confidence, wellbeing, etc.) can become obsessed with this new image every bit as much as those who suffer from eating disorders. With a condition like anorexia, the belief on the part of the sufferer is that they are too big, whatever they actually weigh; on the part of the user, the obsession can be a belief that they can never be big enough. Apart from escalating dosage levels, dissatisfaction with body image, referred to as "reverse anorexia," is one of the most powerful predictors of dependence.

THE LAW

Action against the use of anabolic steroids takes a number of different

forms. In the US, AS are Schedule III drugs under the Controlled Substances Act. Those convicted of a Federal trafficking offense could be jailed for a maximum of five years for a first offence. The situation in the individual states is quite confusing, with different states taking their own view as to whether possession of AS is a misdemeanor or a felony. For example in Ohio, up to 200 tablets or 16 ml is a misdemeanor, but more is a felony. In North Carolina, it's up to 100 tablets. In Hawaii, it's up to only twenty-five tablets. In Alabama, simple possession has a statutory maximum sentence of ten years.

In the UK, there is no possession offence for AS, just a trafficking offence under Class C of the Misuse of Drugs Act with a maximum of fourteen years imprisonment. Across Europe, the laws are similar, in that it is not illegal to possess AS, but trafficking is banned.

BELOW: There are a whole range of serious physical and mental health problems for both men and women who are long-term anabolic steroids users. Some of these side effects are irreversible.

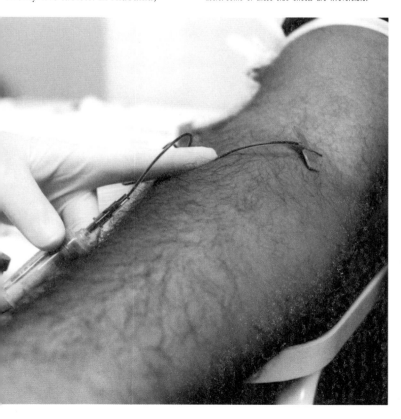

4-MTA

Flatliners

WHAT IS IT?

4-MTA (4-methylthioamphetamine) is a synthetic drug that is chemically and pharmacologically similar to amphetamine and club drugs like MDMA. It is generally found in the form of cream colored pills or tablets. It is also known as para-methylthioamphetamine (p-MTA), MTA, or "Flatliner."

MEDICAL USES

4-MTA was first developed in 1992 as a slimming aid or anti-depressant, and as a potential replacement for Prozac. This new drug originated from research conducted by Professor Dave Nichols of Purdue University in Indiana. His team had been looking for drugs that cause the release of serotonin in the brain, with the expectation that they might have a therapeutic value similar to the SSRI anti-depressants like Prozac.

HISTORY

It was legally on sale in Amsterdam until 1998 at which point it was taken out of the stores when owners and retailers realized that it had only ever been tested on rats—no official medical testing on humans had ever been carried out. Since then the drug has found its way onto the dance scene in Europe and Australia. It is often sold as ecstasy or "Flatliners," with many users unaware that they had been sold 4-MTA in the place of ecstasy.

British authorities recently seized a consignment of 25,000 tablets that probably originated from the Netherlands. As of June 1999, at least fifteen overdoses, five of which were fatal, were reported in Europe. Anecdotal information from people who have knowingly taken 4-MTA, suggests that it has not gained in popularity because its effects are not as pronounced as MDMA.

To date, the drug does not seem to have a notable presence on the American drug scene.

METHOD OF USE

Swallowed as a tablet.

EFFECTS

The drug's effects are very similar to ecstasy except that they come on much more slowly. Users have described 4-MTA as giving a steady increase in energy and a Prozac-like mental calm. Reports suggest that one 125 mg dose of 4-MTA delivers a mild stimulant effect without the charged or euphoric buzz experienced with speed or MDMA, with no hallucinations or visual distortions reported. The effects can last up to twelve hours.

HEALTH RISKS

Because of the slow onset of its effects, users might think that the drug is not working and take more—which is where the risk of overdose lies. This may happen because the effect of 4-MTA is similar to that of taking an MAOI anti-depressant drug along with Prozac, a combination that is known to be very toxic and has also led to deaths. There are also risks resulting from mixing the drug with alcohol, MDMA, amphetamines, ephedrine, and certain foods.

THE LAW

In March 2001, the United Nations Commission on Narcotic Drugs voted to include 4-MTA in Schedule I of the 1971 Convention on Psychotropic Substances. The drug is banned in the UK and some other European countries, but is still legal in the US probably due to its lack of presence on the country's drugs scene.

BELOW: There is a whole "alphabet soup" of MDA-related drugs. They range from relatively mild types like MDMA (ecstasy) to much more toxic varieties. Some of these are "designer drugs"— "designed" in the laboratory to evade the drug laws by changing the chemical composition while retaining all the psychoactive effects.

PMA

Red mitsubishi, killer, death, mitsubishi turbo, double-stacked, chicken yellow, chicken fever, para-methoxyampethamine, para-methoxymethyamphetamine

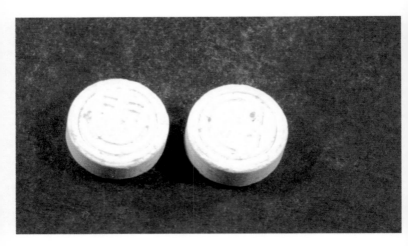

WHAT IS IT?

PMA (or para-methoxyamphetamine to give it the correct medical name), is a synthetic amphetamine with stimulant and hallucinogenic properties related to MDMA (ecstasy) and the rest of the MDA family, but much more potent. Pure PMA is a white powder, but can appear beige, pink, or yellowish on the street. It's usually made into pressed pills and sold as MDMA (ecstasy). There have been several cases of "Mitsubishi's" or ecstasy tablets that have been found to contain PMA.

The drug may well in fact be one of the most dangerous and toxic hallucinogens ever to be available on the drug scene.

ABOVE: This is a highly dangerous drug which can cause dramatic rises in body temperature, heart rate, and blood pressure to the point where the user may go into convulsions, coma, and even die. It can be very hard to distinguish it from ecstasy in dark corners where illegal drugs are dealt.

HISTORY

Until recently, PMA was only briefly encountered during the early 1970s in the US and Canada. However, since February 2000, the significant presence of PMA has been noted in Florida, Illinois, Michigan, Virginia, and Canada.

Since May 2000, PMA ingestion has been associated with three deaths in Chicago and Illinois, and seven deaths in central Florida. The drug has also been identified on the dance scene in the Europe, and Australia, where other PMA-related deaths have occurred. This is the real clue to the drug's return to the drug scene. The PMA precursor chemicals are far easier for the producers in the illegal market to obtain and are not so strictly controlled like those for ecstasy. It is most likely the case that anybody taking PMA these days is doing so accidentally, thinking that it is ecstasy.

METHOD OF USE

The drug has been sold in tablet, capsule, and powder form for oral ingestion. So far all of the PMA tablets sold on the ecstasy market around the world have been white or tan "Mitsubishi" tablets. They are often underscored, have a diameter of 0.28 to 0.3 inches (7 to 7.5 mm), and are thicker than most other pills— about 0.24 inches (6mm) thick, unusually thick compared to ecstasy tablets. They weigh about 230 mg and have gained the nickname "double-stacked" because of its thicker appearance.

EFFECTS

At lower doses (less that 50 mg or roughly a quarter of a tablet, depending on body weight) PMA produces an increase in energy, minor visual hallucinations, and a mild euphoric state, similar in many respects to the effects of ecstasy.

HEALTH RISKS

The initial effects of a low dose of PMA might feel a little bit like MDMA, but PMA takes more than half an hour or sometimes longer for the effects to come on. This may possibly prompt some people to take another pill thinking that they have bought "weak ecstasy." But by taking successive tablets the person may well take a lethal dose.

At slightly higher doses it causes a sudden increase in heart rate, blood pressure, and body temperature to dangerously high levels that can cause the user to suffer convulsions, coma, and even death. A person who has ingested a high enough dose of PMA has difficulty breathing, develops muscle spasms and nausea, and starts vomiting. Still higher doses can also produce cardiac arrhythmia and arrest, pulmonary congestion, renal failure, hyperthermia, convulsions, coma, and eventually death.

THE LAW

In the US, UK, and elsewhere, PMA is controlled under the most stringent category of drug laws. For example, in the UK, PMA is catagorized as a Class A drug—meaning it is illegal to have possession of it, give it away, or sell it. Possession can mean the individual might be sentenced for up to seven years in jail. Supplying the drug to others has more serious consequences and can result in a life sentence and an unlimited fine.

STP

WHAT IS IT?

STP and DOM (2.5-dimethoxy-4-methyl-amphetamine) are chemically identical hallucinogenic amphetamines related to the MDA-MDMA group of drugs.

HISTORY

The chemist responsible for creating a huge range of hallucinogens and stimulant-hallucinogens (and tried them all himself) was Dr. Alexander Shulgin, a man who has acquired a legendary status among drug users across the world.

He has written two books which are no less than recipe books (assuming you have all the background chemistry knowledge of course) which are also required reading for enforcement agencies looking for information on new designer drugs which come onto the drug scene.

In 1964, Shulgin synthesized DOM, an incredibly powerful drug—at 5 mg the experience could last up to three days. Two years later, another powerful drug, STP, appeared on the scene. It turned out to be identical to DOM, but had been produced independently by an underground chemist experimenting with MDA derivatives. STP stood for "Serenity, Tranquillity, and Peace" and was unleashed on the world when 5,000 10 mg tablets were circulated at the "Human Be-In" in San Francisco's Golden Gate Park in January 1967 (a prelude to San Francisco's Summer of Love"). Dr. Shulgin consequently went onto develop less dramatic versions of STP such as DOB and DOET.

Many of these disappeared from the drug scene, but the advent of rave culture has witnessed a renewed interest in all types of hallucinogen. For example, it was reported in the British press that a consignment of 35,000 DOM/STP tablets were seized in France bound for the UK.

METHOD OF USE

Swallowed as a tablet.

EFFECTS

A dose of less than 1 mg acts as a euphoriant, while larger doses produce trips similar to those from LSD or mescaline. As with LSD, set (the user's psychological frame of reference) and setting (his or her physical surroundings) profoundly effect the course of the trip. The user's visual perception is altered; colors create a new world of brilliance and clarity; shapes and forms evolve and change. Users also report that time and space interweave while the self stands apart and observes it all. The trip is usually long and intense, effects begin to surface in about an hour from ingestion and last from anywhere between eight and twenty-four hours.

HEALTH RISKS

Physical responses are similar to those of amphetamines, as it stimulates the sympathetic nervous system and causes increased heart rate, blood pressure, reduction of appetite, tremors, sweating, and pupil dilation. Amphetamine-like effects are less pronounced than the psychological responses. The adverse mental fall-out from an experience like this can be very serious, especially for anybody with a pre-existing or latent mental health problem. The lethal dosage level has not yet been determined.

DEPENDENCE

Tolerance develops rapidly if STP is frequently used. Physical dependence has not been demonstrated and the drug does not appear to cause any withdrawal symptoms.

THE LAW

STP and similar compounds are all controlled as Schedule I drugs in the US and are similarly strictly controlled across Europe.

BELOW: Known as the "father of ecstasy," Dr. Alexander Shulgin has actually discovered many E-type drugs and tested them all out on himself.

SECTION 5

Hallucinogenics

LSD
Mushrooms
Ketamine
DMT
Ibogaine
Mescaline
PCP

This group of drugs cover a wide range of chemically dissimilar substances which act on the brain to alter our perceptions of what is real. They break down or bypass the mechanisms which filter the sounds, thoughts, and images which crowd into our brain on a daily basis. Users of any of these drugs may claim to "see" colors or "hear" sounds as part the effects experienced when taking them. Under the influence of these very powerful drugs, the visions can be awesome and life-enhancing or, just as easily, terrifying. In most cases, the user will know that the hallucinations are not real, but with some types of hallucinogens this is not so. How an individual reacts to these drugs is very much dependent on the drug/set/setting equation explained on pages 8–11.

Many of these drugs occur naturally in plants found in woodlands, deserts, and jungles, and especially in the south American rain forest where most of the world's species of hallucinogenic plants originate from. The best known synthetic hallucinogen is LSD, but other drugs have similar properties, notably the anaesthetic drugs, phencyclidine and ketamine. Marijuana is not included

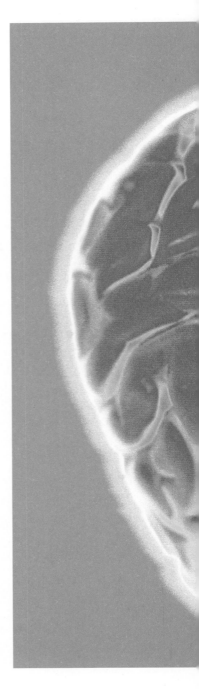

RIGHT: How these drugs actually work on the brain is little understood. What they seem to do is break down the normal filters of ordinary consciousness allowing a torrent of images and sound to flood the brain.

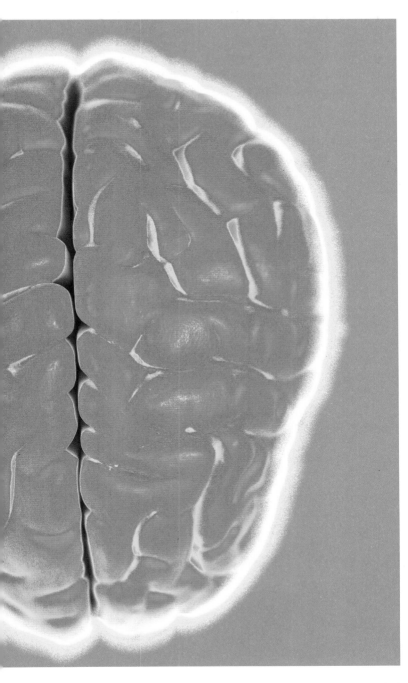

in this section but it has been known to produce hallucinogenic effects in certain circumstances. In high doses and with certain varieties, marijuana shares similar properties with the other drugs listed in this section, however, in normal doses, it acts more like a depressant causing the user to feel relaxed.

HISTORY OF USE

Due to the fact that many hallucinogenic drugs exist as plants in many different regions across the world, their use probably goes back beyond recorded history. Some writers have even suggested that the discovery of the mind-altering properties of these plants by early hominids may have accelerated human development—although they offer up no evidence for this. Early religious scripts do speak of various herbs and

plants which may well have had hallucinogenic properties and medieval stories of flying witches have also been linked to the use of certain plants by what the texts have referred to as "wyse women."

Anthropologists and other researchers who have ventured into the south American jungle in the twentieth century discovered a wealth of hallucinogenic plants used by

LEFT: The Amazonian rain forest has over eighty different species of hallucinogenic plant, the largest concentration of this type of plant in the world.

native tribes for rituals, rites of passage for young men, and as medicines. Many of the active ingredients of these plants were later synthesized in modern laboratories. It was in such a lab in 1943, that the properties of LSD were discovered—one of the most powerful hallucinogenic drugs on the planet.

ACTION ON THE BODY

The "true" hallucinogenic drugs like LSD, mescaline, and psilocybin "magic" mushrooms all have a range of relatively minor physical effects on

ABOVE: Many very powerful hallucinogenics have been synthesized in the laboratory for experimental research, only to find their way onto the streets.

the body including raised blood pressure and heart rate, stomach cramps, and nausea. Minor, that is, compared to the percussive effects on the brain. Marjiuana combines the action of a depressant, a mild to moderate hallucinogen and even a painkiller while at the other end of the scale, phencyclidine and ketamine combine anaesthetic properties with those of the strongest hallucinogens.

LSD

Acid, trips, tabs, boomers, doses, plus other names associated with the designs on LSD-impregnated blotting paper, e.g. Bart Simpson, Darth Maul, Easy Rider, Buddha, Strawberries, etc.

WHAT IS IT?

LSD (or d-lysergic acid diethylamide) is a hallucinogenic drug originally manufactured from ergot—a parasitic fungus found growing naturally on rye and other grasses. The name comes from the German abbreviation of the drug, *lyserg saeure diaethylamid.*

MEDICAL USES

Currently under American law, there are no recognized medical uses for LSD. However, beginning as early as 1950 in the US and 1953 in the UK, LSD was used extensively in the treatment of alcohol and drug addiction, and for those with disturbed personalities and severe mental health problems. It was also used with terminally ill patients to alleviate pain and help them cope with facing death. LSD was also valued for its ability to deliver what one writer referred to as "a big bang" to the memory of a repressed neurotic, in

whom it could release a stream of buried recollections and suppressed responses.

Medical opinion remained divided on the efficacy and (to a lesser extent) the safety of LSD psychotherapy. A major British survey conducted in 1968 used questionnaire returns from

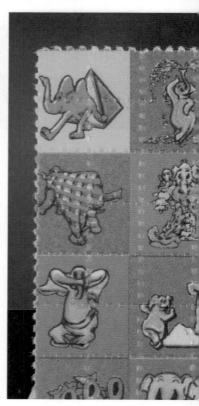

RIGHT: LSD was discovered in 1943 by a Swiss research chemist whose skin accidentally came in contact with a minute amount of the drug. He had a very illuminating bike ride home that day.

clinicians engaged in LSD therapy to construct a bank of information from some 50,000 sessions. The research concluded that LSD's potential benefit was restricted to "substantially strong people whose neurosis is of a kind dimming their enjoyment of life." Other practitioners reported apparent successes with a far wider range of personality disorders up to and including patients suffering from various long-term, severe mental disorders.

Fears about the rapid rise in casual use and concerns about public safety led to the drug being restricted in both in the US and UK, and by 1971, British officials stated that therapists were required to have a license to use LSD clinically, which consequently stopped legitimate use almost completely. In 1995, a number of patients who had received LSD psychotherapy in the UK during the 1950s and 1960s, claimed that they had suffered subsequent mental illness, raising the possibility of legal action against the responsible health authority. Medical opinion remains divided as to it benefits to this day.

HISTORY

LSD was discovered in 1938 by Albert Hofmann then employed as a chemist at Sandoz Pharmaceuticals in Geneva. The drug was first made in the course of an attempt to prepare new therapeutic drugs from ergot. The work had been the main concern of Sandoz's Natural Products Division since the discovery of ergotamine in 1918. LSD was the twenty-fifth (hence "LSD 25") in a series of drugs prepared from lysergic acid, the original aim being to make a new stimulant drug.

Military use

Disappointing preliminary tests on animals meant that further work on its research was shelved until in 1943. During these later tests, Hofmann unwittingly ingested the tiny amount necessary to trigger the first ever LSD "trip." Suspecting LSD as the cause of his strange experience, Hofmann began a series of experiments on himself and colleagues. Confirmation was swift. With only a tiny dose of LSD needed to produce an effect, Hofmann had stumbled upon one of the most potent mind-altering drugs

LEFT: LSD is often sold as impregnated blotting paper called "tabs." The sheets (as pictured here) are dipped in the drug solution and the drug tends to sink to the bottom of the sheets when they hung up to dry. Therefore the dosage strength of the tabs can differ widely within the same sheet, with some tabs containing hardly any while others are very potent.

ever developed. He quickly saw that the drug might have some uses in psychiatry as discussed earlier, but LSD also attracted the American military and intelligence services as a potential brainwashing and truth drug and one that could disable an army in a non-combative way.

Military personnel were given the drug without being told and tragically a few committed suicide in the belief they had gone mad. These tests were eventually abandoned in the 1960s. But in the process of military testing, some of America's most prestigious universities and hospitals had played host as test centers using volunteer students and graduate assistants. One such hospital was attached to Harvard University. When students and academics began feeding back their experiences it attracted the attention of two Harvard psychologists, Timothy Leary and Richard Alpert.

Counter-culture

Leary and Alpert conducted their own experiments on the nature and value of the "psychedelic" experience (a term first coined in 1957 by Dr. Humphrey Osmond, one of the pioneers of research into LSD). They conceived LSD as a "chemical key" that could open up the mind to new experiences of self-awareness and enlightenment. Taken by sufficient numbers of people joined together in a "Brotherhood of Love," they believed that LSD could benefit human kind as

a whole. By making his opinions public, however, Leary donned the mantle of public crusader under the banner "Turn on, tune in, and drop out." The university authorities took fright and subsequently sacked both Leary and Alpert. Leary was to later renounce his earlier stance as naive and became a devotee of cyberspace as the great liberalizing force for humanity.

His legacy was the launching of LSD into the public domain. Through the endeavors of underground chemists, LSD circulated freely among student groups, intellectuals, artists, and musicians and the idea of LSD as a means to self-improvement caught on. Inevitably, the use of LSD spread to a wider and predominantly younger age group who were not so interested in "finding themselves" but simply liked taking it for the effects it produced. LSD became yet another street drug to "threaten" the world's youth, meeting public disdain of its use as a consequence.

So the drug came under public scrutiny. Concerns were expressed about its health impact. Fears included brain damage, deformed babies, psychosis, homicide, suicide, and stories of people believing they could fly. Some of these dangers were real, others were simply without foundation, as discussed further on. However, publicity over these concerns catapulted LSD to the status of a first division media "horror"

ABOVE: The Brotherhood of Eternal Love formed in California in 1966, was credited with generating $200 million and responsible for widely distributing LSD and marijuana in the United States.

drug, much as cannabis had been in the 1930s, heroin in the 1950s, phencyclidine (angel dust or PCP) in the 1970s, and then crack in the 1980s and 1990s.

Modern day use

During the 1970s, interest in LSD diminished considerably as the supporting hippy ideology lost credibility within western culture and the alternative communities (real or imagined) on both sides of the Atlantic broke up. During the 1990s, there was a surge in interest in LSD connected to dance culture, but recent research suggests a dramatic drop in the use of LSD. In the American

household surveys from 2000 and 2001, 6.6 percent of high-school seniors reported that they had used LSD in the previous year. In 2002, the figure dropped to 3.5 percent, and in the most recent survey, from 2003, only 1.9 percent of high-school seniors claim to have "dropped" acid. The US Drug Enforcement Administration reports that there has been a decline in the strength of LSD over the years, from 100–200 micrograms in the 1960s and 1970s now down to 20–80 micrograms today. LSD is also very difficult to make and there may be less than a dozen laboratories in the whole of the US that make the drug.

In 2003, two LSD producers were sentenced to life imprisonment without parole after the DEA made the single largest seizure of an operable LSD lab in its history. During

A black market LSD blotter generally has art or a design printed on the paper. The paper is perforated into individual "tabs" or "hits" approximately ¼ inch by ¼ inch (6 x 6 mm). The sheets (usually divided into 100 perforated squares) are then dipped in a solution containing a known quantity of LSD or have LSD applied with a dropper creating a relatively consistent dosage per tab.

LSD can also be bought as microdots or as liquid. The liquid is usually sold in a small pipette bottle, containing tens or even hundreds of doses. Microdots are small grains of LSD about 0.08 inches (2 mm) long. Prices can range from $1–$10 a dose.

EFFECTS

LSD is an incredibly powerful drug. Enough LSD for 2,500 doses weighs about as much as a postage stamp. Two gallons of pure LSD could dose the whole of the US. LSD is effective in doses as small as 25 micrograms (or twenty-five millionths of a gram) although the average dose for a full-blown psychedelic experience is between 100–150 micrograms.

A trip begins about half an hour to an hour after taking LSD, it then peaks after two to six hours, and fades out within eight to twelve hours,

the trial, it was stated that there had only ever been four seizures of complete LSD labs and three of those were run by these same two defendants. This large dent in the supply of LSD across the US coupled with poor quality, the complex production process, and the increasing difficulty of obtaining the chemicals necessary for production may certainly account for the decline in the use of the drug.

METHOD OF USE

LSD comes in various forms. Most common are stamps or blotters, made by impregnating a sheet of paper with a solution of LSD in alcohol, often vodka. Each paper usually has its own brand design covering the whole sheet or just one dose (usually 0.28 by 0.28 inches or 7 mm by 7 mm). Designs have included a lightning flash, rainbows, smilies, ohm, strawberries, and Buddhas.

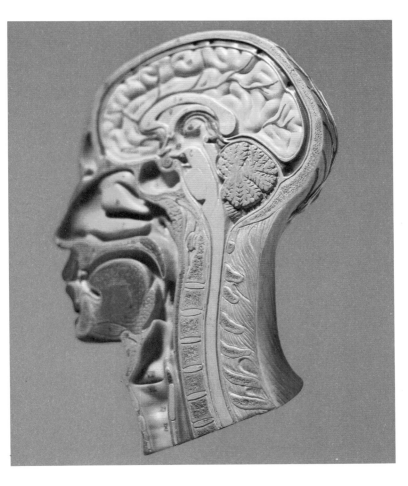

depending on the dose taken. Exactly what happens when a drug is taken is often determined by what the user expects will happen and the situation in which the drug is used. Once a trip is underway, it cannot be stopped even if the experience is be unpleasant.

Users often report visual effects such as intensified colors, distorted shapes and sizes, and movement in stationary objects. Distortions to

hearing occur, as can changes in sense of time and place. Generally the user knows these effects to be unreal. True hallucinations (ones the user believes to be real) are relatively rare. Physical effects (such as dilation of pupils, slight rise in body temperature, goose bumps) are so slight compared with

273

psychological or emotional effects that they are of little importance.

Emotional reactions vary, but may include heightened self-awareness and mystical or ecstatic experiences. Feelings of dissociation from the body are commonly reported. Unpleasant reactions are more likely if the user is unstable, anxious, or depressed. They may include anxiety, depression, dizziness, disorientation, and sometimes a short-lived psychotic episode including hallucinations and paranoia, commonly known as a "bad trip." The same person may experience good and bad trips on different occasions, and even within the same trip.

While the LSD experience is variable compared with many other drugs, it is also relatively more open to the user's intentions and to the suggestions of others. Hence friendly reassurance is an effective antidote to a bad trip. Experienced users can often "steer" the trip toward the area they wish to experience or explore.

HEALTH RISKS

It is difficult to combine a trip with a task requiring concentration and driving will almost certainly be impaired. Suicides or deaths due to LSD-induced beliefs or perceptions, although much publicized, are rare. Incidents of fatal overdose were unreported in medical literature until as recently as 1985 when twice the amount ever found in a post-mortem

was detected in a subject's body with no other drug present.

There are no known physical dangers attributable to long-term LSD use. In particular there is no reliable evidence that LSD causes brain damage or damage to future children. Adverse psychological effects are possible after one trip but are more common in regular users. For some users, the experience of hallucinating can be acutely distressing and include feelings of paranoia, phobia, and delusion. These will take time to subside once the user has comedown from the drug experience. Case studies of prolonged, serious adverse psychological reactions are reported in the literature but appear to be rare.

Mental health

Reactions to LSD use can be psychotic but this usually only occurs among users who already have existing or latent mental illness. This is more common after repeated LSD use, when the drug has perhaps pushed the individual mentally too far. Among drug users such individuals are marked out as acid casualties—those who have taken so much LSD over a period of time and spent so much time tripping that they never quite come back to "normal" consciousness.

Flashbacks

A number of LSD users report a short-lived, vivid reliving of a past trip without use of the drug known as a

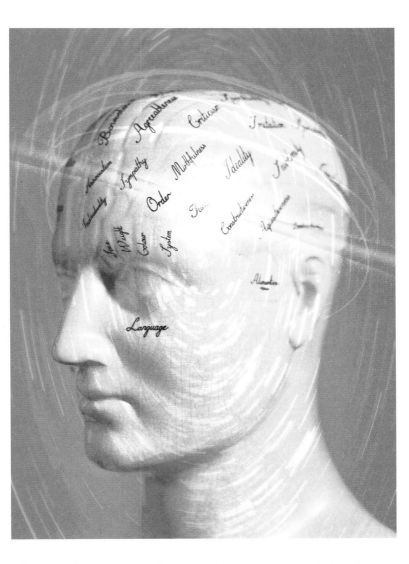

"flashback." Part of LSD's media portfolio as a horror drug were claims that users could have flashbacks lasting days or even weeks. In truth an LSD flashback (which can occur months after using the drug) normally only lasts a few minutes and is rarely

ABOVE: It is not just the chemistry which dictates how a person will react to LSD. What the user's expectations of the effects will be, the mood of the user, and the environment are all important.

dangerous although it can leave the person feeling anxious, disorientated,

275

or distressed, especially if they are unaware that flashbacks can happen. These incidents are most likely to happen in situations reminiscent of past LSD experiences or sometimes when a past user is smoking cannabis or using other drugs.

DEPENDENCE

There is no physical dependence with LSD, but tolerance builds up rapidly. After twenty-four hours, achieving the same effect requires a much larger dose. After three to four days of increasing the dosage, a limit is reached whereby no dose would be effective. A break of around three days would be required for LSD sensitivity to return. Only a small minority of those who use LSD become psychologically dependent.

THE LAW

LSD is a Schedule I drug under the Controlled Substances Act. Under Federal trafficking laws in the US, anybody convicted of supplying 1–9 g as a first offense can expect a jail term of not less than five years. LSD was banned in the UK in 1966, the same year as the US, and is controlled worldwide under the 1972 UN Convention on Psychotropic Substances. All countries put LSD in the most strict category of control.

RIGHT: In the 1960s, LSD became synonymous with the colours, sounds, images and politics of youth culture and the alternative society.

Mushrooms

Magic mushrooms, mushies, shrooms

WHAT IS IT?

There are around two dozen species of mushroom which contain the hallucinogens known as psilocin and psilocybin. The most common are stropharia (psilocybe) cubenis, psilocybe semilanceata (or Liberty Cap), and psilocybe subbaltteatus. Psilocybe cyanesens (or Wavy Caps) are the most potent of this mushrooms. There is another group of mushrooms from the Amanita family like Amanita muscaria (known commonly as Fly Agaric) which are also psychedelic, but their chemical make-up is notably distinct from the psilocybin varieties.

Mushrooms prefer moist, often dark areas, usually in fields or, more specifically in the case of the Fly

BELOW: R. Gordon Wasson, a retired merchant banker, and his wife were the first westerners of modern times to witness the ancient Mexican mushroom ceremonies when they traveled there in the mid-1950s.

Agaric, near birch trees. The mushrooms grow in autumn, usually between August and October, particularly after periods of heavy rainfall. Once picked, the funghi are often dried and kept for later use or the user passes them onto friends or buyers. Because of their wide availability, there is no significant black market in mushrooms. In fact, in most countries it is not illegal to pick and consume raw "magic" mushrooms and there is a thriving mail order and internet industry supplying fresh mushrooms and mushroom spore kits.

HISTORY

A bewildering array of hallucinogenic plants were known to be used by ancient tribes and civilizations for a variety of reasons—and many are still used actively by their successors to this day. Generally, these plants were used as a means of visionary divination and to enable the user to gain access to the "spirit" world.

Psilocybian mushrooms were used for thousands of years by Native Americans living in central America, but the West knew very little about the plants until some botanists began to explore Mexico in search of plants written about in old Spanish texts.

It was R. Gordon Wasson, an American banker who, with his wife Valentina, developed a passion for mushrooms and traveled to Mexico in the mid-1950s in search of fabled

TYPES OF MUSHROOM

B+

Cambodia

Koh Samui

psychedelic mushrooms and the tribes who still performed sacred mushroom ceremonies. He was successful in his quest; Wasson and Valentina were probably the first white people (at least in modern times and almost certainly in his wife's case) ever to have taken part in such a tribal ceremony. Their tale was written up in *Life* magazine in 1957 and sparked a huge interest among psychedelic researchers.

One such researcher was Aldous Huxley, and he was an early experimenter in the awesome mind expanding properties of these innocuous-looking little plants and before Timothy Leary became a champion of LSD, he set up a research programme at Harvard University studying the effects of hallucinogenic mushrooms. Since then, mushroom hunting has been a regular pastime in the Western world among recreational drug users as a legal and more "organic" alternative to LSD.

METHODS OF USE

Psilocybin mushrooms can be eaten fresh, or alternatively they can be cooked or brewed into a tea. They may also be preserved by drying.

EFFECTS

The effects of these mushrooms can start anywhere between as little as seven minutes to an hour depending on the potency of the mushroom and the method of ingestion. The

BELOW: Many people experience nausea and/or vomiting during psychedelic mushroom experiences, especially with higher doses. Other possible effects include anxiety and frightening thoughts and visions.

experience generally peaks within three hours and will last four to nine hours, but sometimes longer with a higher dose. The individual's heart rate, blood pressure, and pupil size all increase. At low doses, euphoria and detachment predominate; at higher doses, visual distortions progress to vivid "pseudo-hallucinations" of color and movement where what the user sees is not real.

The Fly Agaric mushroom reportedly delivers a more intense and introspective experience than the psilocybin mushrooms. The effects of the Fly Agaric are also associated more with a feeling of drowsiness followed by a stimulation of the senses. Users in the Siberian north also talk of its ability to prolong physical endurance, a feeling which is possibly related to a heightening of the senses as a result of the drug.

ABOVE: The main danger from ingesting mushrooms is eating a poisonous variety by mistake. About ninety percent of deaths from mushrooms in the US and western Europe result from eating *Amanita phalloides.*

Health risks

Infrequently (but especially after repeated or unusually high doses, if the user is inexperienced, or if they are anxious or unhappy to start with) "bad trips" characterized by deep fear and anxiety can occur, and may develop into a psychotic episode. These can usually be dealt with by friendly reassurance and leave no persistent effects, though there have been reports of longer-lasting disturbances, such as recurrent anxiety attacks and flashbacks to the original experience. Again, after a time, these almost invariably fade of their own accord.

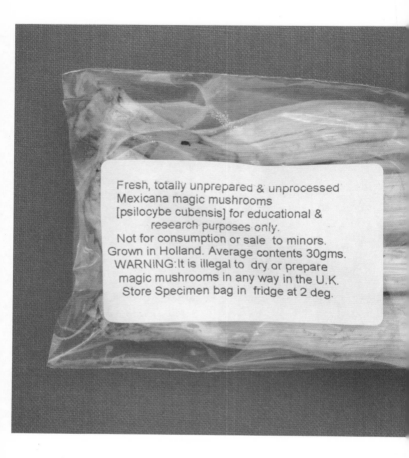

Fresh, totally unprepared & unprocessed
Mexicana magic mushrooms
[psilocybe cubensis] for educational &
research purposes only.
Not for consumption or sale to minors.
Grown in Holland. Average contents 30gms.
WARNING:It is illegal to dry or prepare
magic mushrooms in any way in the U.K.
Store Specimen bag in fridge at 2 deg.

ABOVE: A substantial online market has developed in the sale of "magic" mushroom growing kits. However, in 2003, one of the largest retailers in the US was raided by federal agents. This caused many other retailers, who were selling similar kits, to stop trading.

Mixing drugs

As the mushrooms in which the drugs occur naturally are seasonal, magic mushrooms tend to be taken on their own and usually on an irregular basis. Similarly, users in general tend to be teenagers experimenting with drugs, usually one at a time.

If taken with another drug, which is commonly alcohol or cannabis, the effects can be highly unpredictable. Alcohol will usually exaggerate feelings of confusion and disorientation, whilst cannabis may enhance the intensity of the hallucinatory experience.

Those who attempt to grow their own mushrooms from kits are warned never to eat them if they have gone

taken in small amounts. In fact, mushroom connoisseurs do not regard Fly Agaric as being a "real" magic mushroom even though it is psychedelic. This is because the active ingredient of Fly Agaric is not psilocybin but muscarine, which even in small doses can cause a variety of rather unpleasant side-effects such as nausea, vomiting, diarrhoea, headache, and bronchospasm. With larger doses of this particular mushroom there is also a risk of reduced pulse rate, low blood pressure, and even shock.

Reports of the correct dosage for the Fly Agaric vary. There are some records of experienced users eating up to seven caps without any ill effects but some people have died from consuming considerably less. In contrast, it would take large amounts of Liberty Cap mushrooms to cause a fatal overdose.

moldy or discolored as harmful bacteria could make the individual very ill.

Poisoning

The greatest potential danger arises from the possibility of mistakenly picking poisonous varieties of mushrooms instead of the hallucinogenic ones, for example consuming Amanita phalloides or Amanita virosa (instead of muscaria or Fly Agaric) can be fatal even when

DEPENDENCE

Like LSD, tolerance develops rapidly and the next day it might take twice as many Liberty Caps to repeat the experience. Full sensitivity is restored after about a week, so there is a natural discouragement to daily use. There are no significant withdrawal symptoms and no physical dependence, though, of course, individuals may become psychologically attached and feel a desire to repeat their experiences. At present, no serious lasting sequels to

ABOVE: A mushroom "trip" tends to last about four to five hours. Users often report the mushroom experience to be more "earthy" than other psychedelics, increasing emotional awareness and causing less psychological confusion.

the long-term use of hallucinogenic mushrooms have been reported, but there are no studies which might permit an assessment of the effects of extended, frequent use.

THE LAW

In the US, UK, and elsewhere world wide, it is usually not illegal to pick and eat raw mushrooms, although the

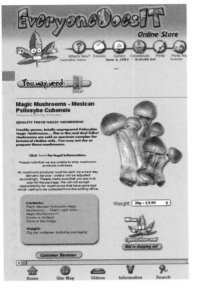

ABOVE (LEFT AND RIGHT): The Federal case against mushroom kit sellers in the US (see page 282) is that while growing the spores themselves is not illegal, producing detailed instructions on how to do it is conspiracy to manufacture a controlled substance.

Japanese government have proposed to ban possession of raw mushrooms. It is the psychoactive ingredients like psilocybe and psilocybin which are illegal and controlled with much the same severity as LSD.

In the US, there have been various state legislature interpretations of the word "container" where some people have argued that the raw mushroom is a "container" for the banned psychoactive ingredients, which in turn makes the mushroom as much a banned item in its own right as the marijuana joint which "contains" marijuana. Just such a judgement passed on one user in Indiana who was found guilty of possessing psilocybin "contained" inside a mushroom.

But where a user could more obviously fall foul of the law is if they try and prepare these mushrooms in any way, such as boiling or crushing. Even simply drying the mushrooms could be construed by some laws and authorities as attempting to extract the psychoactive ingredient. Until November 2002, it was legal to possess dried mushrooms in the Netherlands, but the law has since been changed to fall in line with most other countries. Even so, the law remains complex and open to interpretation in many countries.

Ketamine

K, special K, super K, vitamin K, tekno ("on ket" written backwards), green

WHAT IS IT?

Ketamine is a strange drug. It is a powerful anaesthetic with hallucinogenic properties, but it is also both a stimulant and a pain-killing opiate-type drug as well. It is known as a dissociative anaesthetic meaning that patients feel detached and remote from their immediate surroundings. It is classed in the same family of drugs as phencyclidine (also referred to as PCP or Angel Dust).

BELOW: Ketamine is the only hallucinogenic drug which can be said to be addictive. At one point in his life, ketamine researcher Dr. John Lilly went on a thirteen month injecting binge.

MEDICAL USES

Ketamine was invented in 1962 at the Parke-Davies laboratories in Michigan. Because of its special properties of inducing a sense of detachment in patients and because it is fast acting, ketamine was used for emergency surgery and in field hospitals during the Vietnam War. Ketamine is still used medically for humans under the brand name Ketalar because very young children and the elderly seem less affected by the hallucinogenic effects of the drug than the rest of the patient population. Ketamine is also used in veterinary surgery.

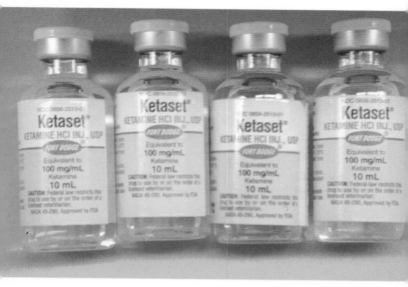

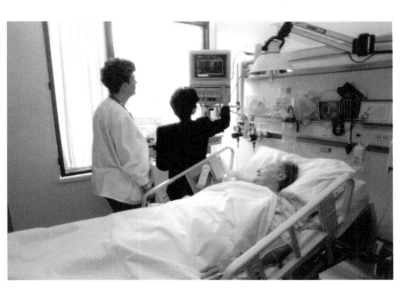

HISTORY

Recreational use was first reported in the US 1965 and word quickly spread around the world about this legal drug and its amazing effects. Two books published in the late 1970s increased interest still further; *Journeys into the Bright World* by Marcia Moore and *The Scientist* by John Lilly. Moore's story ended tragically when she went out into the woods near her home and injected herself with all the ketamine she had. Her body was not discovered for two years.

As well as ketamine, Lilly experimented with the use of flotation tanks for inducing hallucinogenic states, brought to the silver screen by Ken Russell in the film *Altered States*. By the early 1990s ketamine found its way on to the club

ABOVE: Ketamine is no longer used as an anaesthetic for adult surgery. As they woke, patients reported bizarre and sometimes frightening out of body sensations and hallucinations.

and rave scene in the US and the UK. Use is more prevalent among students, particularly medical students who have access to medical supplies of the drug. A survey of British club goers in 2000 revealed that in total thirty percent of them had tried the drug.

METHOD OF USE

Ketamine comes in powder and tablet forms. Some tablets have motifs on and may be indistinguishable from ecstasy tablets. As a white powder it is snorted. It can also be injected in liquid form and sometimes comes in small phials. A gram sells for about $80 in the US.

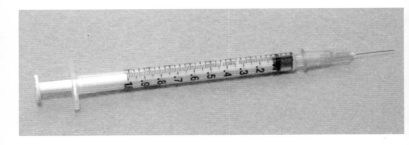

EFFECTS

The effects of ketamine vary with the method of administration and on the dose. The dose for snorting ketamine powder is usually about 60–200 mg. For tablet or oral use it is about 350–500 mg and doses for injecting are usually about 75–150 mg. When snorted in powder form, the effects begin within a few minutes and last for up to an hour. When swallowed, effects begin after about fifteen minutes and last from between one and four hours. When injected, effects

ABOVE: Ketamine can be injected but this method obviously brings with it all of the subsequent dangers of infections and transmitted diseases such as HIV, if needles and syringes are shared.

begin almost immediately and can last for one to four hours.

The initial effects of ketamine when used in moderate doses are usually the experience of stimulation and feelings of energy and euphoria. This has been compared to taking ecstasy and cocaine. Many people will initially dance under the influence, especially if the ketamine has been taken with stimulants. The initial speedy effects are often followed by experiences similar to those of sedative and hallucinatory drugs. Physical sensations may include nausea and vomiting, slurring of speech, lack of coordination, and numbness. Users commonly experience temporary paralysis and find it difficult to move or speak.

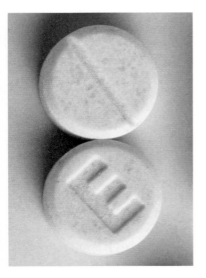

LEFT: Clubbers are sometimes sold ketamine as ecstasy. But the effects are very different: the naïve user would be taken by surprise by the strong sensations of ketamine.

Higher doses

With higher or repeat doses hallucinations can occur. Hallucinatory experiences often include floating sensations, loss of the sense of time, and feeling disconnected from the body. Users report feelings of being very alone and having out-of-body and near death experiences. This seems to be different from the effects of LSD.

High ketamine doses seem to deprive the brain of all senses and result in people filling the vacuum by creating their own, often bizarre, worlds from memories, fantasies and dreams. While some people have positive, almost spiritual experiences for others it can be very frightening.

These effects usually come on and recede faster than with LSD but can be very powerful, especially if a large dose is taken. As with other hallucinogens a good or bad trip depends on the user's mood, expectations, and the environment in which they use.

HEALTH RISKS

Powerful hallucinations and possible numbing effects can be very frightening and disorientating. This can be a particular problem if the

BELOW: The DEA have field testing kits for a whole range of drugs. The testing kits shown here are used to detect Ketamine, as well as Valium (diazepam) and Rohypnol (flunitrazepam).

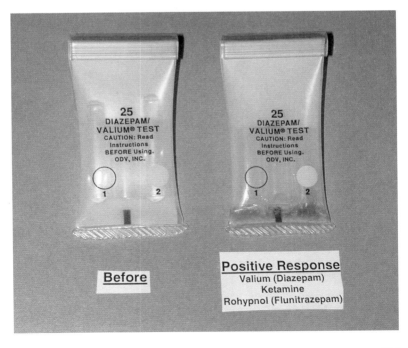

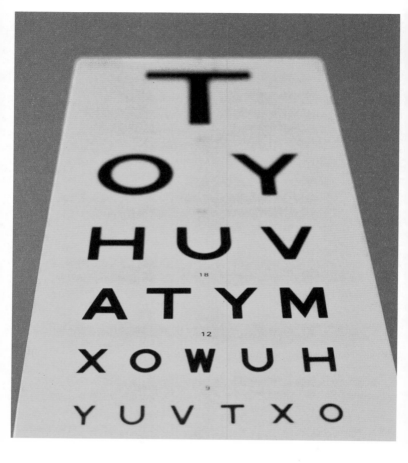

ABOVE: Long-term use can impair vision.

person has inadvertently bought ketamine expecting it to be ecstasy, which is always an inherent risk on the illicit market.

The fact that ketamine is an anaesthetic poses particular dangers. When on ketamine people are less likely to experience pain. Combined with the fact that some people may not realize they are hallucinating and think the trip is real, there is the potential for serious injury. As with any anaesthetic, eating or drinking prior to use may induce vomiting, which can be very dangerous if the user falls unconscious.

Overdoses

If a very large amount is taken there is a risk of respiratory collapse or heart failure—a few people have died after injecting large doses. Users are often warned not to combine ketamine with alcohol or other sedative-type drugs. Despite this ketamine-related deaths appear to be relatively rare.

Injecting ketamine can cause damage to veins and lead to abscesses and possibly thrombosis. Sharing of injecting equipment can lead to the spread of hepatitis and HIV.

As with LSD, flashbacks can occur. They are relatively rare and repeated experiences are typical to other hallucinatory drugs. Users report re-living a feeling or hallucination they associate with a previous trip. Flashbacks tend to occur when using other drugs like cannabis or in similar environments, and tend to fade.

Long-term use

Long-term use can lead to impairment of memory, attention, and vision, which may not completely return to normal. Long term, regular ketamine use has also been linked to a range of mental health problems including psychosis and delusions, panic attacks, depression, insomnia, and suicide. Whether ketamine itself can cause such problems or whether it merely exacerbates existing conditions is as yet unclear.

DEPENDENCE

Physical dependence and withdrawal are not a feature of ketamine use. Tolerance can develop with regular use so people need to take more to get a similar effect. Some people say ketamine tolerance is different from other drugs in that once people need larger doses they continue to need the same level even after they have had a break from use.

There is evidence that some users can develop psychological dependence. While dependence on LSD is rare some people have been seduced by the ketamine experience and become compulsive users. This may have something to do with the anaesthetic effect that users may become accustomed to. John Lilly actually became so obsessed with ketamine that during one three week period, he injected 50 mg every hour, for nearly twenty-four hours a day.

THE LAW

In the US, ketamine is a Schedule III drug under the Controlled Substances Act and is regarded similarly by most states, although these is little consistency in sentencing for possession and dealing in the drug. In the UK, ketamine is not controlled under the Misuse of Drugs Act and therefore legal to possess. It is, however, controlled under the Medicines Act and people can be prosecuted for unauthorized manufacture or supplying it to others.

Globally, despite its powerful effects, there do not appear to be specific laws against its recreational use or possession although there are regulations governing import and manufacture in many countries.

DMT

Businessman's Lunch, fantasia

WHAT IS IT?

DMT (or N,N- dimethyl-tryptamine) is a very powerful hallucinogen that is derived from *cohoba* snuff from the seeds of the yopo tree which can be found in Central and South America.

Similar compounds to DMT have been found not only in plants, but also toads and fish. One such compound is Bufotenine which is named after the toad which secretes it. In its natural state this compound is not hallucinogenic—it needs to be combined with other compounds to become so. However, this apparently did not stop (presumably desperate) 1960s drug experimenters in Australia who reportedly went on "toad-licking" expeditions after having read and believed a newspaper story which stated that the toad slime from the Bufo marinus variety actually contained mind-altering properties. In reality, all it did was make them extremely sick.

Nevertheless the practice spread briefly to the US where in the 1980s,

people apparently tried smoking the the dried secretions. This actually worked, but the experience was too intense and ever really caught on.

HISTORY

As with many of the hallucinogenic plants of central and South America, it was the sixteenth century Spanish conquerors who first reported their existence to the wider world, having witnessed their use in tribal

RIGHT: From 1990 to 1995, Dr. Rick Strassman investigated the role of the body's natural DMT (in the pineal gland) in abnormal experiences like alien abduction using human volunteers. This was the first research of its type to be conducted in the the US for over twenty years.

ceremonies. A friar, Ramon Paul, who accompanied Christopher Columbus on his second voyage, became the first white observer of the power of *cohoba* snuff. He wrote:

> "This powder they draw up through the nose and it intoxicates them to such an extent that when they are under its influence, they know not what they do."

There is just such a scene of ceremonial snuff use, reported by Paul, in John Boorman's film about the threat to the Amazon tribes, called the *Emerald Forest* (1985).

The drug was first synthesized in the laboratory in 1957 and for the next decade or so was the subject of experimental use by the usual suspects of academic and artistic "psychonauts" including, Richard Alpert, Allen Ginsberg, Timothy Leary, and William Burroughs most of whom found the drug far too intense for comfort. By 1969, the drug was banned in the US, but not before it had found its way into the wider world of recreational drug use.

METHODS OF USE

DMT is usually smoked or injected in doses ranging from 20–50 mg,

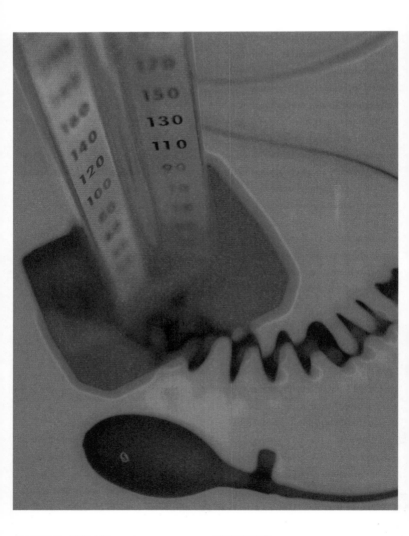

ABOVE: The DMT "trip" is very intense, even more than LSD, but brief and can be quite frightening because it kicks in so quickly. Those individuals with high blood pressure or heart problems are warned to steer clear of DMT as they are much more likely to experience to suffer harm.

although as little as 5 mg will have a major effect.

EFFECTS

The nickname "Businessman's Lunch" comes from the fact that the drug works very quickly and can produce a very strong trip that usually lasts from between ten to thirty minutes. This is in contrast to a drug like LSD, where the trip takes time to come on and then lasts for hours.

Unlike most psychedelic drugs where the hallucinations are in fact "pseudo-hallucinations" (meaning that the person taking the drug consciously knows that what they are seeing is not real), the visions seen under the influence of DMT can appear totally lifelike. Heart rate and blood pressure increase dramatically and there are feelings of both exhilaration and confusion.

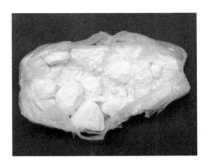

Health risks

Anybody with high blood pressure or heart problems would be well advised to steer clear of DMT: mixing it with stimulants like cocaine, ecstasy, or amyl nitrite could prove fatal to individuals suffering with these conditions.

Some drug users have described their DMT trip as the most terrifying experience of their lives and it can create significant panic, confusion, and paranoia.

There is another version of DMT called 5-methoxy DMT which is actually five times stronger than DMT. One user described its effects as similar to having an elephant sit on your head. Another researcher observed that the phrase "mind-blowing" might well have been invented for this group of drugs. Much of the anxiety experienced while under the influence of this drug is caused by the fact that the onset of its effects is so rapid that user has no time to get used to what is happening.

ABOVE: Mixing the use of DMT with other drugs such as Amyl nitrite or cocaine (as pictured above) increases the inherent risks of taking the drug and could prove to be fatal, especially to those with pre-existing medical conditions.

DEPENDENCE

This is generally not associated with hallucinogenic drugs.

THE LAW

Worldwide, DMT is generally catagorized in the drug schedules reserved for the most dangerous drugs with no recognized medical uses.

Ibogaine

WHAT IS IT?

Ibogaine is a psychoactive chemical derived from the root bark of a bush found in Central Africa—*Tabernanthe iboga*. There are five species in the family of which two are known to have psychedelic properties.

It is traditionally associated with the Bwiti religion. There are an estimated two to three million Bwiti members scattered in groups throughout the countries of Gabon, Zaire, and the Cameroon. The plant has stimulant properties used to fend off tiredness and hunger during starvation. It is also used as a hallucinogenic plant in Bwiti initiation ceremonies.

MEDICAL USES

In the tribal communities, it is used as an aphrodisiac and a cure for impotence. Early western doctors used it to treat a number of conditions including influenza, depression, and some cardiac disorders.

More recently there has been intense interest in this drug among a group of dedicated enthusiasts as a means of combating drug and alcohol addiction. Self-help groups claim that ibogaine reduces withdrawal symptoms and that even a single dose can reduce cravings for periods of up to six months. At the moment there are no conclusive answers as to how this works, but it may be that the drug acts on those parts of the brain most associated with influencing addiction and temporarily overwhelms craving and learned behavior patterns. The theory goes on to suggest that besides blocking opiate withdrawal, and "interrupting" craving, the visionary state induced by ibogaine (which can

RIGHT: There are those who make claims for the value of ibogaine in the treatment of chemical dependence including reduction in opioid withdrawal and interruption of drug craving.

last for up to two days) helps the individual to explore their past, providing insight into the source of their compulsive behavior, and helps to break their pattern of addiction.

METHOD OF USE

The bark can be eaten in its natural state or ground up into a powder to make a tea.

EFFECTS

Doses of less than 100 mg have an effect similar to amphetamine. At 150 mg, the hallucinogenic properties of the drug take over with a psychedelic experience similar to mescaline. At one gram, the hallucinations could last for days.

Health risks

People taking this drug can suffer from nausea and vomiting. At excessive dose levels, there have been reports made of convulsions, paralysis, and even death due to respiratory collapse.

DEPENDENCE

There have been no reports on dependence on ibogaine.

THE LAW

Ibogaine is not listed under the Misuse of Drugs Act in the UK and so it is therefore legal to possess but not to supply. It is a restricted substance in some countries, including the US, Switzerland, Sweden, and Belgium.

Mescaline

WHAT IS IT?

Mescaline is a naturally occurring hallucinogen derived from the Mexican peyote cactus (also found in the south-western US) and the San Pedro cactus found in Peru. The psychoactive part of the cactus is called the mescal button. This contains at least fifteen pharmacologically active substances of which mescaline is the most important.

HISTORY

The cactus has been used for centuries by a number of Mexican tribes as an integral part of their religious ceremonies. The "peyote cult" crossed into the US and was adopted by a number of tribes, especially the Plains Indians, and became the ritual sacrament of the Native American Church of North America. Mescaline was popularized in the West by Aldous Huxley whose landmark book *The Doors of Perception* (1954) detailed his experiences under the influence of the drug.

METHOD OF USE

The traditional tribal method of ingesting the buttons is to dry them until completely brown, chew and swallow. But they are very bitter and non-tribal users are more likely to grind the buttons up and then dissolve them in tea or fruit juice. Between three to five buttons are ingested for a full psychedelic experience.

EFFECTS

The effects start one or two hours after ingestion. The visual distortions, vivid images and hallucinations, and synaesthesia (where one sense combines with another, so that colors are "heard" and sound is "seen") are similar to LSD. There is also a sense of detachment from the world and distortions of time and space. Users report that they experience what they regard as profound mystical revelations.

HEALTH RISKS

Nausea and vomiting are the most unpleasant physical effects. With a substance that has such a percussive impact on the mind, there is always the risk of an equally disturbing downside. The visions can be terrifying and anybody with a latent mental health condition could be badly affected by the experience.

DEPENDENCE

Tolerance, withdrawal, and dependency are not normally associated with hallucinogenic drugs (with the exception of ketamine).

THE LAW

The Native American Church won a landmark legal battle to have peyote recognized as a religious sacrament, like wine is for the Christian church, and so for that group, mescaline is legal. Otherwise, however, it is a Schedule I drug under the Controlled Substances Act and is similarly controlled in other countries.

BELOW: Aldous Huxley's major contribution to the modern literature of altered states was based on his experiences with mescaline.

Phencyclidine

PCP, angel dust, wacky dust, dust, hog, shermans, sherms (PCP laced cigarettes)

WHAT IS IT?

Phencyclidine is an anaesthetic with hallucinogenic, stimulant, and depressant properties. It is chemically close to ketamine (see page 286) in that it is a dissociative anaesthetic. As patients emerge from anaesthesia under its influence, they feel remote and detached from their surroundings, which helps them to remain feeling calm and sedated. The drug also produces changes in perception similar to that of LSD.

HISTORY

PCP was first synthesized in 1926, but remained as an experimental drug in the laboratory until 1957 when the pharmaceutical company Parke-Davis marketed the drug as an anaesthetic called Seryl. PCP looked useful because it did not depress the central

nervous system or inhibit breathing and so was safer than other anaesthetics. However, reports emerged of psychotic behavior by some patients and the drug was withdrawn for human use in 1962, but reintroduced for veterinary purposes in 1967. Since then, it has had no recognized medical uses.

Inevitably the drug found its way onto the street, specifically at rock music festivals on the US west coast in the late 1960s where it was sold as a "PeaCe pill." From there use spread quickly, as did its reputation as a highly unpredictable drug which caused violent reactions in some users and (because they could feel no pain) incredible feats of superhuman strength in others. The American media had a field day with horrendous stories of people gouging out their own eyes and pulling out their nails with pliers, murdering their relatives, and strange tales of people walking out onto the freeway and doing push-ups—all under the influence of PCP. Because of its bizarre side effects, PCP never became a major drug on the recreational scene, nor did its use spread much beyond the US.

The latest American government statistics from 2003 on PCP show that 2.5 percent of high school seniors say they have used PCP, 1.3 percent say they have used it in the past year, with less than one percent saying they used it in the month prior to the survey. Across the general population, 3.2 percent aged twelve and older have used PCP at least once. Lifetime use of PCP was highest among those aged twenty-six or older (3.5 percent). Although generally, the drug is not so prevalent as it used to be, nevertheless, incidents of PCP patients in emergency departments increased twenty-eight percent from 1995 to

LEFT: PCP or Angel Dust has a fearsome reputation as a drug which can drive certain individuals to believe they are invincible and have superhuman strength. This can lead to senseless acts of violence to themselves and others.

2002. There was a forty-two percent increase from the 5,404 reports in 2000 to 7,648 in 2002. There were significant increases in PCP incidents in Washington DC, Newark, Philadelphia, Baltimore, and Dallas.

METHOD OF USE

Almost all the PCP currently available is illicitly manufactured. In its pure form, it is a white crystalline powder, but on the street, the impurities from manufacture render it various shades of dirty brown. It can be obtained as tablets, capsules, liquid, and powder, but is usually smoked—users sprinkle powder or liquid on tobacco, marijuana, or make herb cigarettes with oregano or parsley. In the Denzil Washington movie *Training Day*

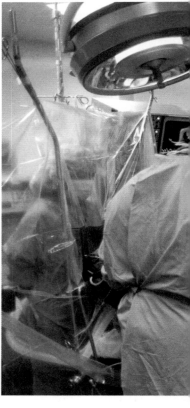

BELOW: In its liquid or powder form, phencyclidine can be mixed in with tobacco, herbs, or marijuana and rolled into a cigarette.

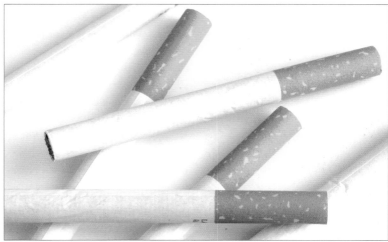

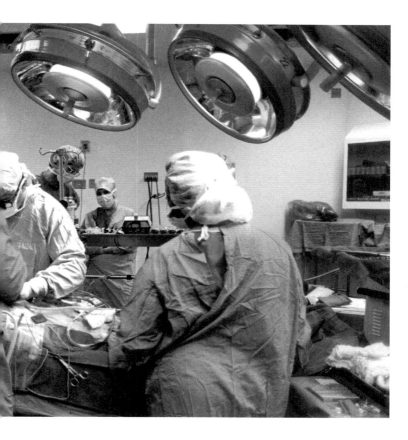

ABOVE: The post-surgery effects of PCP as an anaesthetic were even more bizarre than those of ketamine and it has even been discontinued for veterinary purposes.

(2001) where he plays a corrupt narcotics officer, he gives rookie cop, played by Ethan Hawke, a PCP-laced cigarette on his first day.

A typical dose would be 5–10 mg, but when sprinkled on cigarettes, users might ingest 80–100 mg two or three times a day over consecutive days. There have been reports of the drug being injected intravenously.

EFFECTS

The effects of PCP kick-in after a few minutes, peak around thirty minutes, and last from four to six hours. At low doses (5 mg or less taken orally by an occasional user) there is mild to intense euphoria, pleasant stimulation, a sense of relaxation, weightlessness, hallucinations, and distortions of time and space.

The physical effects of PCP include a slight increase in breathing rate and

ABOVE: Although there is little media coverage of PCP these days, mentions in emergency departments in the US increased by forty-two percent from the 5,404 mentions in 2000 to 7,648 in 2002.

a pronounced rise in blood pressure and pulse rate. Breathing becomes shallow, and flushing and profuse sweating occurs. The extremities become numb with some loss of muscular coordination.

HEALTH RISKS

At high doses of PCP (about 10 mg or more taken orally by an occasional user) blood pressure, pulse rate, and respiration drop. This may be accompanied by nausea, vomiting, blurred vision, flicking up and down

of the eyes, drooling, loss of balance, and dizziness. High doses of PCP can also cause seizures, coma, and death (though death more often results from accidental injury or suicide during PCP intoxication). High doses can cause symptoms that mimic schizophrenia, such as delusions, hallucinations, paranoia, disordered thinking, a sensation of distance from one's environment, and catatonia. There are many accounts of violence (some of it extreme) and general aggression among some individuals at these higher doses.

As documented with the use of amphetamines and cocaine, chronic PCP users tend to go on runs where the drug is used almost constantly for up to two or three days with no sleep and hardly any food, which could occur two to four times a month.

People who use PCP for long periods report memory loss, difficulties with speech (stuttering or even no speech at all) and thinking, depression (sometimes to the point of suicidal thoughts), and weight loss. These symptoms can persist up to a year after stopping PCP use.

DEPENDENCE

Tolerance can occur with prolonged use where users have to increase the dose to get the desired effects and chronic users report a psychological craving for the drug similar to that experienced by crack users.

THE LAW

PCP is a Schedule I drug under US Federal law and in the UK and Europe it is classed in the most dangerous category of drugs.

BELOW: One of the reported long-terms effects of PCP is weight loss and, together with other symptoms, can last for anywhere up to year after the drug has stopped being used.

SECTION 6

Marijuana

Marijuana

Blow, bud, weed, blunt, chronic, grass, herb, joint, hash, ganja, skunk, draw, dope, puff, pot, and smoke among many other names

WHAT IS IT?

Marijuana (or cannabis) refers to the leaves and flowering tops of the cannabis plant. There are two species, the most common being *cannabis sativa* which can grow up to fifteen feet high. The plant flourishes in temperate climates all over the world, including, for example, California and other parts of the US. In fact, about a third of the marijuana consumed in the US is actually home-grown—most of the rest comes from Mexico.

The active ingredient of marijuana is THC (tetrahydrocannabinol) and different varieties of marijuana have different strengths or levels of THC content. In the mid-1990s, the THC content of home-grown marijuana was about five percent. However, as law enforcement began to crack down on the drug, growers were forced to cultivate their crops indoors. Ironically, this produced more crop because growing could take place all year and it allowed for the cultivation of more potent varieties like sinsemilla, which now accounts for over three quarters of American home-grown and has a THC content

BELOW: There have always been strong varieties of marijuana, but indoor growing has increased the availability of marijuana with a higher THC content.

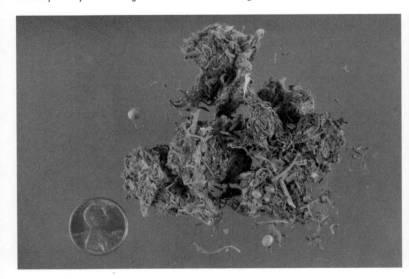

of around ten percent. In Holland, super-strength varieties have been developed with names like Netherweed, Northern Lights, and Skunk where the THC levels can approach twenty percent (see the following pages for a more extensive list of varieties).

HISTORY

Marijuana has been used as a herbal medicine since ancient times. Assyrian stone tablets from the seventh century BC make reference to marijuana and it is documented as a herbal remedy in a Chinese pharmacy text dating from about 2700 BC. It has a long history as a medicine in the Middle East, India, China, and North Africa, and has also been used for religious ceremonies and for pleasure. Hemp, derived from marijuana plants which usually have little or no psychoactive effect, was used to manufacture a range of products including clothing, fishing nets, ropes, sacks, and oils. Hemp was so valuable as a commercial crop to seafaring nations that the first colonists to the US were commanded to grow it by the British authorities. But they soon realized how useful it was and needed no encouragement.

The recreational use of marijuana developed in the 1920s mainly among the black community, musicians, gamblers, and others who were on the edges of society. The head of the newly-formed Federal Bureau of Narcotics in the US started a marijuana scare campaign in the 1930s blaming the drug for violent murders, so-called "reefer madness"—in an attempt to keep Congressional funds coming into their department in the wake of Depression. But it wasn't

BELOW: Anybody with a mental health problem would be ill-advised to use marijuana, but whether the drug actually causes psychosis is controversial.

BELOW: Hashish, produced mainly in Morocco and Afghanistan, is the sticky resin which is scraped from the leaves and compressed into solid blocks.

ABOVE: Marijuana/hemp has a long history as a herbal remedy and an important commercial plant for the production of cloth, rope, and paper.

until the drug "came out of the ghetto" in the 1960s and onto white university campuses that its use spread to all sectors of society. Currently in the US, there are an estimated ten million regular users and twenty million people say they have used the drug at least once in the past year while a third of all adults say they have tried marijuana at least once.

In the UK, marijuana use came to popular attention during the late 1960s as spread among students and then more widely in the 1970s and 1980s among young people. Within Europe, the Netherlands has become synonymous with a more liberal approach to marijuana.

MEDICAL USES

Increasingly clinical research is demonstrating that marijuana has a range of possible medical uses including reducing eye pressure in glaucoma, as an anti-nausea drug in chemotherapy, and more recently as a pain-reliever for musculo-skeletal disorders such as Multiple Sclerosis. However, the US Federal authorities refuse to acknowledge that marijuana has any medical benefits. Even so, thirty-six states have passed laws allowing medical use and many doctors argue that marijuana should be recatagorized as a Schedule II drug to allow use as a prescription medicine while still remaining illegal.

Trials for the medical use of marijuana are under way in the UK, and research is also being conducted in Canada and Australia.

METHOD OF USE

The most common way of using marijuana in the US is by smoking it either in a pipe or rolling it up in cigarette paper, usually called a joint. Alternatively, a cigarette or cigar may have the tobacco removed and replaced with marijuana, called a blunt.

By contrast in the UK, because the most common form of cannabis used is hash (resin scrapped off the leaves), this is sprinkled into a cigarette and rolled up with the tobacco still inside. Marijuana can also be brewed into a drink, eaten on its own, or cooked in food, especially cakes or biscuits. It can sometimes be smoked between two hot knives, and occasionally it may also be mixed with drinks or yoghurts.

BELOW: There is a growing body of international clinical evidence indicating that marijuana has a number of medical applications including pain relief for multiple sclerosis and other musculo-skeletal condition and reducing chemotherapy-induced nausea.

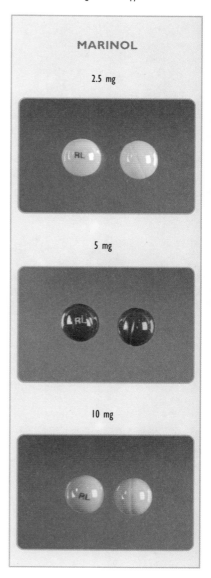

MARINOL

2.5 mg

5 mg

10 mg

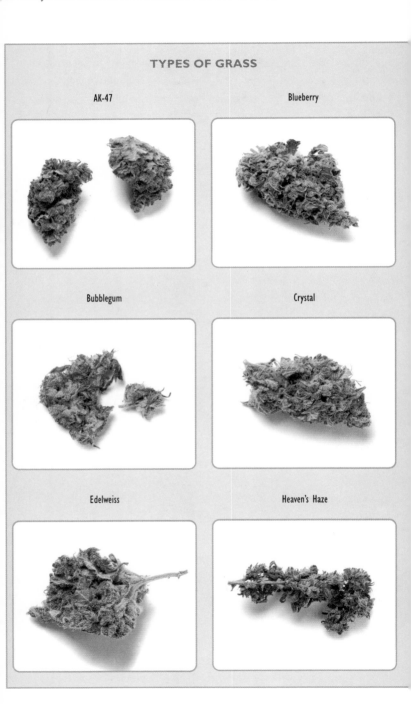

TYPES OF GRASS

AK-47

Blueberry

Bubblegum

Crystal

Edelweiss

Heaven's Haze

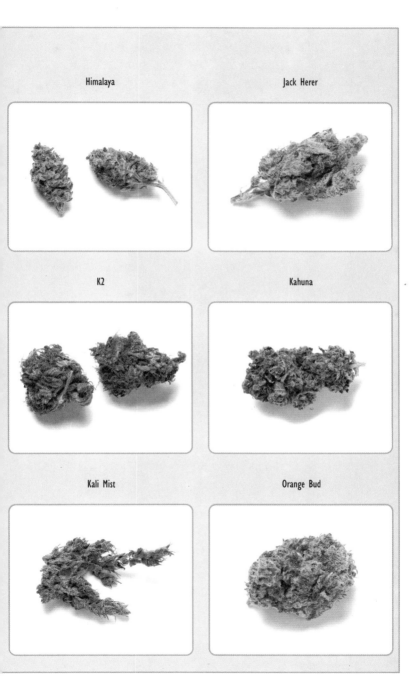

Himalaya

Jack Herer

K2

Kahuna

Kali Mist

Orange Bud

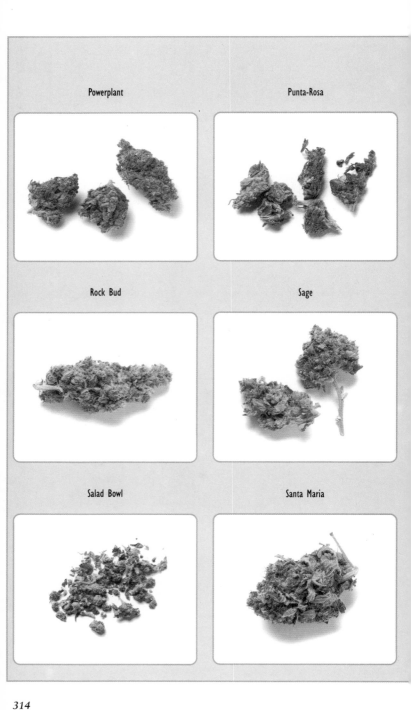

Powerplant

Punta-Rosa

Rock Bud

Sage

Salad Bowl

Santa Maria

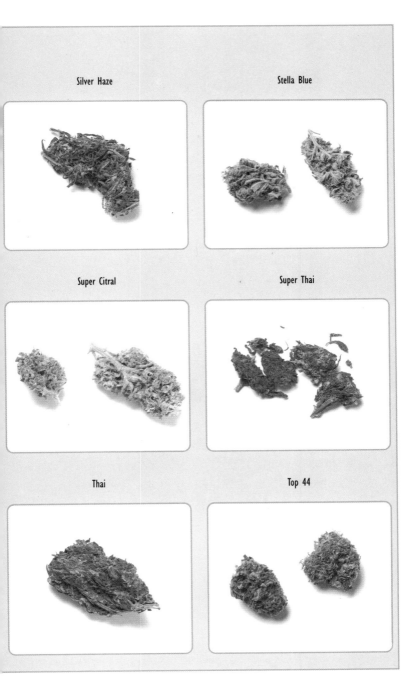

Silver Haze

Stella Blue

Super Citral

Super Thai

Thai

Top 44

TYPES OF HASH

Afgani Black

Afghani Pollon

Indian Hand-Rubbed

Melana Cream

Cream

Gold Lebanese

Nepalese

Royal Nepalese

Nepalese Temple Balls

Caramello

Huevos

Marrakesh I

Ketama

King Hassan

King Muhammed

Tangier Tiger

Casablanca Gold

Super Ketama

Zero-Zero

Moonshine

Northern Lights

White Widow

Sheeba

Jellyhash

ABOVE: Marijuana is not physically addictive, but some regular smokers feel that cannot give up easily and seek treatment.

EFFECTS

The effects generally start a few minutes after smoking, and may last up to an hour with low doses and for up to two or three hours with higher doses. When eaten or drunk, marijuana takes an hour or more to have an effect and cannot be regulated as well as if smoked in measured doses over a period of time. The effects after swallowing can last twelve hours or longer. Marijuana causes a number of noticeable but usually mild physical effects, including increased pulse rate and later decreased blood pressure (so those with heart complaints may be at special risk), bloodshot eyes, dry mouth, mild pain reduction, and occasional dizziness. Marijuana use also often increases appetite. Users may feel hungry once "stoned"—the "munchies" as it is often called—and may particularly crave sweet foods such as chocolate.

The acute toxicity of marijuana is very low and there are no records of anyone suffering a fatal overdose. Animal studies have shown a very large gap between an effective and lethal dose. The few cases of human drug-related deaths involving marijuana and no other drug have been due to inhalation of vomit.

With normal doses, usually 10–20 mg THC or one regular joint, the psychological effects of marijuana are subtle and hard to classify. The effects of the cannabinoids are similar to those that are also produced by the use of alcohol, tranquillizers, opiates, and at stronger doses, hallucinogenic drugs like LSD. Marijuana is usually used to promote relaxation, sociability, talkativeness, hilarity, or, alternatively, episodes of introspective reflection.

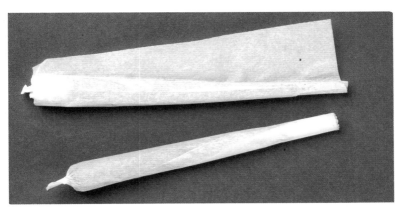

There are feelings of enhanced awareness and appreciation of the inner feelings of other people, of music and other sensory experiences. In this state of increased attention to the immediate inner and outer environment, time often seems to stand still. The situation in which marijuana is often used—in comfortable, warm surroundings, with friends, during a period given over to leisure and relaxation—probably serves to encourage these kinds of responses. The subtlety of these effects mean that they can be interpreted by the user in a wide variety of ways depending on experience, what they expect or want to happen, and on the reactions of other people around them. Novice users who do not know what to expect may find the experience of using marijuana particularly distressing, especially if strong variants are involved. On the other hand many people report that nothing much happened.

HEALTH RISKS

Respiratory system

Frequent inhalation of marijuana smoke over a period of years can exacerbate bronchitis and other respiratory disorders and can also cause cancer of the lung and parts of the upper digestive tract. Smoked marijuana contains high concentrations of carcinogenic tar and toxins. Smoking marijuana and tobacco together may be more damaging than smoking either alone.

It is not known whether regular marijuana smoking will turn out to cause more or less risk to health than regular tobacco smoking. It does appear that marijuana users inhale less frequently, but more deeply and for longer, therefore possibly exposing the lungs less frequently but more intensely to harmful smoke.

ABOVE: Probably the most serious long-term danger of smoking marijuana is the possible impact on the respiratory system.

Marijuana use has also been shown to weaken the lungs' ability to fight infection. Tests have indicated that cannabinoids can impair the functioning of the lungs' immune cells. Most of the effects are small and reversible, suggesting that only in very heavy smokers may any degree of mutation be significant. However, large population studies have shown that incidences of lung infections are somewhat more common in marijuana smokers than in tobacco only smokers.

Reproductive function

It has been suggested that regular marijuana use effects sex drive. While this may not hold true for all users, regular, heavy use can lower oestrogen and testosterone levels, which leads to reduced sperm count and a shortening of the menstrual cycle. Claims that marijuana use definitely reduces fertility have not been substantiated by research.

Lack of motivation

A lot of attention has been paid to the apparent tendency of marijuana to precipitate a chronic lack of motivation and bouts of apathy. Amotivational syndrome, as it is referred to, was one of the inherent dangers highlighted in the early 1970s and 1980s depicting intoxicated and permanently unmotivated youth. Closer examination has found that while heavy use may be linked to some behavioral disorders, they are not long-term. These types of disorders appear to be linked more to psychotic incidences that could have been triggered by the effects of marijuana.

A heavy user chronically intoxicated on marijuana may appear apathetic, lack energy, and perform poorly at their work or education due possibly to marijuana-related problems involving memory and attention span. This state may persist for weeks after stopping use. However, such a condition seems rare and little different from what might be expected of someone chronically depressed or intoxicated on alcohol or other sedative-type drugs such as benzodiazepines.

Concern has been raised that heavy marijuana use during early adolescence may have some effect on social or cognitive development. Adolescence is typically defined as a time when biological and social changes are at there most pervasive, impacting on future mental capabilities and lifestyle choices. Research in the US has shown that while marijuana use during this period might lead to poorer academic results, it does not predict intellectual development.

With higher doses or if stronger varieties are smoked, there may be

BELOW: As well as being rolled up into cigarettes, marijuana can be smoked in a variety of elaborate and decorative pipes called "bongs"—a vast array of which can be seen here.

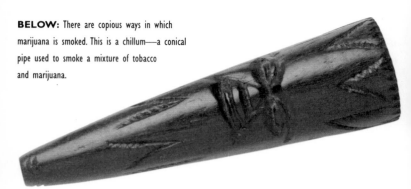

BELOW: There are copious ways in which marijuana is smoked. This is a chillum—a conical pipe used to smoke a mixture of tobacco and marijuana.

perceptual distortions, forgetfulness, and confusion. There may also be varying degrees of temporary psychological distress, especially paranoia and anxiety particularly if the user is already anxious or depressed or taking the drug in a threatening environment.

Mental health

Certain studies undertaken in the UK and the US suggest that marijuana can worsen the condition of some schizophrenic disorders. Individuals who are otherwise reasonably well-controlled on antipsychotic drugs have reported adverse reactions to regular or even sporadic use of marijuana. Some studies have also linked episodes of schizophrenia following the onset of heavy marijuana use. While it is not clear what role marijuana plays in such incidences and on general mental health, it is reasonable to say that those with a history of mental illness may be vulnerable to marijuana induced psychosis. However, there is no convincing evidence of marijuana use causing psychosis in people who do not already have underlying mental health problems. It is also needs to be borne in mind that individuals with mental disorders may be more inclined to use marijuana and to use it heavily, possibly in an attempt to self-medicate.

DEPENDENCE

In a laboratory situation, where people have been exposed to high doses of marijuana every few hours for several weeks, it has been possible to produce a mild withdrawal syndrome consisting of irritability, restlessness, insomnia, and decreased appetite.

The development of a marijuana dependency syndrome in heavy users has been observed, and is associated with an inability to control use of the drug, cognitive and motivational handicaps, lowered self-esteem, and the possible occurrence of depression in long-term users. The extent of these symptoms among users is not clear, but general consensus is that very few experience physical dependence. Regular users can come to feel a psychological need for the drug or may rely on it as a "social lubricant." It is not unknown for people to use marijuana so frequently that they are almost constantly under the influence and feel they cannot face other people or the world without being perpetually stoned.

While the vast majority of drug users who present to drug agencies for help have heroin as their main drug of misuse, surveys show a significant and growing number of people are asking for help with marijuana-related problems.

Tolerance (the need to take more of the drug to produce the same effect) will develop in regular users, though many also become sensitized to its effects. Regular users therefore may often only need a little to enjoy the drugs effects, but will go on to smoke a lot of the drug without becoming overly stoned.

Pregnancy

It is known that THC can cross the placenta and also enters breast milk. Regular, frequent marijuana use during pregnancy increases the risk of premature birth with its attendant complications such as shorter baby length, lighter birth weight, and shorter gestation periods. Consequences such as these have been likened (though not proven) to those associated with tobacco smoking, and are possibly linked to the fact that the growing tissue of the baby might not receive enough oxygen.

Some mothers who use marijuana very heavily (daily) prior to the birth have given birth to babies who temporarily suffer tremor and distress and are easily startled. However, there is no evidence that babies exposed to marijuana before or after birth suffer any adverse effects later in life. It is also unclear as to what role is played by other viable factors such as the use of other types of drugs, poverty, and other aspects of lifestyle and social environment.

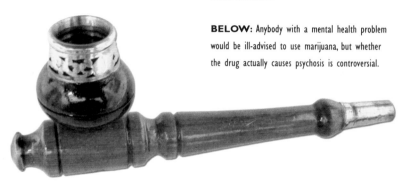

BELOW: Anybody with a mental health problem would be ill-advised to use marijuana, but whether the drug actually causes psychosis is controversial.

THE LAW

In the US, marijuana is a Schedule I drug under the Controlled Substances Act putting it in the highest category for drug control. Under Federal trafficking laws, for example, a second offense for possessing up to fifty marijuana plants could earn the individual anything up to thirty years in jail.

The laws for possession vary widely across the states. In Alaska, for example, the state has decriminalized marijuana to some degree. This means that there is no prison or criminal record for those caught for the first-time possession of a small amount for personal consumption. The conduct is treated as equivalent to a minor traffic violation. By contrast, in Alabama, there is a minimum mandatory sentence policy in operation where the judge cannot impose a sentence less than the one stipulated for the offense

and those caught in possession could face a year in jail.

In the UK in January 2004, marijuana was moved lower down the drug schedules from Class B to Class C. The drug is still illegal, but people over the age of eighteen are unlikely to be arrested for possession of a small amount. However, the

LEFT: Contrary to popular belief, the Dutch have not legalized marijuana. Instead, the police do not enforce the law when a small amount is smoked in certain cafes.

ABOVE: This is one of the more organized dealing counters in one of Amsterdam's numerous coffee shops. There are nearly 300 such cafes across the city.

maximum penalty for dealing has been increased substantially, and the individual caught dealing the drug can now expect to be sentenced to a possible fourteen years in jail opposed to the previous five year sentence.

Contrary to popular belief, the Dutch have not legalized marijuana, although the situation appears confusing. The laws for possession and trafficking remain in place, except that within the confines of designated "coffee shops" customers can buy and consume up to 5 mg of marijuana without fear of prosecution. Nor will the owner be arrested for selling the drug, although the person who sells the supplies to the café owner could be. The laws for possession of a small amount of marijuana differ widely across Europe, but as a whole most countries strictly control its trafficking and supply.

SECTION 7

Legal Highs

Legal Highs

Aphrodesia, Bliss extra, Jamaican Ghanja, Kratom, Cloud 9, Yohimbix 8, Explore XS, Nirvana Plus, Salvia divinorum, and many other products

WHAT ARE THEY?

Legal Highs are a range of substances legally available in certain shops, at music festivals, by mail order, and over the internet which mimic the effects of illegal drugs. These might be herbs with similar (but milder) effects to marijuana, LSD, and ecstasy or they might be preparations with a stimulant effect. There are also a

BELOW: Generally, "legal highs" are substances which are milder version of illegal drugs like ecstasy, marijuana, amphetamine, and the hallucinogens.

number of compound preparations on the market combining stimulant-type drugs with herb extracts and nutritional supplements.

Some legal highs are quite hallucinogenic, like Salvia, and others are very potent (like psilocybin mushrooms) but remain legal because of interpretations of the law. In general, given the huge variety of psychoactive plant species around the world, it is not surprising that a number have been identified which provide something of the desired

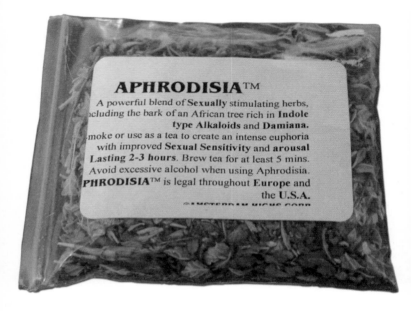

APHRODISIA™
A powerful blend of **Sexually** stimulating herbs,
including the bark of an African tree rich in **Indole** type **Alkaloids** and **Damiana**.
smoke or use as a tea to create an intense euphoria with improved **Sexual Sensitivity** and **arousal**
Lasting **2-3 hours**. Brew tea for at least 5 mins.
Avoid excessive alcohol when using Aphrodisia.
PHRODISIA™ is legal throughout **Europe** and the U.S.A.

effects while remaining outside the control of current laws.

Herbal ecstasy

Herbal ecstasy has been sold freely at raves, clubs, concerts, and festivals. It contains various herbs and extracts that are claimed to be hallucinogenic and/or stimulant. Packaging and vendors claim that it is a natural and safe substitute for ecstasy. However, it often has side effects similar to many synthetic drugs.

Ephedrine and Ma-Huang

Ephedrine is an extract of the Chinese herb Ma-Huang which reportedly has stimulant effects: users feel shivers up and down the spine, sensitive skin and

ABOVE: The internet has seen a boom in the trading of these substances worldwide

BELOW: While possession of some of the chemicals may be illegal, possession of the plant source is not.

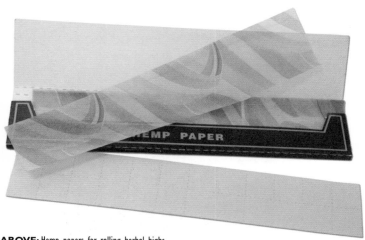

ABOVE: Hemp papers for rolling herbal highs.

ABOVE AND BELOW: There is a herbal
form of ecstasy available for smoking.

BELOW: Because these substances act in similar ways to illegal drugs, there may be similar (if less acute) risks in using them.

muscles, and feelings of exhilaration. In China, the herb Ma-Huang is sold as a medicine and as an aphrodisiac. In the West, it is sold as Cloud 9, Nirvana Plus, and other herbal highs said to mimic ecstasy. Higher doses can be quite unpleasant, possibly causing muscle spasms and even heart attack.

Yohimbe

This is said to be an aphrodisiac and is sold as a hallucinogenic with stimulant effects (also spelled yohimbine). It is marketed as Yohimbix8 or as an additive to other herbal highs. The drug is derived from the yohimbe tree roots. As with ephedrine, higher doses can be quite

RIGHT: Legal High advertising often hints at the aphrodisiacal properties of many of the products.

unpleasant, possibly causing muscle spasms and even heart attack.

The principle alkaloid in Kratom is mitragynine, an indole alkaloid superficially resembling yohimbine. Kratom is a very popular legal high, usually taken as a tea in doses ranging from 5–50 g. The effects last for four to six hours. In low doses it induces mild euphoria and reduces fatigue. At strong doses (20–50 g) typically people describe the effects as dreamy, ecstatic, and blissful. Many people experience closed-eye visuals.

Packaging often states that these drugs, because they are natural and herbal, are safe or non-addictive, but any drug which has a psychological effect can prove difficult to stop if used regularly. Proper controlled research on these drugs is sparse, and therefore side effects and possible dangers when taken with other drugs, and even foods, are not fully known.

BELOW: The advice is that these substances should not be used by anybody who is on medication or who is pregnant or breast-feeding.

Salvia

Salvia is derived from the American plant Salvia divinorum, a member of

the mint family. It is used in shamanic rituals by the Mazatecs and other groups in Meso-America. Salvia is marketed in the UK as herbal ecstasy, as for example Eclipse, or a legal hallucinogen. It is sold as a herbal remedy in health food shops and chemists under its botanical name. Its effects are more hallucinatory than the other legal highs and it has some stimulant properties. The drug is swallowed as a capsule or smoked in its dried leaf form (albeit in large quantities).

EFFECTS

Within approximately forty-five minutes of being eaten, yohimbe raises blood pressure and increases heart rate. The drug has alleged aphrodisiac properties, increasing sensuality and sexual desire. The hallucinations are said to be quite strong and the effects on the body similar to that of ecstasy.

Ephedrine has effects similar to ecstasy also, although physical sensations are more pronounced. Side effects include racing heart, dry throat, possible anxiety, tremor, and cold feet and hands. Salvia must be smoked in large quantities, usually

BELOW: With pills and capsules, the effects last from two to eight hours. Drinking alcohol may mask some of the effects. Mixing products is not recommended unless the user is experienced.

ABOVE: Legal Highs are very close in effect to banned drugs. As the law catches up with the market, some ingredients are changed or removed while some products disappear.

two or three large pipefuls, and held in the lungs for up to forty-five seconds. A trip lasts up to forty-five minutes. The effects are said to similar to LSD, although more introspective with a slight stimulatory effect. The effects when swallowed are less profound and longer lasting.

HEALTH RISKS

According to health experts, these drugs should not be used by people with heart disease, diabetes, hypertension, or kidney disease. Generally, they have no listing of the ingredients on the label or packaging—and even if they did, almost all of the chemicals and ingredients listed would be unknown to most of its buyers.

BELOW: One possible advantage of these products is that they are "pure," meaning that they are not cut with potentially hazardous substances and most companies list the ingredients and the effects on the packaging.

The Herbal High Company

Bliss EXtra

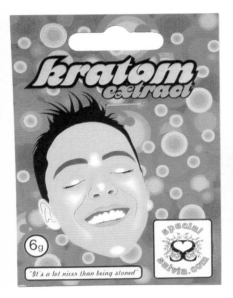

ABOVE: Kratom is indigenous to the rain forests of South East Asia, mainly Thailand and Malaysia. It is a large tree that can reach fifteen meters. Over twenty-five alkaloids have been isolated from kratom, the most important being mitragynine.

Mixing with other drugs

Concern has been raised that ephedrine, and in particular yohimbe, when taken with some drugs and a number of amine-specific foods, can prove to be toxic to the user. Cases of individuals collapsing after taking yohimbe and foods such as chocolate, cheese, sherry, pineapple, bananas, and other foods containing tryptophans, have been reported. Combinations with LSD, MDA, and MMDA are also not without serious risk. MAOI drugs may also contribute to high blood pressure.

Long-term use

The long-term effects of yohimbe, salvia or ephedrine use are not well documented. Regular use can lead to problems associated with hypertension such as dizziness, glaucoma and heart disease. As with most stimulants, repeated use can result in users feeling fatigued, possibly anxious and paranoid, leading to psychotic episodes.

THE LAW

As their name suggests, these substances remain outside national and international laws, although it is possible that at least under UK laws, they could be classed as medicines because they have a psychoactive effect (a fact which is heavily promoted)—and in which case they would come under the UK Medicines Act which has penalties for supply, but not possession. So far there has been no government action.

However, in the US, the Food and Drug Administration (FDA) issued a recent warning against legal highs. They found some products containing high levels of the over-the-counter drugs diphenhydramine and dextromethorphan and the controlled substances GBL and GHB as well.

The products included in the FDA warning are Trip2Night, Invigorate II, Snuffadelic, Liquid Speed, Solar Water, Orange Butterfly, Schoomz, and Green Hornet Liquid. The FDA says it considers any product that is promoted as an alternative to any street drug to be an unapproved new drug and therefore a misbranded drug marketed in violation of the Federal Food, Drug, and Cosmetic Act. Also, any product containing undeclared active drug ingredients violates the law. Such violations may result in enforcement action, including seizure and injunction. As the law catches up with the market these drugs will have to be changed or will just disappear.

BELOW: Some substances will potentiate the action of other drugs, for example atropine will increase the potency of marijuana. Also they are often MAO inhibitors and taking them in combination with certain foods can be dangerous.

Glossary

Addiction implies that a drug dependency has developed to such an extent that it has serious detrimental effects on the user. They may be chronically intoxicated, have great difficulty stopping the drug use, and be determined to obtain the drug by almost any means. The term addiction is inextricably linked to society's reaction to the user, and so medical experts try to avoid using it, preferring to use the term dependence instead.

Addict is a drug user whose use causes serious physical, social, or psychological problems. As it is a much-abused term, many people prefer to talk of dependent, problem, or chronic drug users instead.

Analgesic is a painkiller.

BELOW: Darvocet-N 100 mg

Benzodiazepines are the most commonly prescribed minor tranquillizers (for daytime anxiety relief) and hypnotics (to promote sleep). They include products such as Valium and Librium.

BELOW: Valium 2 mg

Chaotic use is when an individual is regarded as taking a drug or drugs in a spontaneous way that tends not to follow any typical drug-using pattern. It is generally associated with problematic bouts of heavy use that may cause the user harm.

Controlled drugs in the UK are preparations subject to the Misuse of Drugs Regulations 1985. These drugs are divided into five schedules covering import, export, production, supply, possession, prescribing, and appropriate record keeping. The first schedule deals with drugs such as LSD and ecstasy for which medical prescription is not available. The strictest schedules for prescribed drugs are two and three and these include opioids and stimulants.

Come down is the hangover or after-effect of taking a drug. Reflecting the low feeling experienced after the high of taking a drug. A come down is mostly associated with the after-effects of stimulant taking, in particular ecstasy, which can last anything up to four days.

Dependence describes a compulsion to continue taking a drug in order to feel good or to avoid feeling bad. When this is done to avoid physical discomfort or withdrawal, it is known as physical dependence; when it has a psychological aspect (the need for stimulation or pleasure, or to escape reality) then it is known as psychological dependence.

BELOW: Depressant—alcohol

BELOW: Ecstasy in various forms

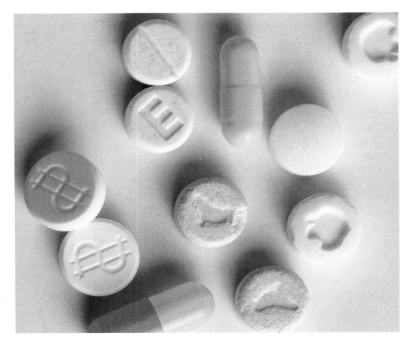

BELOW: A designer drug—fentanyl

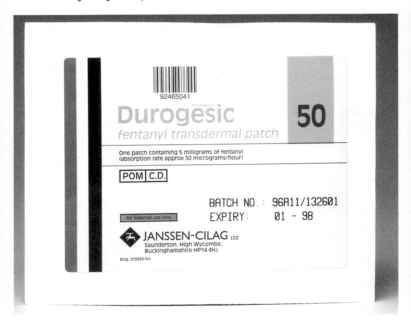

Depressant is a drug that acts on the central nervous system to suppress neural activity in the brain. Opioids and sedatives are both classes of depressants.

Designer drugs is a term coined in the 1980s to describe drugs specifically synthesized to circumvent regulations on controlled substances. Ecstasy is often cited as a designer drug, but this is incorrect. As an analogue of amphetamine, there was no need for new legislation to control its use when it became popular. In the US, fentanyl, a painkilling drug many more times potent than morphine, induced Parkinson's Disease in some users who sampled it. More recently, the anabolic steroid tetrahydrogestrinone (THG) looks to be another designer drug.

Detoxification is the process by which a user withdraws from the effects of a drug. It usually refers to withdrawal in a safe environment (a detoxification or detox center), with help on hand to minimize the unpleasant symptoms.

Drug use/misuse/abuse Drug use is an easy term to understand. Misuse and abuse are more difficult to pin down, as they are highly subjective. In most circles, misuse means using in a socially unacceptable way. However, the definition currently being adopted defines misuse as using drugs in a way that results in experience of social, psychological, physical, or legal problems related to intoxication and/or regular consumption. Many regard the term abuse as too judgmental, as it suggests impropriety regardless of how the drug is being used. In general, abuse means using drugs in a harmful way. As abuse and misuse can be morally "loaded" terms, many people prefer to talk of drug taking, or of harmful or problematic use instead, when appropriate.

Flashbacks are hallucinations that occur a long time after a drug (often LSD) has been used.

BELOW: Hallucinogenic mushrooms

BELOW: Hard drug—cocaine

Hallucinogenic is a drug which induces hallucinations and alters perceptions (e.g. LSD, magic mushrooms—see *Psychedelic*).

Hard drugs usually refer to drugs which are seen to be more dangerous and more likely to cause dependency, such as heroin and crack cocaine, than those designated as "soft," such as cannabis and LSD. Obviously there is an element of truth in the distinction, but it is generally a value judgement used for propaganda purposes by both pro- and anti-drug lobbies and so is best avoided. The terms "hard" and "soft" when applied to drugs have no legal or pharmacological validity.

Harm reduction is a term that covers activities and services that acknowledge the continued drug use of individuals, but seek to minimize the harm that such behavior causes.

BELOW: M.A.D.A. is a herbal high

Narcotics are commonly used to mean any illicit drug, especially in the US. However, the term technically refers to chemicals that induce stupor, coma, or insensibility to pain, such as opiates or opioids.

Opiates are derived from the opium poppy (e.g. morphine and heroin).

Opioids include both opiates and their synthetic analogues (e.g. methadone, pethidine).

BELOW: Opiate—opium poppy

Legal highs are drugs that do not fall under the drug control laws. Most are herbal (also called herbal highs) such as ephedrine, yohimbine, and salvia, but some, such as poppers, are synthetic or processed. Many are sold as legal and safe alternatives to illegal drugs, but are usually retailed without a license, and are not without their own risks to the user's health.

BELOW: Paraphernalia for cocaine use

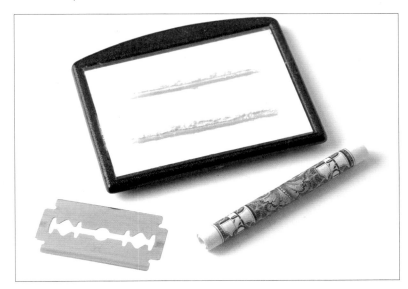

Over-the-counter (OTC) drugs are those which are available from chemists without a prescription.

Overdose (OD) is the use of any drug in such quantities that acute adverse physical or mental effects occur. It can be deliberate or accidental, lethal or non-lethal.

Paraphernalia is the equipment for drug taking (e.g. silver foil, spoon).

Polydrug use is the use of more than one drug, often with the intention of enhancing or countering the effects of another drug. Polydrug use, however, may simply occur because the user's preferred drug is unavailable (or too expensive) at the time.

BELOW: Analgesic—methadone

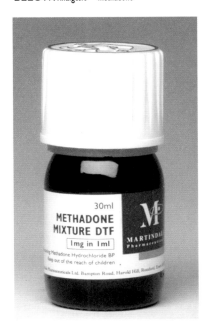

BELOW: Psychedellic—LSD tabs

Prescribed drugs are those drugs obtained on a prescription. May refer to methadone and other opioids or to tranquillizers and antidepressants.

Problem drug use refers to drug use which could be either dependent or recreational. In other words, it is not necessarily the frequency of drug use which is the primary "problem," but the effects that drug taking have on the user's life (i.e. they may experience social, financial, psychological, physical, or legal problems as a result of their drug use).

Psychedelic was a term coined in 1956 by the LSD researcher Humphrey Osmond, and literally means "soul manifesting"—an activation of consciousness. Although virtually synonymous with hallucinogenic, psychedelic implies that the drug acts as a catalyst to further feelings and thoughts, and is not merely hallucinatory.

BELOW: Recreational drugs are often used at clubs and raves

Psychoactive or psychotropic are perhaps the most all-encompassing ways of describing mood-altering drugs in general, though they are more often used to describe LSD and similar hallucinogenic drugs.

Recreational drug use is the use of drugs for pleasure or leisure. The term is often used to denote the use of ecstasy and other so-called "dance drugs," and implies that drug use has become part of someone's lifestyle (even though they may only take drugs occasionally).

Sedative is a depressant which acts on an individual's central nervous system in order to relieve anxiety and induce calm or sleep (e.g. benzodiazapines).

Scheduled drugs These are drugs controlled under US Federal law. Drugs are divided into five sections:

BELOW: Sedative—oxazepam 30 mg

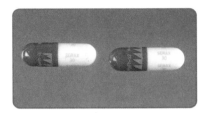

Schedule I: Those drugs considered to have a very high misuse potential and no accepted medical use. Only rarely are doctors allowed to prescribe them. Examples included LSD, marijuana, and heroin.

Schedule II: Those drugs considered to have a very high misuse potential, but also have an accepted medical use. Doctors may prescribe them, but only under very strict conditions. Examples include morphine, cocaine, and amphetamines.

BELOW: Schedule II drug—amphetamine

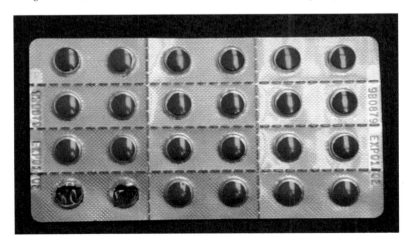

BELOW: Stimulant—caffeine

Schedule III: Those drugs considered to have a high potential for misuse, but also have accepted medical uses. Doctors would routinely prescribe them, including weaker opiate formulations.

Schedule IV: Those drugs considered to have a moderate misuse potential, but also have accepted medical uses. Doctors would routinely prescribe them including Valium and most of the antidepressants.

Schedule V: Those drugs considered to have a low, but significant misuse potential, but also have accepted medical uses. They may be purchased without a prescription like cough and cold remedies.

Stimulant is a drug which acts on the central nervous system to increase neural activity in the brain (e.g. amphetamine, cocaine, caffeine, and—if used in high quantities—antidepressants and certain opioids).

BELOW: Tranquillizer—Midazolam

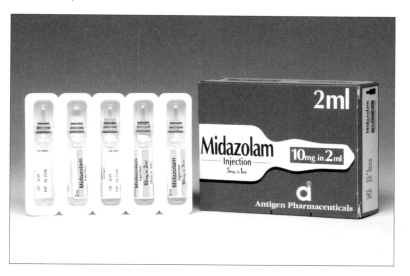

Tolerance refers to the way the body becomes accustomed to the repeated presence of a drug, meaning that higher doses are needed to maintain or achieve the same effect.

Tranquillizers are calming drugs used to manage various mental disorders. They can be differentiated from sedatives in that (unless used in high doses) they do not interfere with the patient's thought processes or send the user to sleep.

Volatile substances refers to all solvents and inhalants—not, as is sometimes thought, to aerosols only.

Withdrawal is the body's reaction to the sudden absence of a drug to which it has adapted. The effects can be stopped either by taking more of the drug, or by stopping the drug completely or going turkey"—which may last for up to a week.

BELOW: Volatile substance—solvent